DAREDEVIL

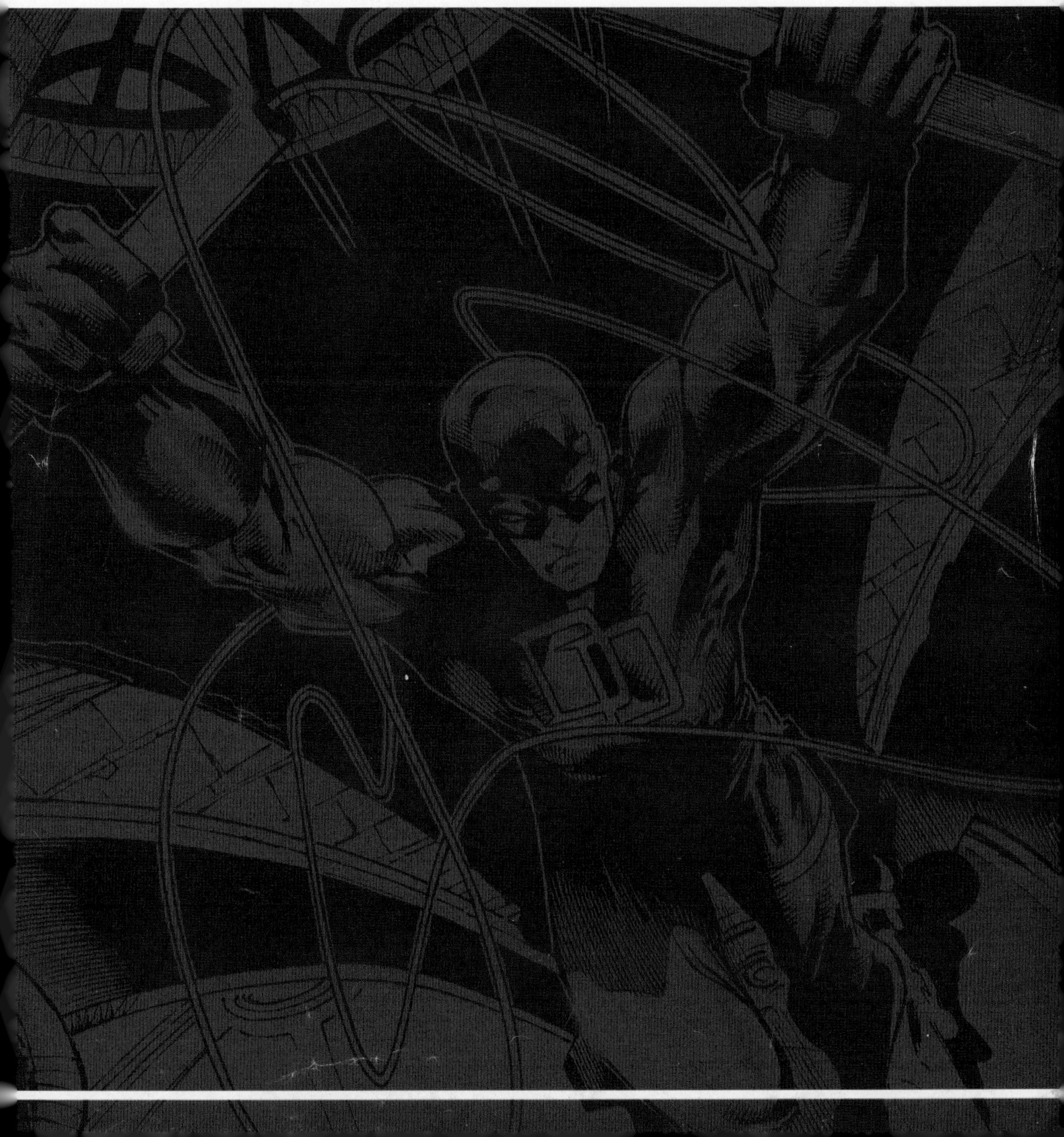

COLLECTION EDITOR: **JENNIFER GRÜNWALD**
ASSISTANT EDITORS: **ALEX STARBUCK & NELSON RIBEIRO**
EDITOR, SPECIAL PROJECTS: **MARK D. BEAZLEY**
SENIOR EDITOR, SPECIAL PROJECTS: **JEFF YOUNGQUIST**
SENIOR VICE PRESIDENT OF SALES: **DAVID GABRIEL**
SVP OF BRAND PLANNING & COMMUNICATIONS: **MICHAEL PASCIULLO**
COVER & BOOK DESIGN: **JEFF POWELL**

EDITOR IN CHIEF: **AXEL ALONSO**
CHIEF CREATIVE OFFICER: **JOE QUESADA**
PUBLISHER: **DAN BUCKLEY**
EXECUTIVE PRODUCER: **ALAN FINE**

DAREDEVIL: SEASON ONE. Contains material originally published in magazine form as DAREDEVIL #1. First printing 2012. ISBN# 978-0-7851-5643-7. Published by MARVEL WORLDWIDE, INC., a subsidiary
MARVEL ENTERTAINMENT, LLC. OFFICE OF PUBLICATION: 135 West 50th Street, New York, NY 10020. **Manufactured between 2/21/2012 and 3/26/2012 by R.R. DONNELLEY, INC., SALEM, VA, U**

10 9 8 7 6 5 4 3 2 1

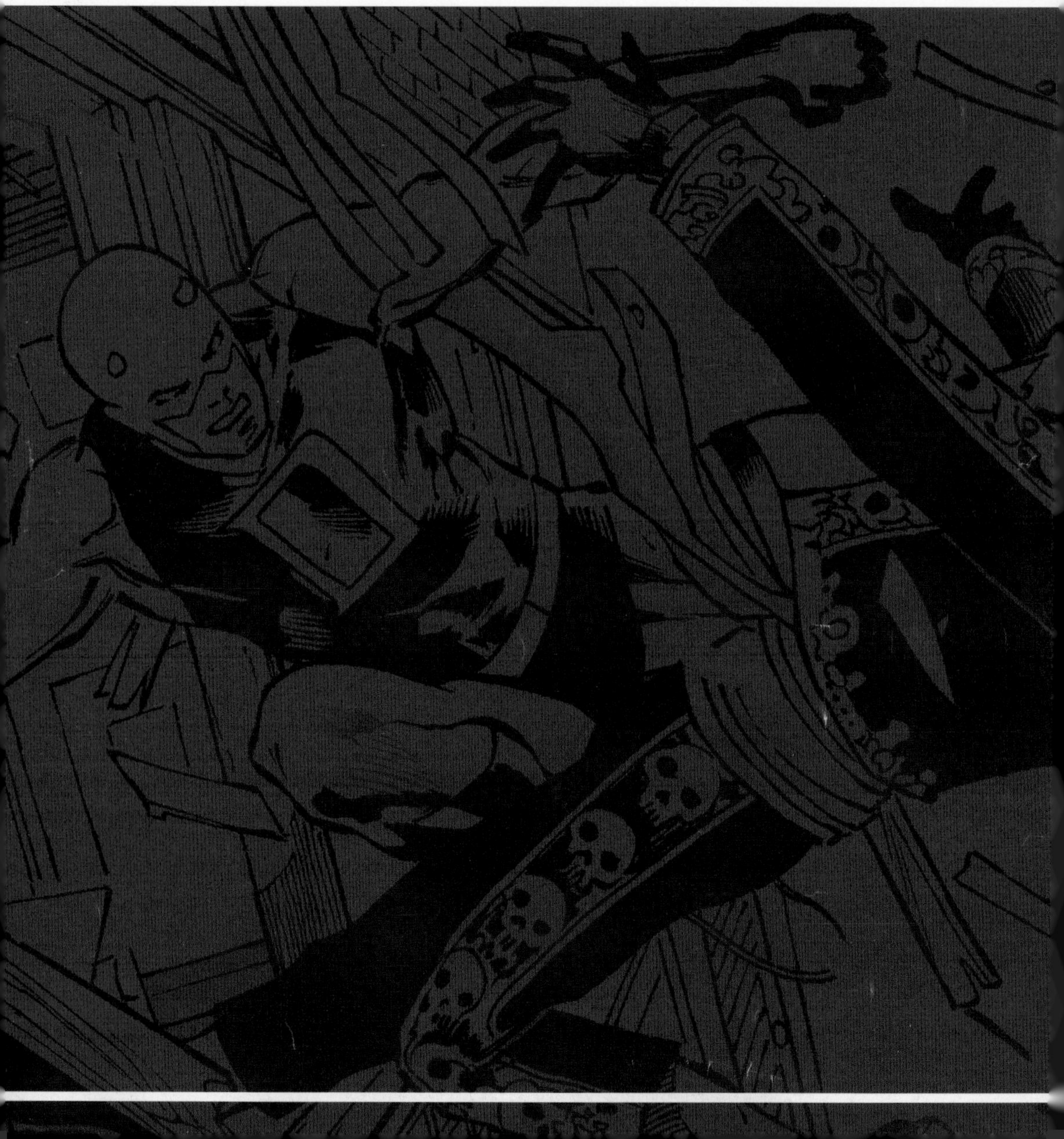

DAREDEVIL

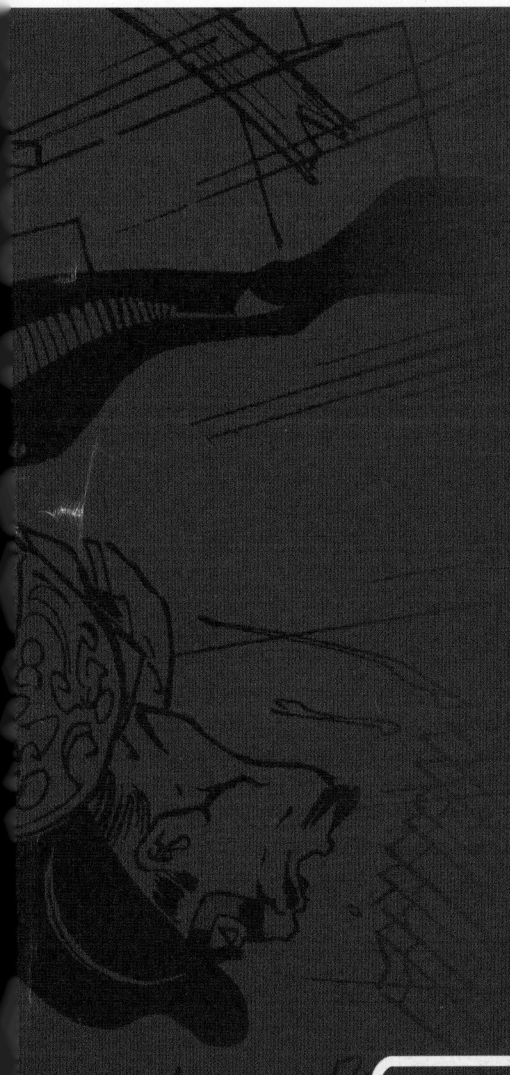

WRITER
ANTONY JOHNSTON

PENCILER
WELLINTON ALVES

INKER
NELSON PEREIRA

COLORIST
BRUNO HANG

LETTERER
VC'S CLAYTON COWLES

COVER ARTIST
JULIAN TOTINO TEDESCO

ASSISTANT EDITOR
RACHEL PINNELAS

EDITOR
TOM BRENNAN

EXECUTIVE EDITOR
TOM BREVOORT

SPECIAL THANKS TO BILL ROSEMANN

SEASON ONE

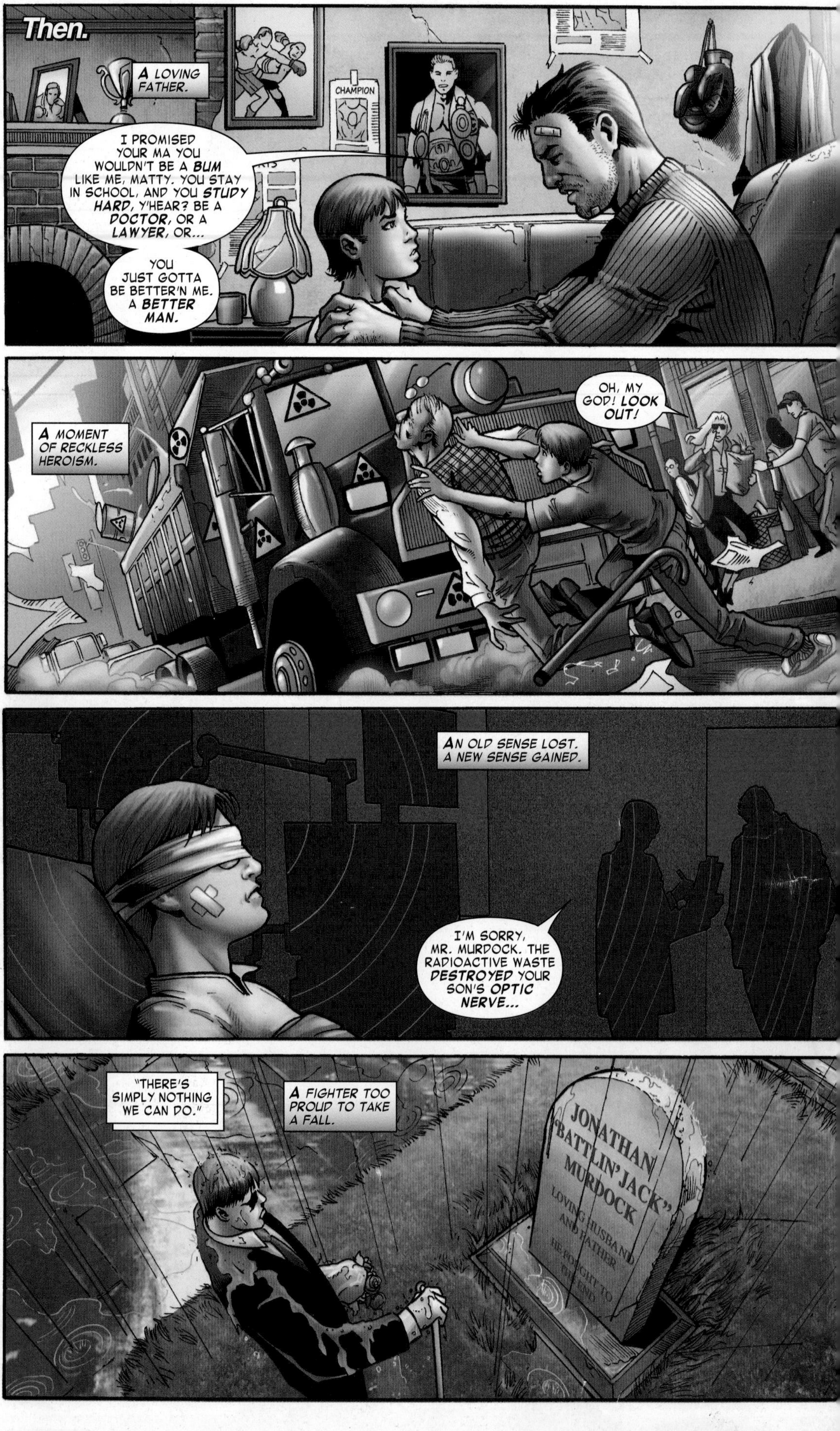

Then.
A LOVING FATHER.
I PROMISED YOUR MA YOU WOULDN'T BE A BUM LIKE ME, MATTY. YOU STAY IN SCHOOL, AND YOU STUDY HARD, Y'HEAR? BE A DOCTOR, OR A LAWYER, OR...
YOU JUST GOTTA BE BETTER'N ME. A BETTER MAN.
CHAMPION
A MOMENT OF RECKLESS HEROISM.
OH, MY GOD! LOOK OUT!
AN OLD SENSE LOST. A NEW SENSE GAINED.
I'M SORRY, MR. MURDOCK. THE RADIOACTIVE WASTE DESTROYED YOUR SON'S OPTIC NERVE...
"THERE'S SIMPLY NOTHING WE CAN DO."
A FIGHTER TOO PROUD TO TAKE A FALL.
JONATHAN "BATTLIN' JACK" MURDOCK
LOVING HUSBAND AND FATHER

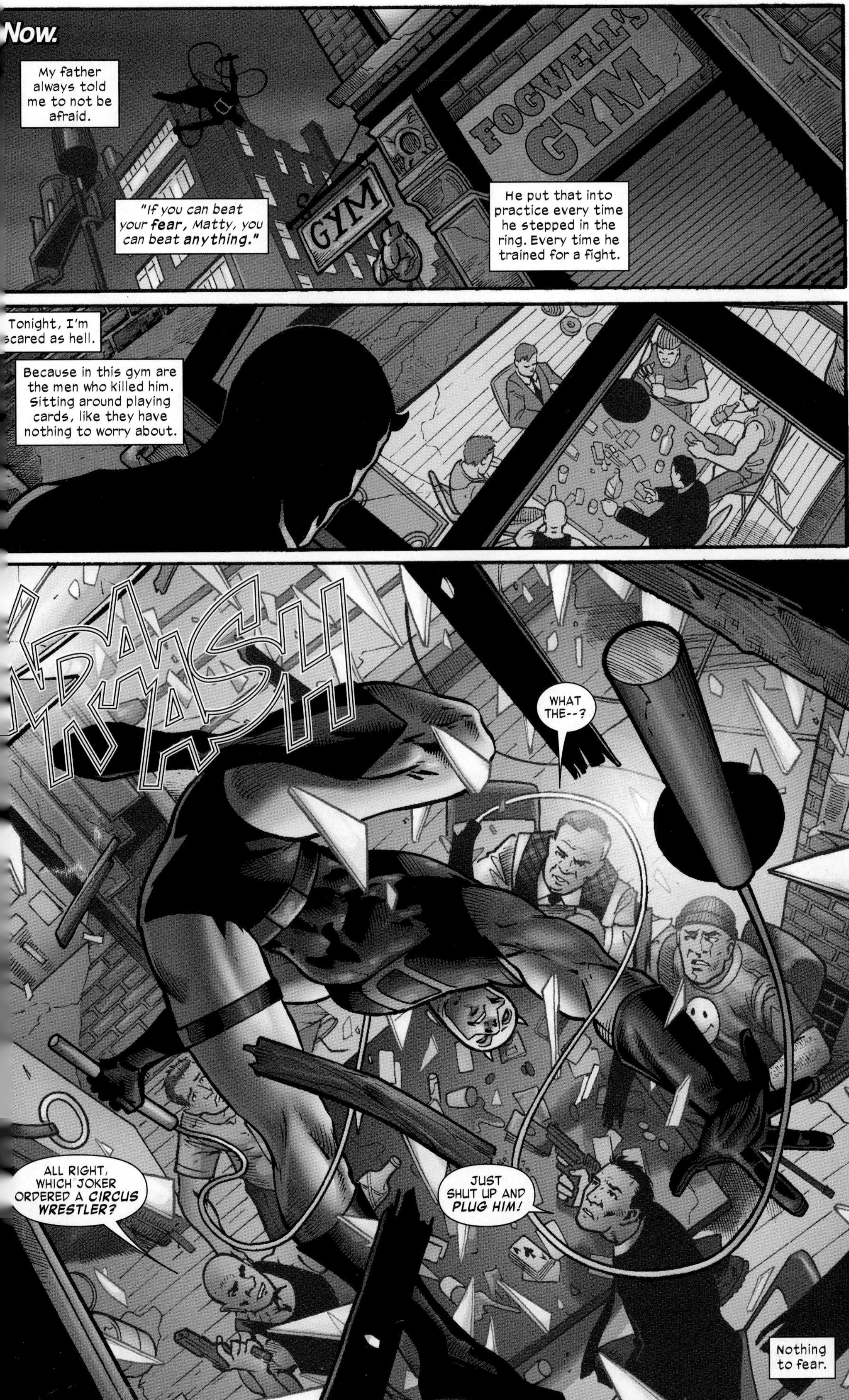

Now.
My father always told me to not be afraid.
FOGWELL'S GYM
GYM
"If you can beat your fear, Matty, you can beat anything."
He put that into practice every time he stepped in the ring. Every time he trained for a fight.
Tonight, I'm scared as hell.
Because in this gym are the men who killed him. Sitting around playing cards, like they have nothing to worry about.
KRASH
WHAT THE--?
ALL RIGHT, WHICH JOKER ORDERED A CIRCUS WRESTLER?
JUST SHUT UP AND PLUG HIM!
Nothing to fear.

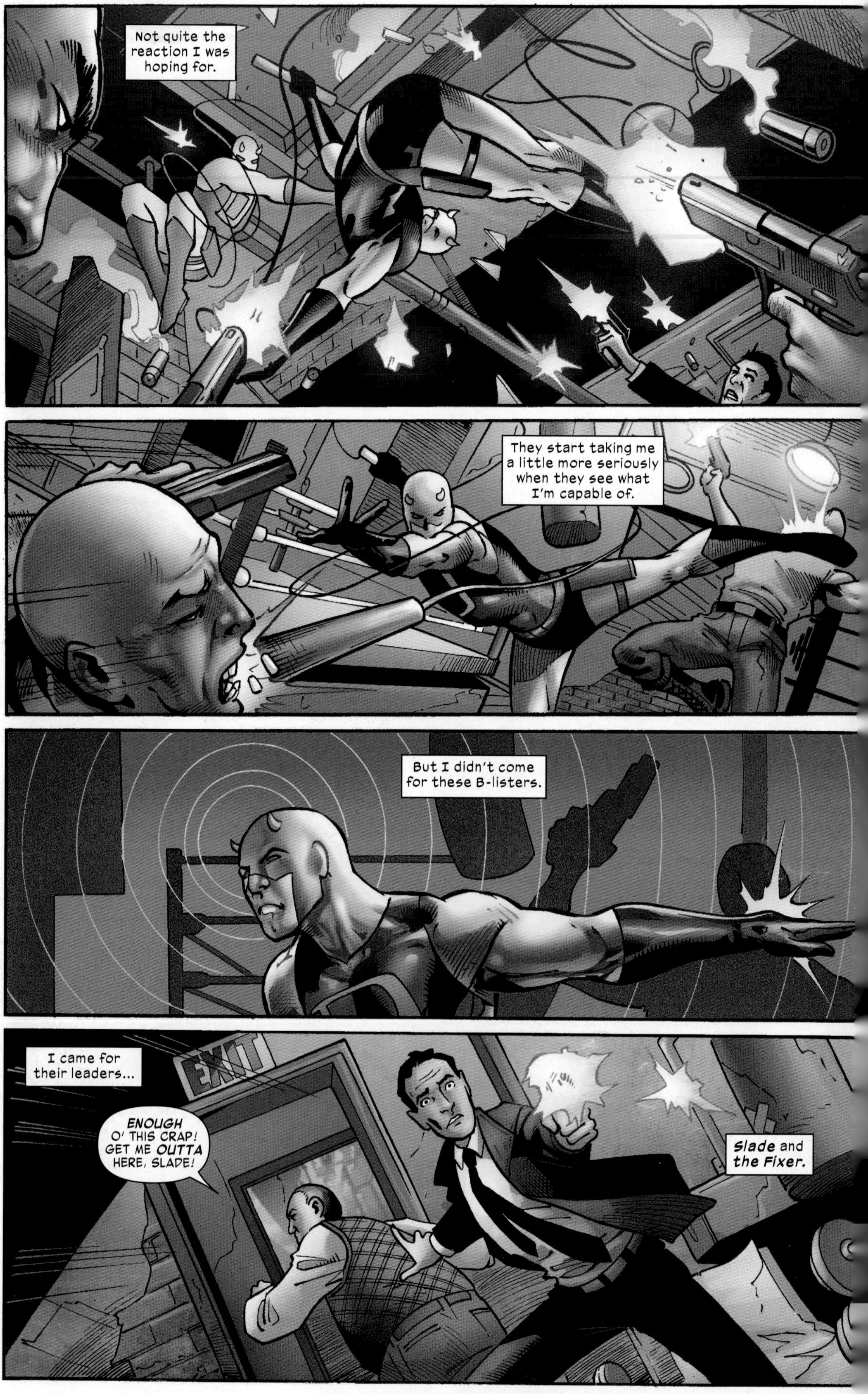
Not quite the reaction I was hoping for.
They start taking me a little more seriously when they see what I'm capable of.
But I didn't come for these B-listers.
I came for their leaders...
EXIT
ENOUGH O' THIS CRAP! GET ME OUTTA HERE, SLADE!
Slade and the Fixer.

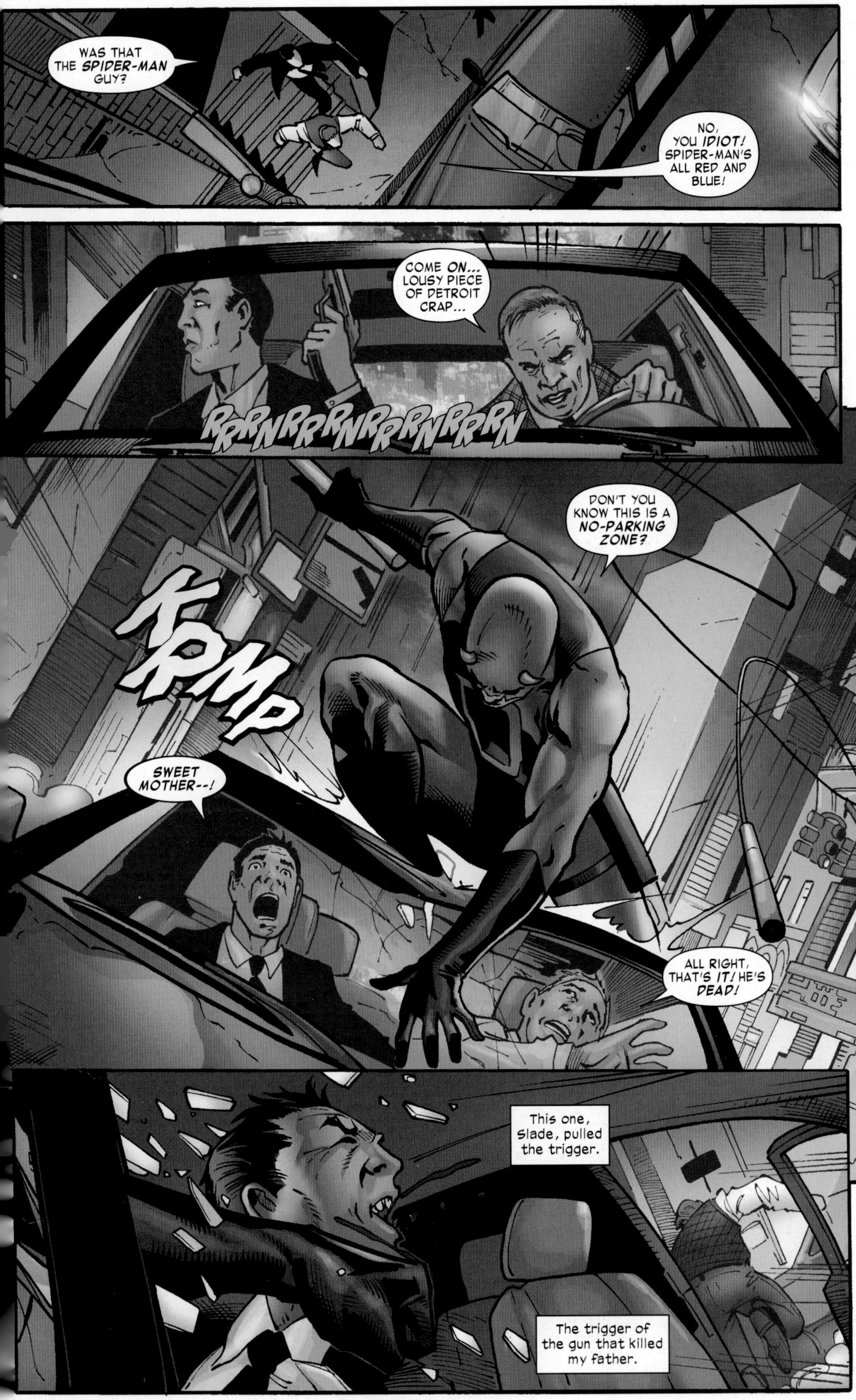
WAS THAT THE SPIDER-MAN GUY?
NO, YOU IDIOT! SPIDER-MAN'S ALL RED AND BLUE!
COME ON... LOUSY PIECE OF DETROIT CRAP...
RRRNRRRNRRRNRRRN
DON'T YOU KNOW THIS IS A NO-PARKING ZONE?
KRMP
SWEET MOTHER--!
ALL RIGHT, THAT'S IT! HE'S DEAD!
This one, Slade, pulled the trigger.
The trigger of the gun that killed my father.

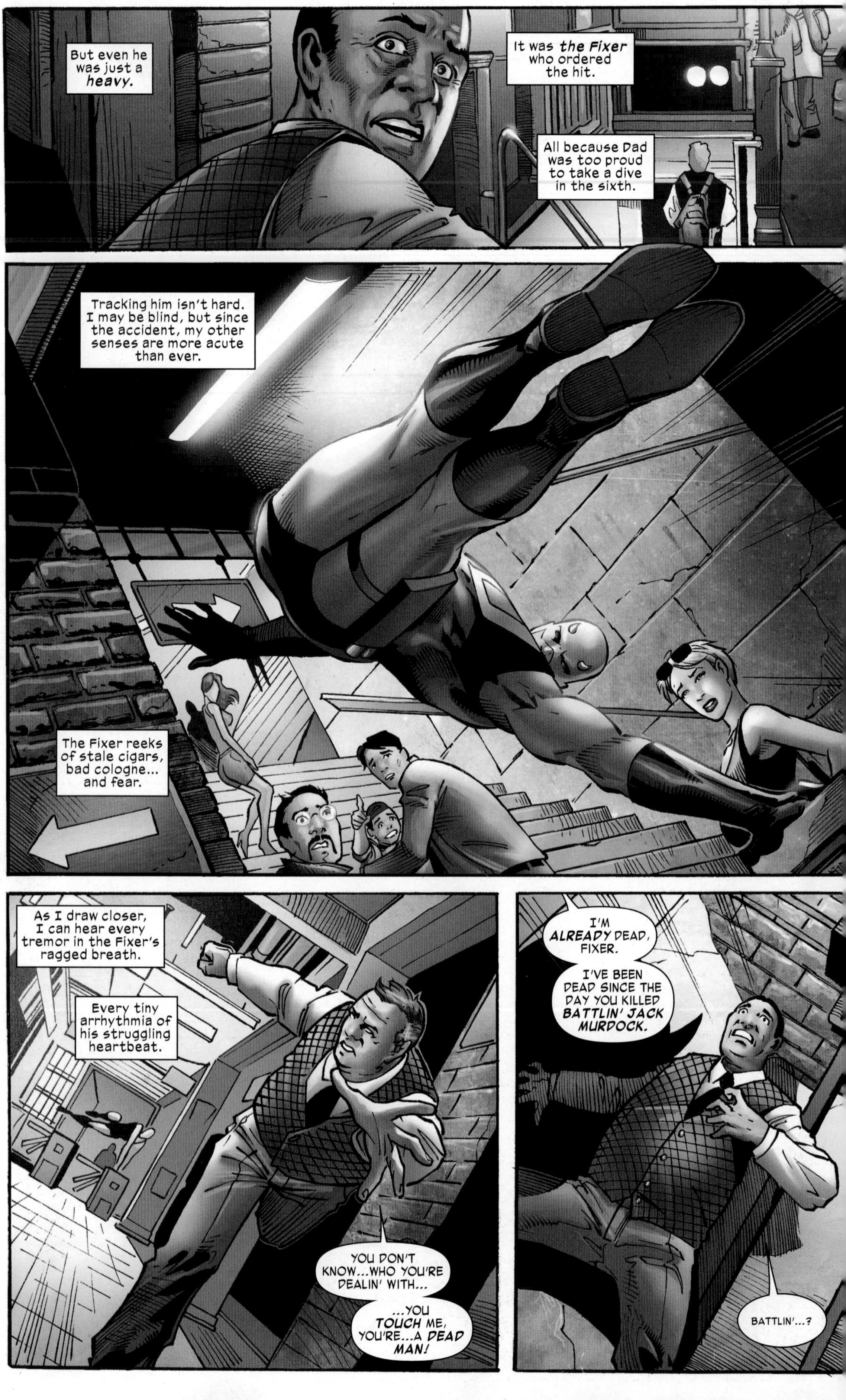

But even he was just a *heavy.*
It was *the Fixer* who ordered the hit.
All because Dad was too proud to take a dive in the sixth.
Tracking him isn't hard. I may be blind, but since the accident, my other senses are more acute than ever.
The Fixer reeks of stale cigars, bad cologne... and fear.
As I draw closer, I can hear every tremor in the Fixer's ragged breath.
Every tiny arrhythmia of his struggling heartbeat.
YOU DON'T KNOW...WHO YOU'RE DEALIN' WITH...
...YOU *TOUCH* ME, YOU'RE...A *DEAD MAN!*
I'M *ALREADY* DEAD, FIXER.
I'VE BEEN DEAD SINCE THE DAY YOU KILLED ***BATTLIN' JACK MURDOCK.***
BATTLIN'...?

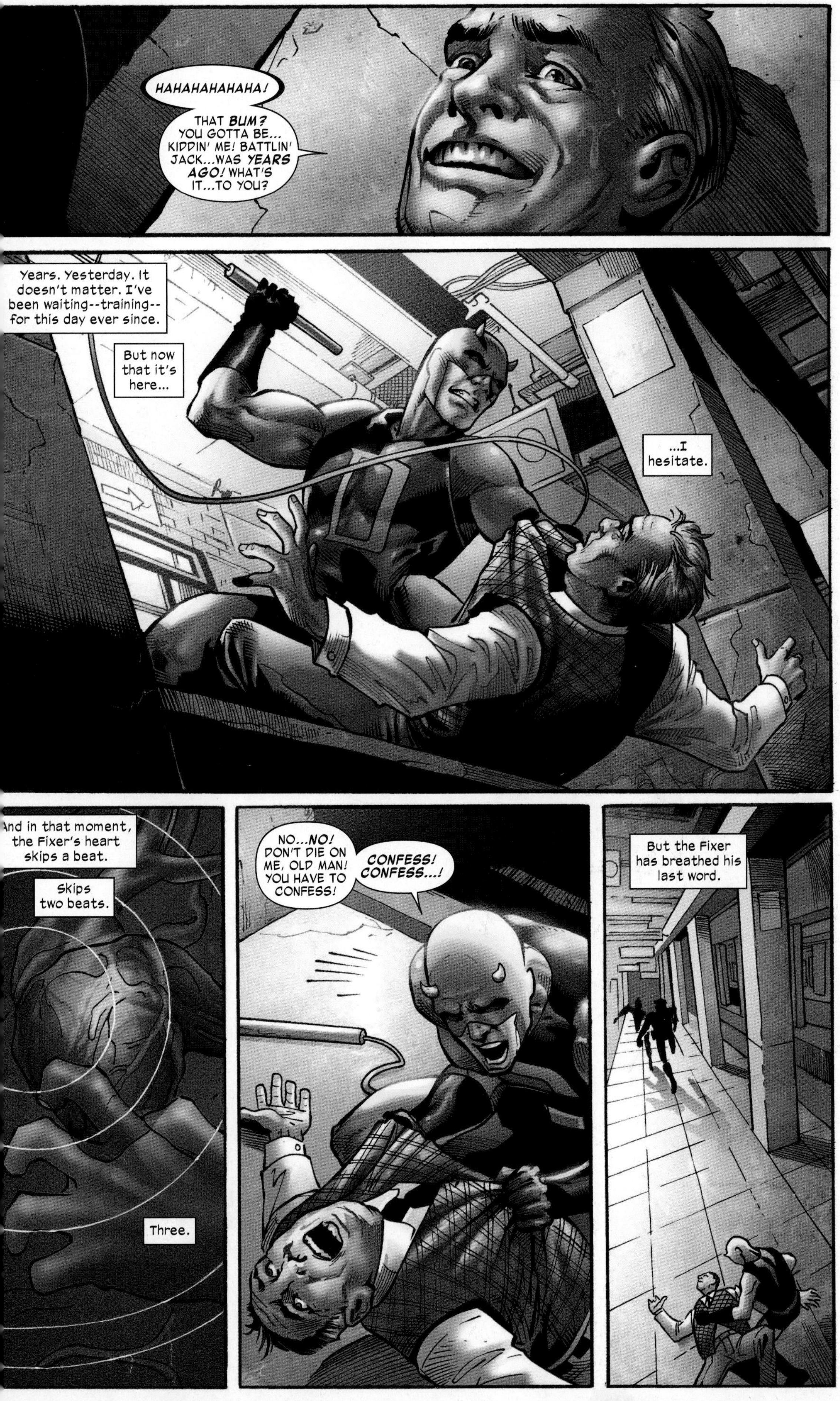
HAHAHAHAHAHA!
THAT BUM? YOU GOTTA BE... KIDDIN' ME! BATTLIN' JACK...WAS YEARS AGO! WHAT'S IT...TO YOU?
Years. Yesterday. It doesn't matter. I've been waiting--training--for this day ever since.
But now that it's here...
...I hesitate.
And in that moment, the Fixer's heart skips a beat.
Skips two beats.
Three.
NO...NO! DON'T DIE ON ME, OLD MAN! YOU HAVE TO CONFESS!
CONFESS! CONFESS...!
But the Fixer has breathed his last word.

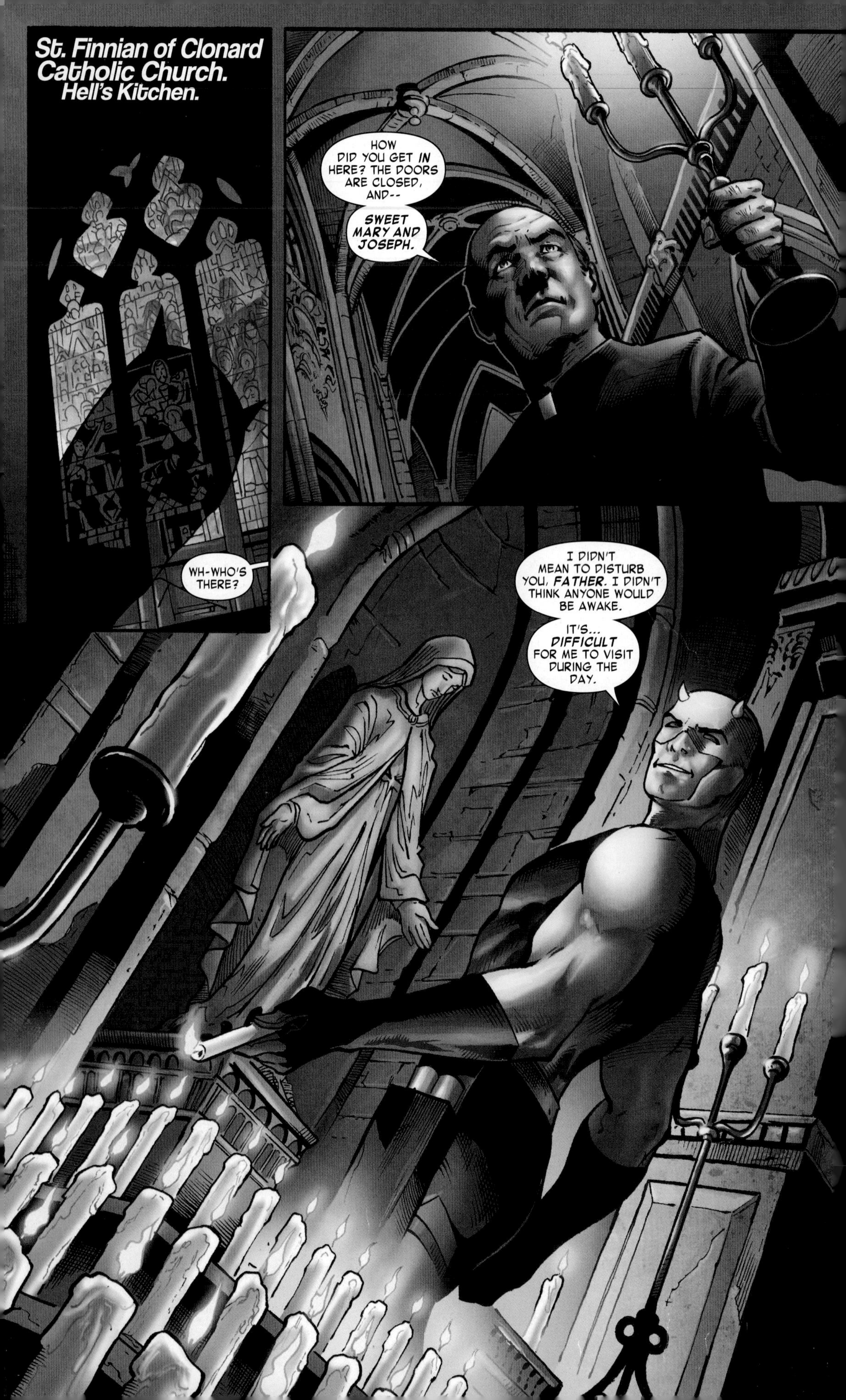
St. Finnian of Clonard Catholic Church. Hell's Kitchen.
HOW DID YOU GET IN HERE? THE DOORS ARE CLOSED, AND--
SWEET MARY AND JOSEPH.
WH-WHO'S THERE?
I DIDN'T MEAN TO DISTURB YOU, FATHER. I DIDN'T THINK ANYONE WOULD BE AWAKE.
IT'S... DIFFICULT FOR ME TO VISIT DURING THE DAY.

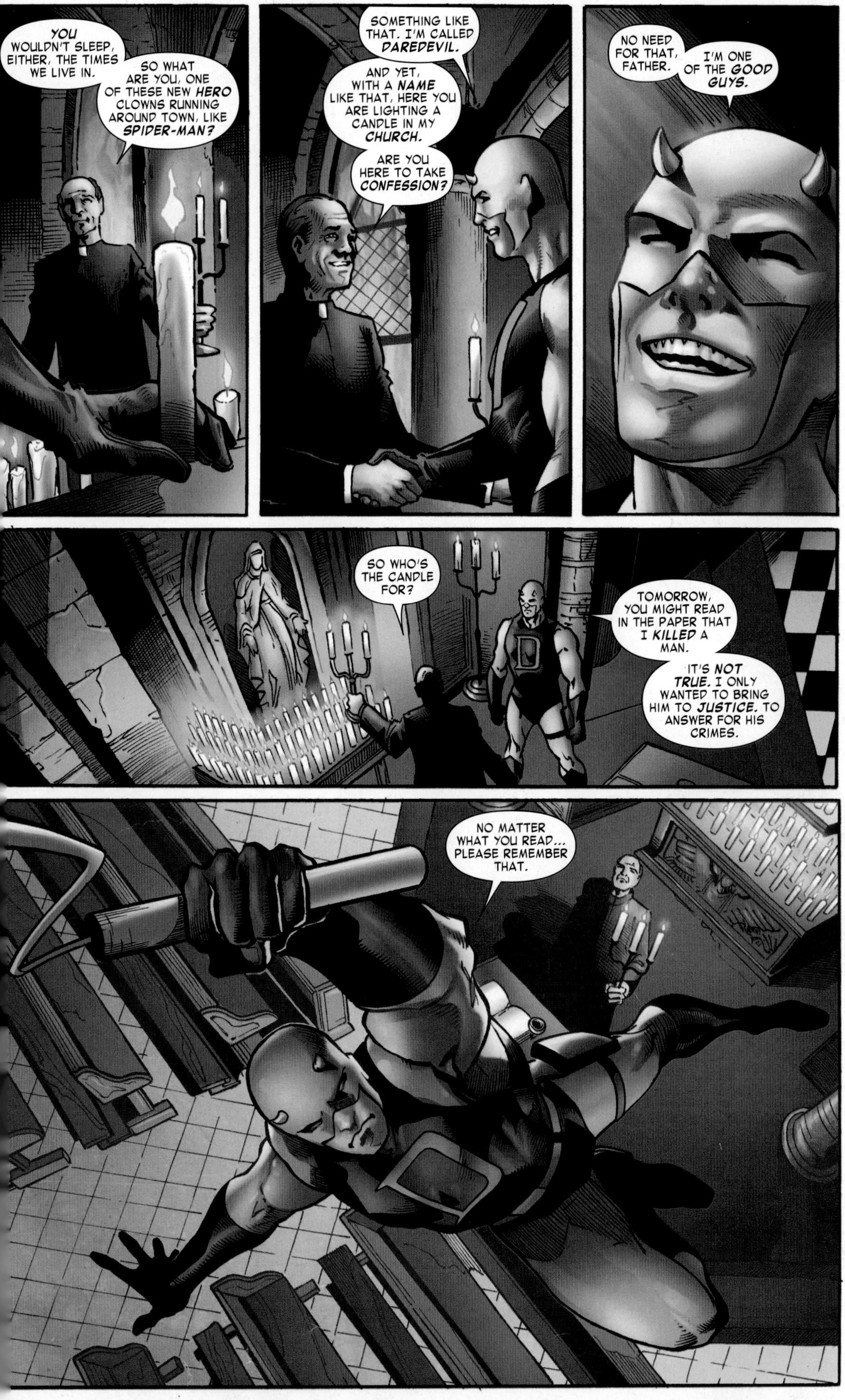
YOU WOULDN'T SLEEP, EITHER, THE TIMES WE LIVE IN.
SO WHAT ARE YOU, ONE OF THESE NEW HERO CLOWNS RUNNING AROUND TOWN, LIKE SPIDER-MAN?
SOMETHING LIKE THAT. I'M CALLED DAREDEVIL.
AND YET, WITH A NAME LIKE THAT, HERE YOU ARE LIGHTING A CANDLE IN MY CHURCH.
ARE YOU HERE TO TAKE CONFESSION?
NO NEED FOR THAT, FATHER.
I'M ONE OF THE GOOD GUYS.
SO WHO'S THE CANDLE FOR?
TOMORROW, YOU MIGHT READ IN THE PAPER THAT I KILLED A MAN.
IT'S NOT TRUE. I ONLY WANTED TO BRING HIM TO JUSTICE. TO ANSWER FOR HIS CRIMES.
NO MATTER WHAT YOU READ... PLEASE REMEMBER THAT.

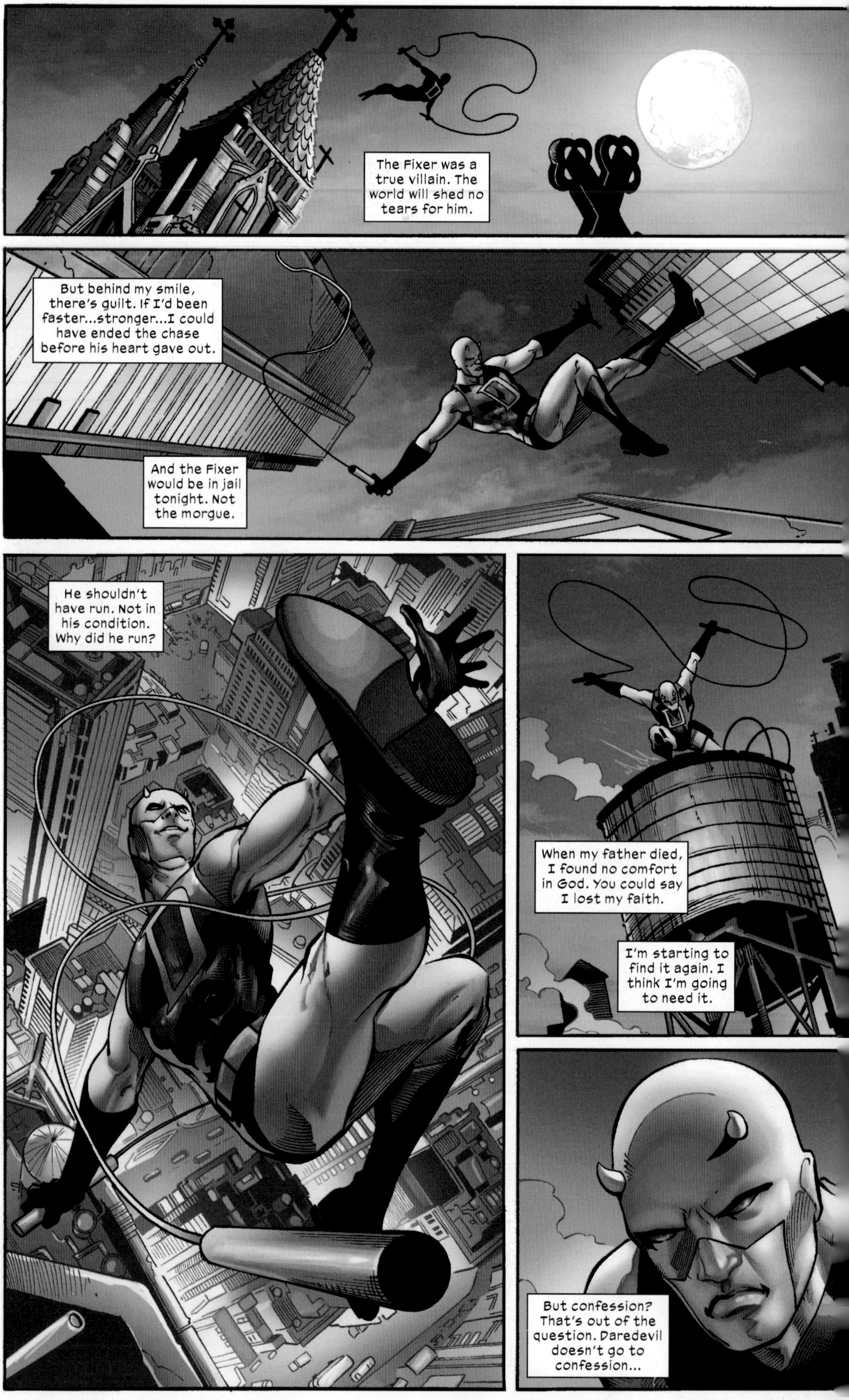

The Fixer was a true villain. The world will shed no tears for him.
But behind my smile, there's guilt. If I'd been faster...stronger...I could have ended the chase before his heart gave out.
And the Fixer would be in jail tonight. Not the morgue.
He shouldn't have run. Not in his condition. Why did he run?
When my father died, I found no comfort in God. You could say I lost my faith.
I'm starting to find it again. I think I'm going to need it.
But confession? That's out of the question. Daredevil doesn't go to confession...

...he leaves that to *Matt Murdock,* the *blind lawyer.*

MATT? ARE YOU *LISTENING* TO ME?

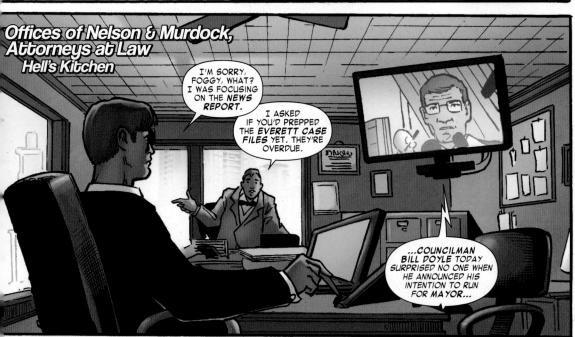

Offices of Nelson & Murdock, Attorneys at Law
Hell's Kitchen

I'M SORRY, FOGGY, WHAT? I WAS FOCUSING ON THE *NEWS REPORT.*

I ASKED IF YOU'D PREPPED THE *EVERETT CASE FILES* YET. THEY'RE OVERDUE.

...COUNCILMAN BILL DOYLE TODAY SURPRISED NO ONE WHEN HE ANNOUNCED HIS INTENTION TO RUN FOR *MAYOR...*

E EVERETT FILES FOR YOU, R. *NELSON.* I FINISHED TYPING THEM UP THIS MORNING.

AS FOR *DOYLE,* I WOULDN'T TRUST HIM AS FAR AS I COULD *THROW HIM.* POLITICIANS ARE ALL THE SAME.

KAREN, *SHHH...!*

NOT *ALL,* KAREN.

DOYLE'S PARENTS WERE POOR IRISH IMMIGRANTS. HIS MOTHER *DIED,* THEN HIS FATHER *DISAPPEARED,* ALL WHEN HE WAS STILL A KID.

DOYLE COULD HAVE WOUND UP *WARMING CELLS* MOST OF HIS LIFE. INSTEAD, HE'S RUNNING FOR *MAYOR.*

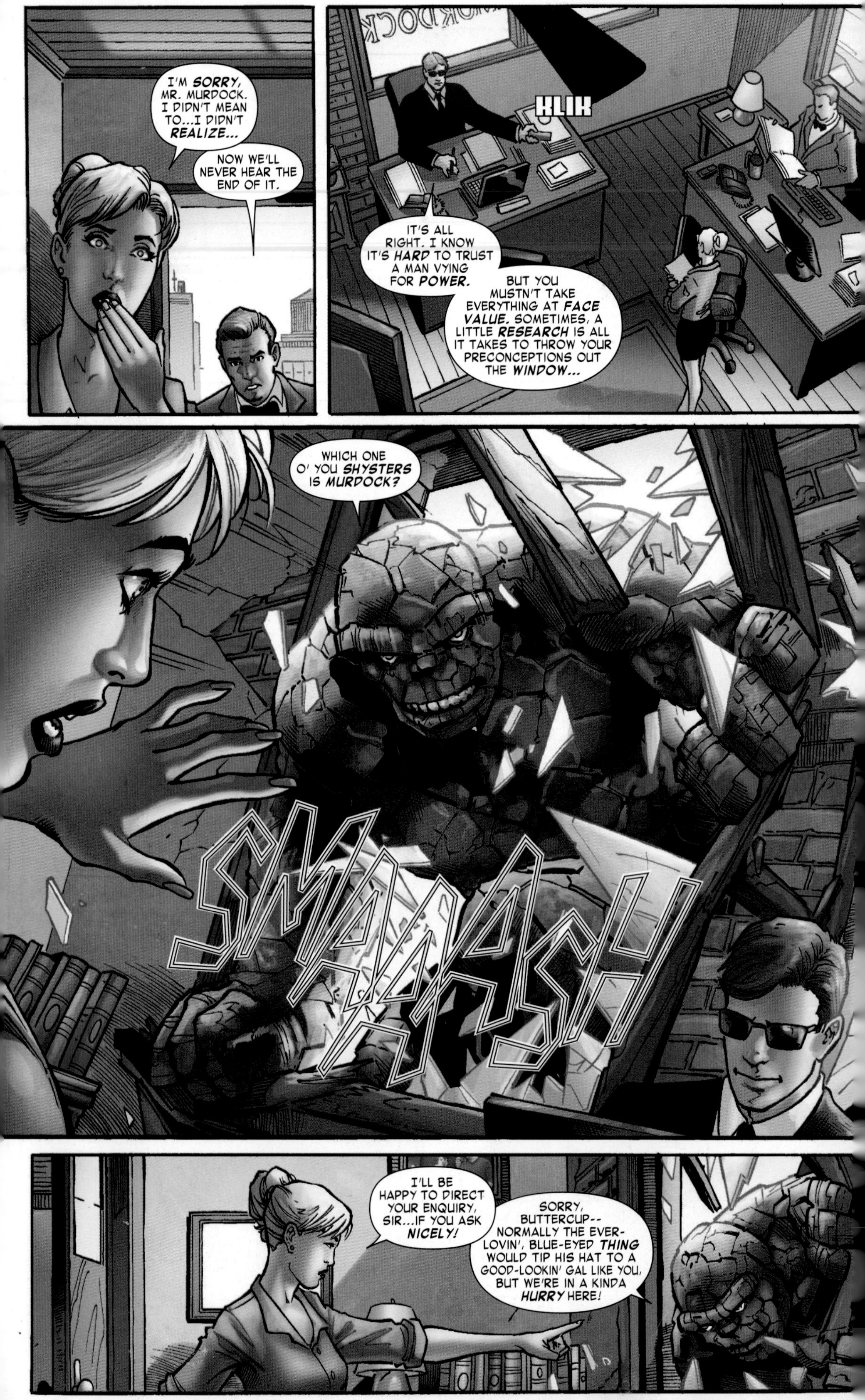

I'M SORRY, MR. MURDOCK. I DIDN'T MEAN TO...I DIDN'T REALIZE...
NOW WE'LL NEVER HEAR THE END OF IT.
KLIK
IT'S ALL RIGHT. I KNOW IT'S HARD TO TRUST A MAN VYING FOR POWER.
BUT YOU MUSTN'T TAKE EVERYTHING AT FACE VALUE. SOMETIMES, A LITTLE RESEARCH IS ALL IT TAKES TO THROW YOUR PRECONCEPTIONS OUT THE WINDOW...
WHICH ONE O' YOU SHYSTERS IS MURDOCK?
SMAAASH
I'LL BE HAPPY TO DIRECT YOUR ENQUIRY, SIR...IF YOU ASK NICELY!
SORRY, BUTTERCUP-- NORMALLY THE EVER-LOVIN', BLUE-EYED THING WOULD TIP HIS HAT TO A GOOD-LOOKIN' GAL LIKE YOU, BUT WE'RE IN A KINDA HURRY HERE!

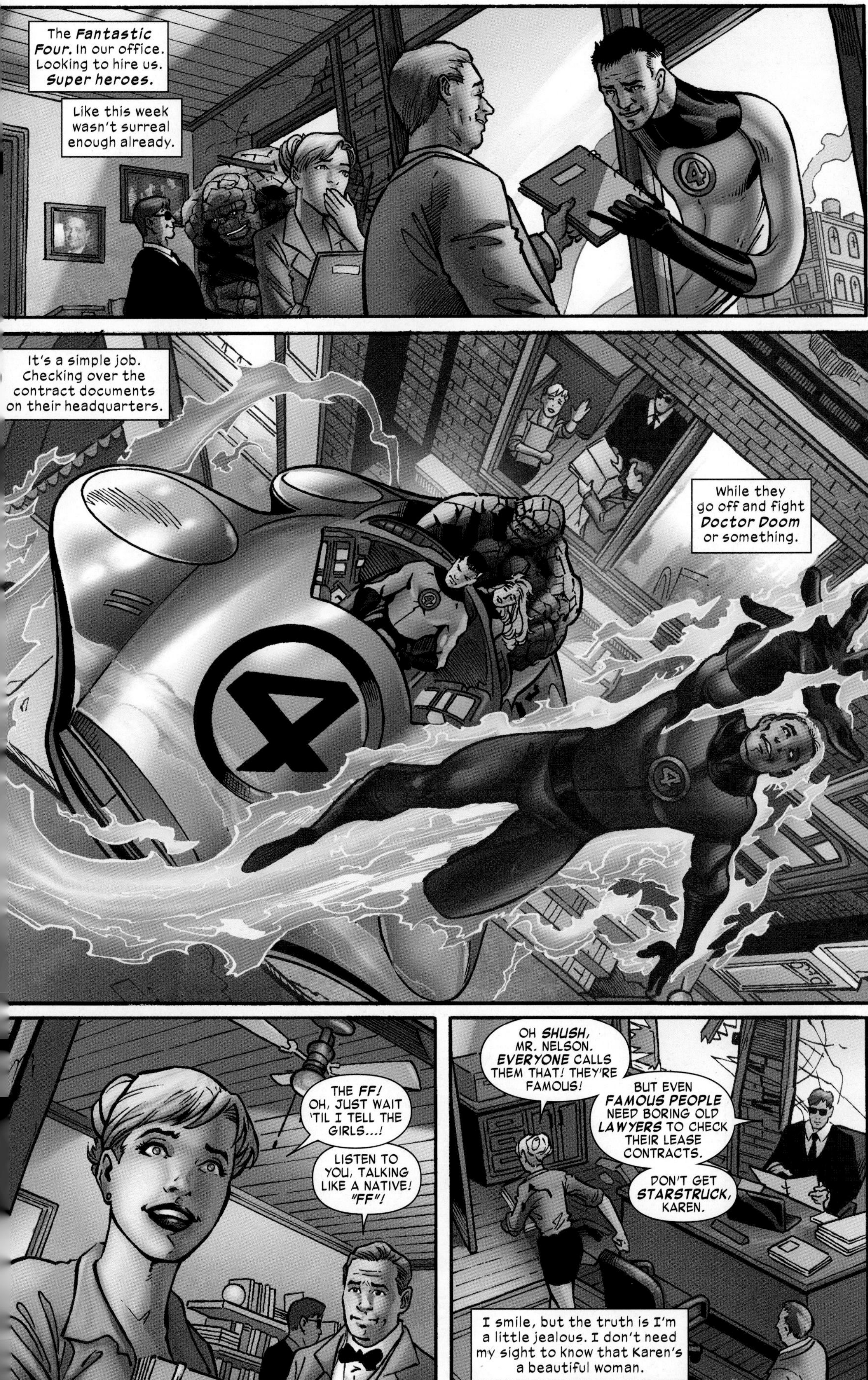

The *Fantastic Four.* In our office. Looking to hire us. ***Super heroes.***
Like this week wasn't surreal enough already.
It's a simple job. Checking over the contract documents on their headquarters.
While they go off and fight ***Doctor Doom*** or something.
THE ***FF!*** OH, JUST WAIT 'TIL I TELL THE GIRLS...!
LISTEN TO YOU, TALKING LIKE A NATIVE! ***"FF"!***
OH ***SHUSH,*** MR. NELSON. ***EVERYONE*** CALLS THEM THAT! THEY'RE FAMOUS!
BUT EVEN ***FAMOUS PEOPLE*** NEED BORING OLD ***LAWYERS*** TO CHECK THEIR LEASE CONTRACTS.
DON'T GET ***STARSTRUCK,*** KAREN.
I smile, but the truth is I'm a little jealous. I don't need my sight to know that Karen's a beautiful woman.

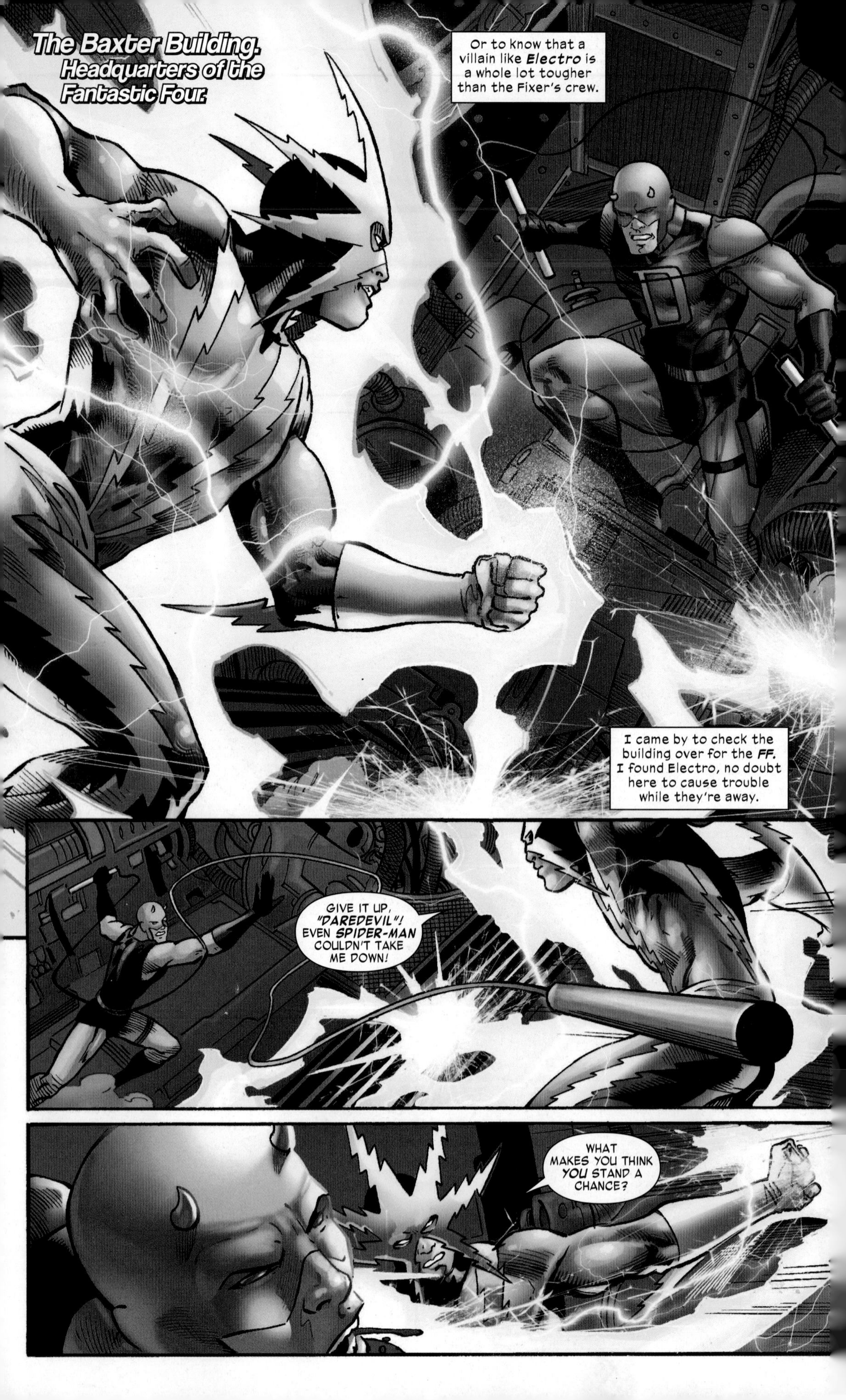
The Baxter Building. Headquarters of the Fantastic Four.
Or to know that a villain like Electro is a whole lot tougher than the Fixer's crew.
I came by to check the building over for the FF. I found Electro, no doubt here to cause trouble while they're away.
GIVE IT UP, "DAREDEVIL"! EVEN SPIDER-MAN COULDN'T TAKE ME DOWN!
WHAT MAKES YOU THINK YOU STAND A CHANCE?

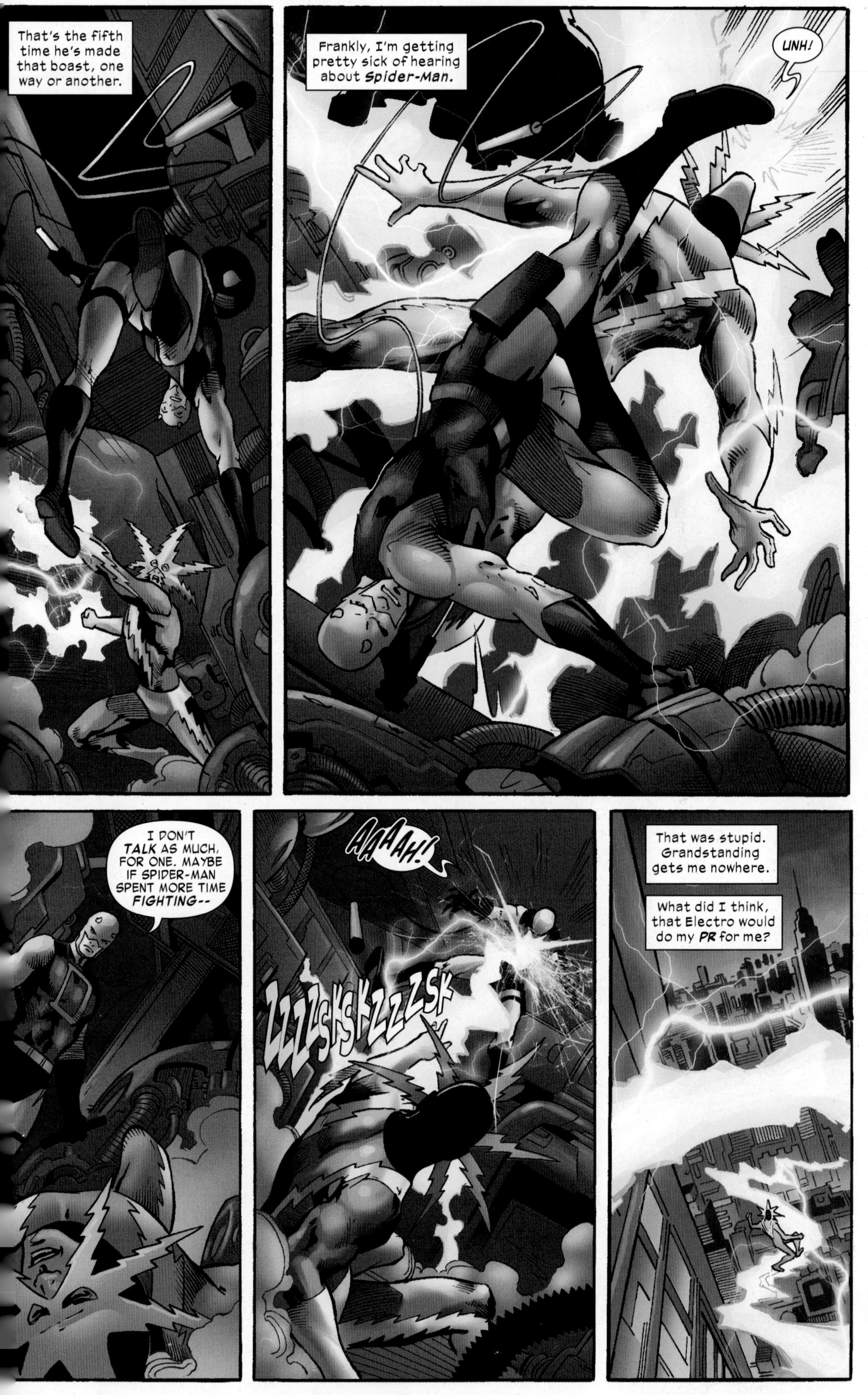
That's the fifth time he's made that boast, one way or another.
Frankly, I'm getting pretty sick of hearing about Spider-Man.
UNH!
I DON'T TALK AS MUCH, FOR ONE. MAYBE IF SPIDER-MAN SPENT MORE TIME FIGHTING--
AAAAAH!
ZZZZSKSKZZZZSK
That was stupid. Grandstanding gets me nowhere.
What did I think, that Electro would do my PR for me?

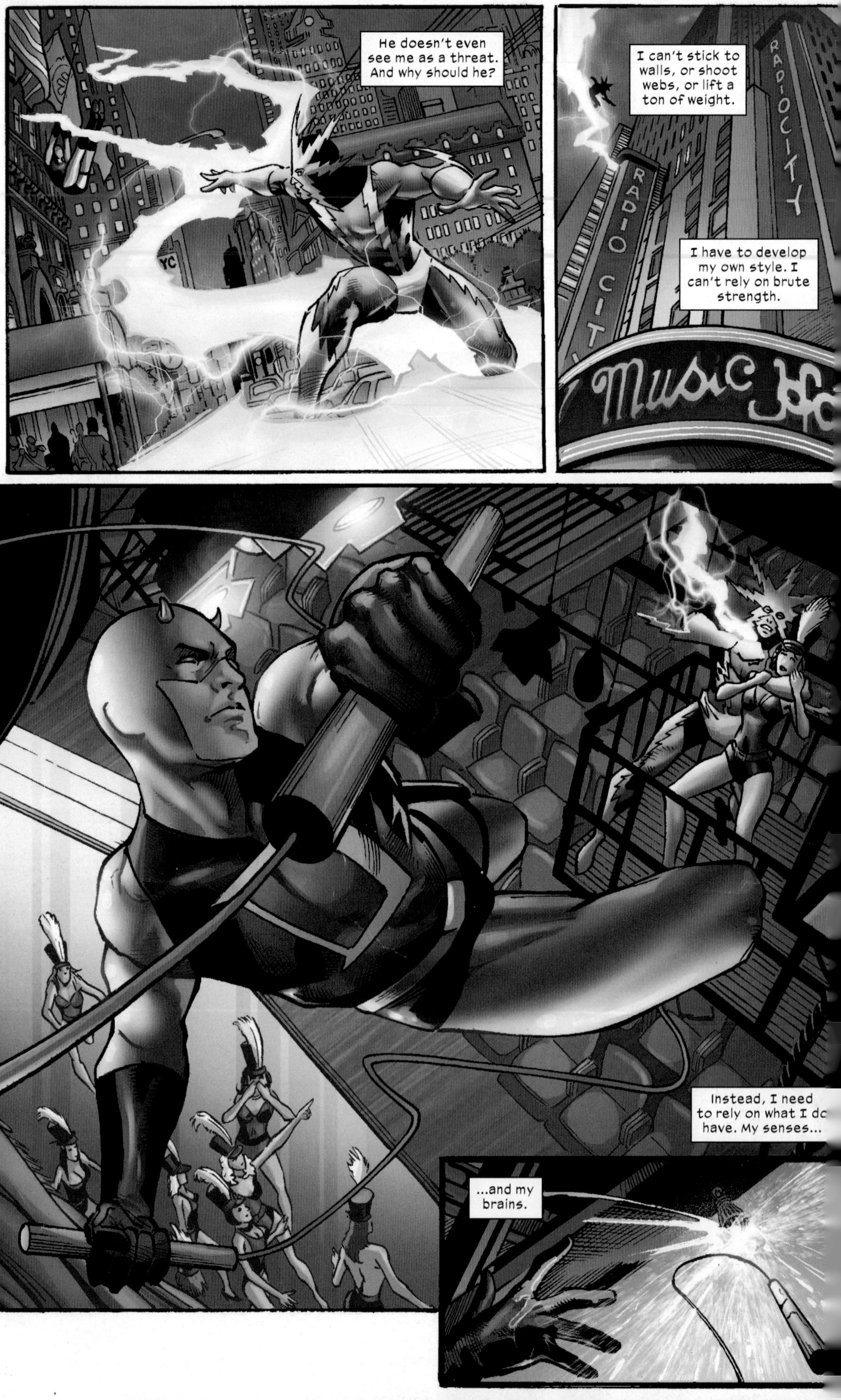
He doesn't even see me as a threat. And why should he?
I can't stick to walls, or shoot webs, or lift a ton of weight.
RADIOCITY
RADIO CITY
Music
I have to develop my own style. I can't rely on brute strength.
Instead, I need to rely on what I d
have. My senses...
...and my brains.

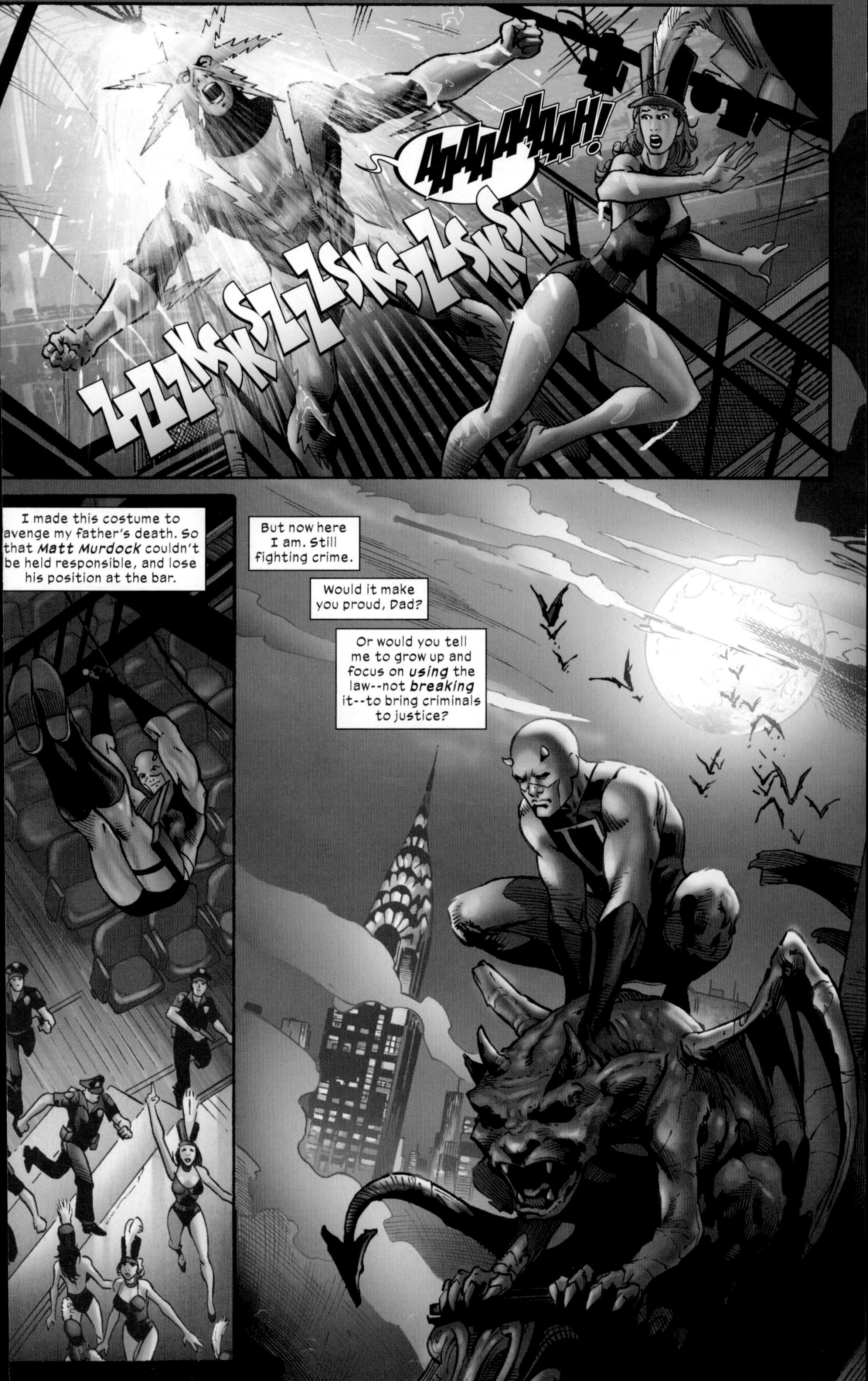
AAAAAAAAH!
I made this costume to avenge my father's death. So that *Matt Murdock* couldn't be held responsible, and lose his position at the bar.
But now here I am. Still fighting crime.
Would it make you proud, Dad?
Or would you tell me to grow up and focus on *using* the law--not *breaking* it--to bring criminals to justice?

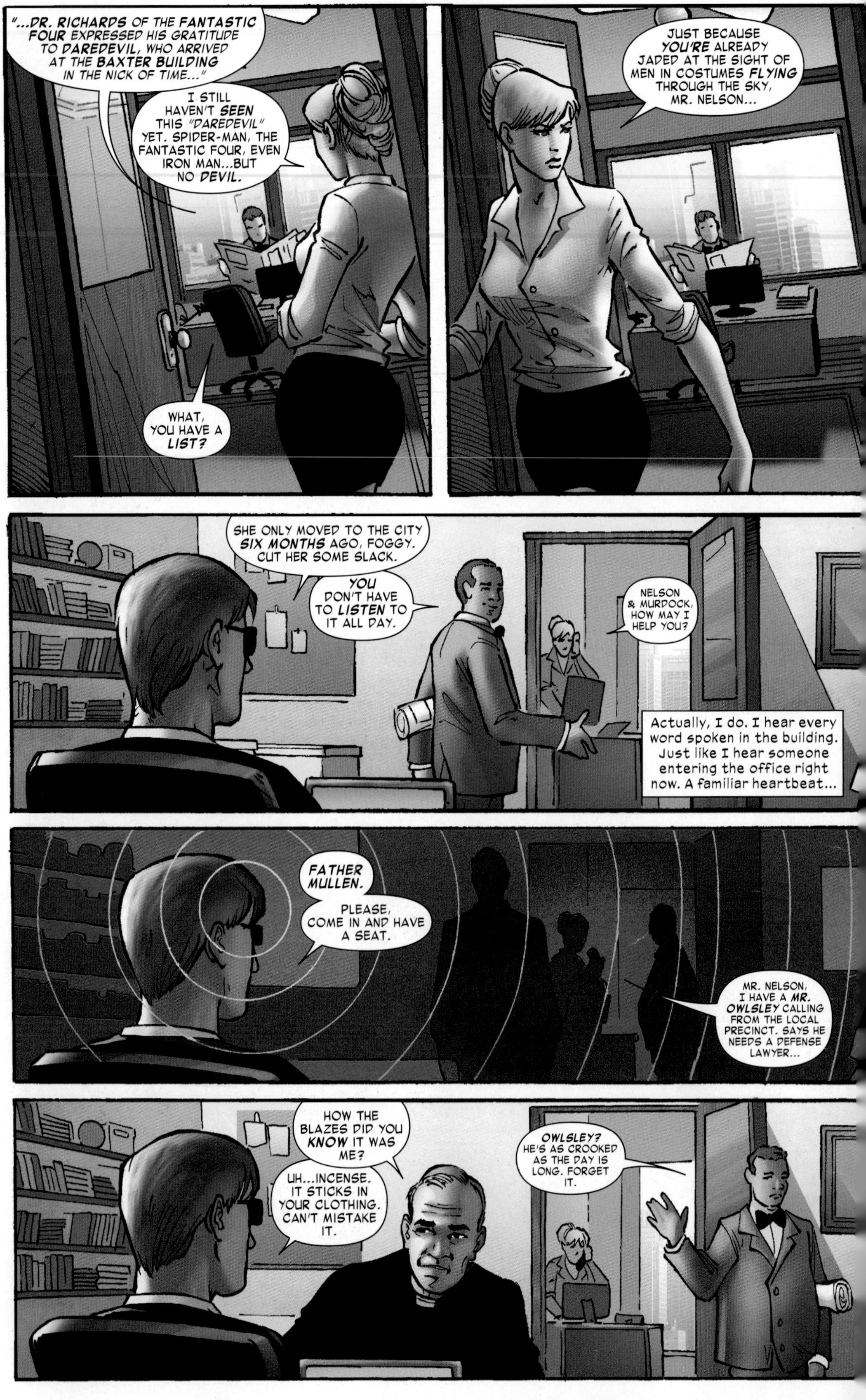
"...DR. RICHARDS OF THE FANTASTIC FOUR EXPRESSED HIS GRATITUDE TO DAREDEVIL, WHO ARRIVED AT THE BAXTER BUILDING IN THE NICK OF TIME..."
I STILL HAVEN'T SEEN THIS "DAREDEVIL" YET. SPIDER-MAN, THE FANTASTIC FOUR, EVEN IRON MAN...BUT NO DEVIL.
WHAT, YOU HAVE A LIST?
JUST BECAUSE YOU'RE ALREADY JADED AT THE SIGHT OF MEN IN COSTUMES FLYING THROUGH THE SKY, MR. NELSON...
SHE ONLY MOVED TO THE CITY SIX MONTHS AGO, FOGGY. CUT HER SOME SLACK.
YOU DON'T HAVE TO LISTEN TO IT ALL DAY.
NELSON & MURDOCK, HOW MAY I HELP YOU?
Actually, I do. I hear every word spoken in the building. Just like I hear someone entering the office right now. A familiar heartbeat...
FATHER MULLEN.
PLEASE, COME IN AND HAVE A SEAT.
MR. NELSON, I HAVE A MR. OWLSLEY CALLING FROM THE LOCAL PRECINCT. SAYS HE NEEDS A DEFENSE LAWYER...
HOW THE BLAZES DID YOU KNOW IT WAS ME?
UH...INCENSE. IT STICKS IN YOUR CLOTHING. CAN'T MISTAKE IT.
OWLSLEY? HE'S AS CROOKED AS THE DAY IS LONG. FORGET IT.

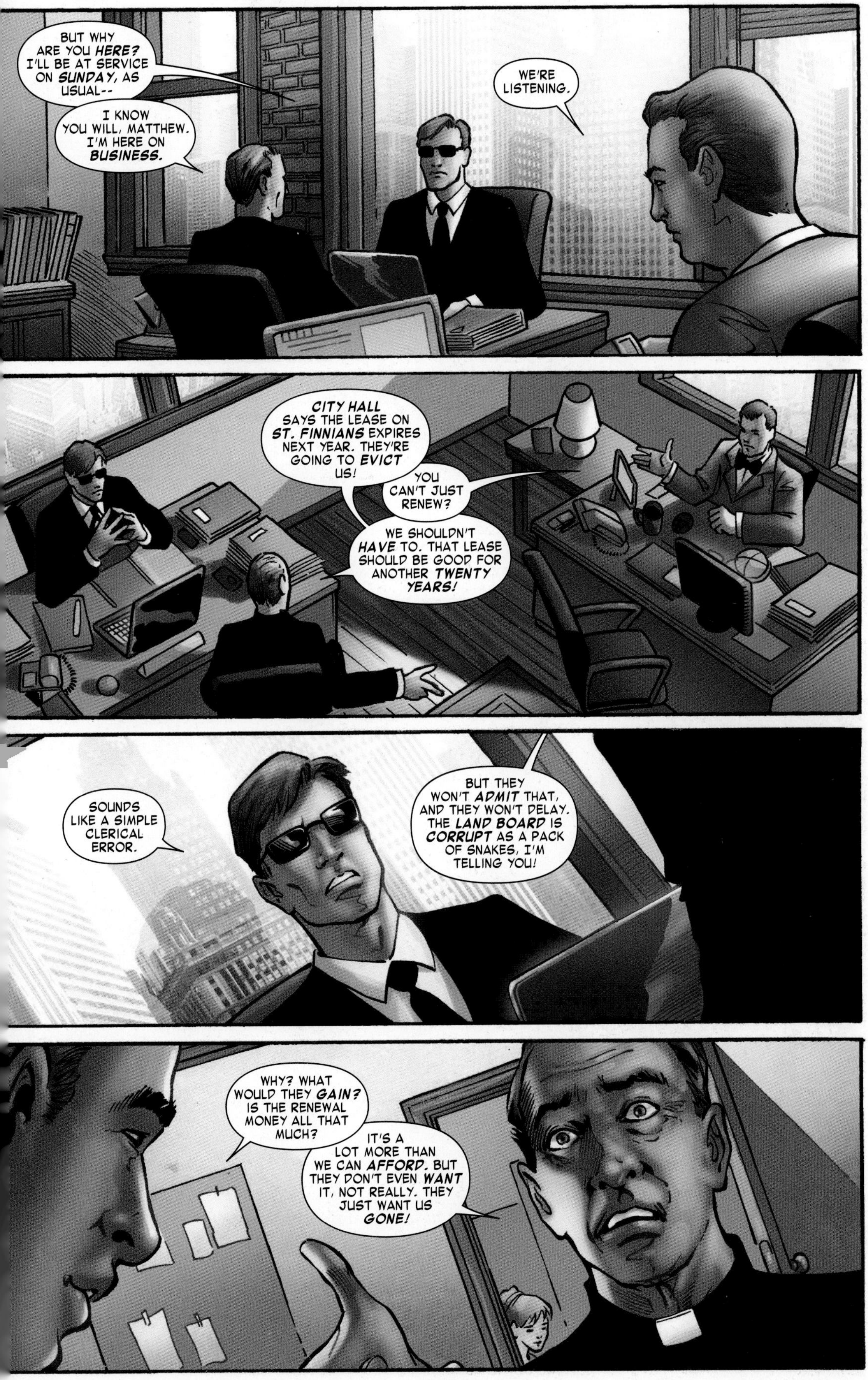
BUT WHY ARE YOU HERE? I'LL BE AT SERVICE ON SUNDAY, AS USUAL--
I KNOW YOU WILL, MATTHEW. I'M HERE ON BUSINESS.
WE'RE LISTENING.
CITY HALL SAYS THE LEASE ON ST. FINNIANS EXPIRES NEXT YEAR. THEY'RE GOING TO EVICT US!
YOU CAN'T JUST RENEW?
WE SHOULDN'T HAVE TO. THAT LEASE SHOULD BE GOOD FOR ANOTHER TWENTY YEARS!
SOUNDS LIKE A SIMPLE CLERICAL ERROR.
BUT THEY WON'T ADMIT THAT, AND THEY WON'T DELAY. THE LAND BOARD IS CORRUPT AS A PACK OF SNAKES, I'M TELLING YOU!
WHY? WHAT WOULD THEY GAIN? IS THE RENEWAL MONEY ALL THAT MUCH?
IT'S A LOT MORE THAN WE CAN AFFORD. BUT THEY DON'T EVEN WANT IT, NOT REALLY. THEY JUST WANT US GONE!

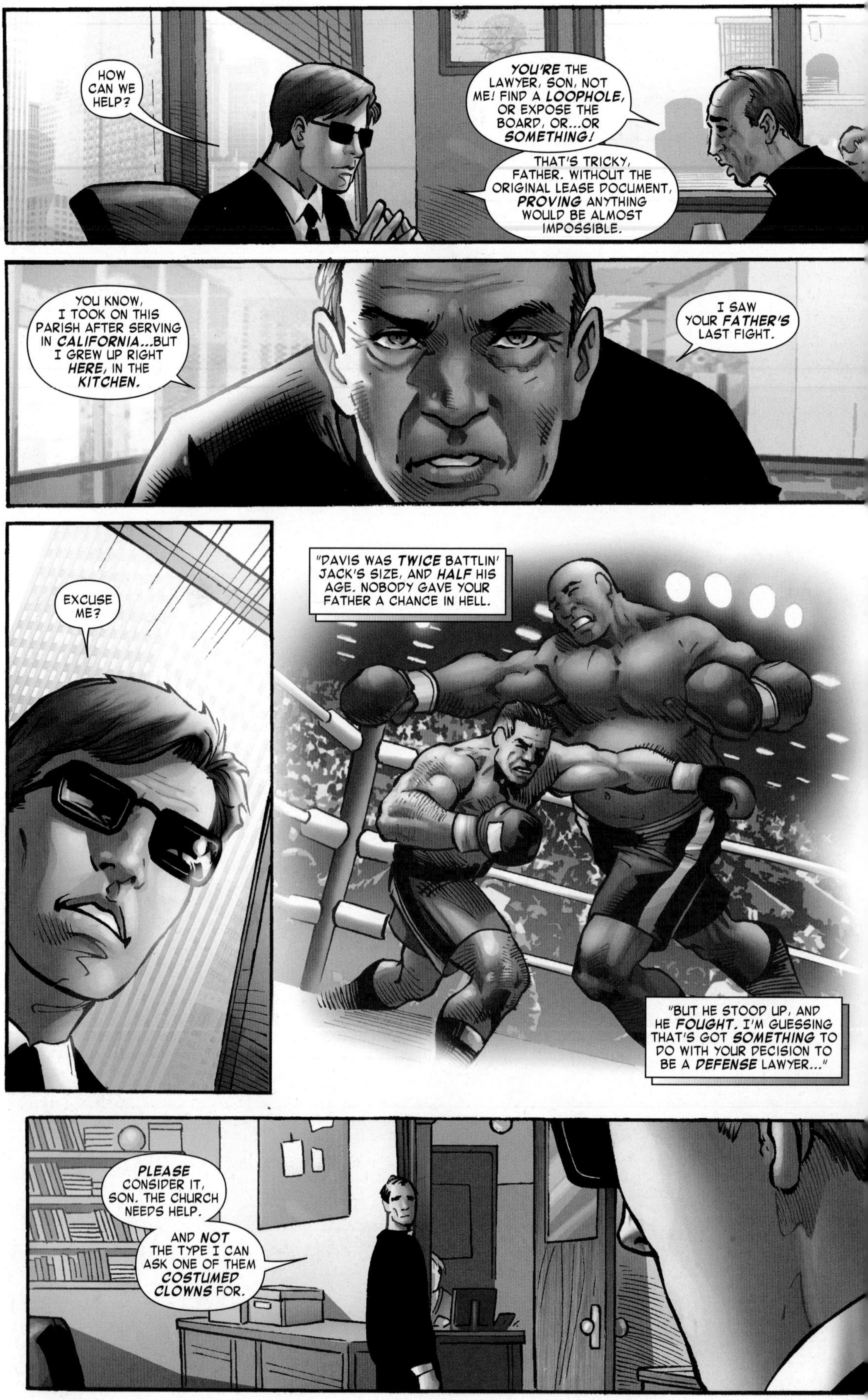
HOW CAN WE HELP?
YOU'RE THE LAWYER, SON, NOT ME! FIND A LOOPHOLE, OR EXPOSE THE BOARD, OR...OR SOMETHING!
THAT'S TRICKY, FATHER. WITHOUT THE ORIGINAL LEASE DOCUMENT, PROVING ANYTHING WOULD BE ALMOST IMPOSSIBLE.
YOU KNOW, I TOOK ON THIS PARISH AFTER SERVING IN CALIFORNIA...BUT I GREW UP RIGHT HERE, IN THE KITCHEN.
I SAW YOUR FATHER'S LAST FIGHT.
EXCUSE ME?
"DAVIS WAS TWICE BATTLIN' JACK'S SIZE, AND HALF HIS AGE. NOBODY GAVE YOUR FATHER A CHANCE IN HELL.
"BUT HE STOOD UP, AND HE FOUGHT. I'M GUESSING THAT'S GOT SOMETHING TO DO WITH YOUR DECISION TO BE A DEFENSE LAWYER..."
PLEASE CONSIDER IT, SON. THE CHURCH NEEDS HELP.
AND NOT THE TYPE I CAN ASK ONE OF THEM COSTUMED CLOWNS FOR.

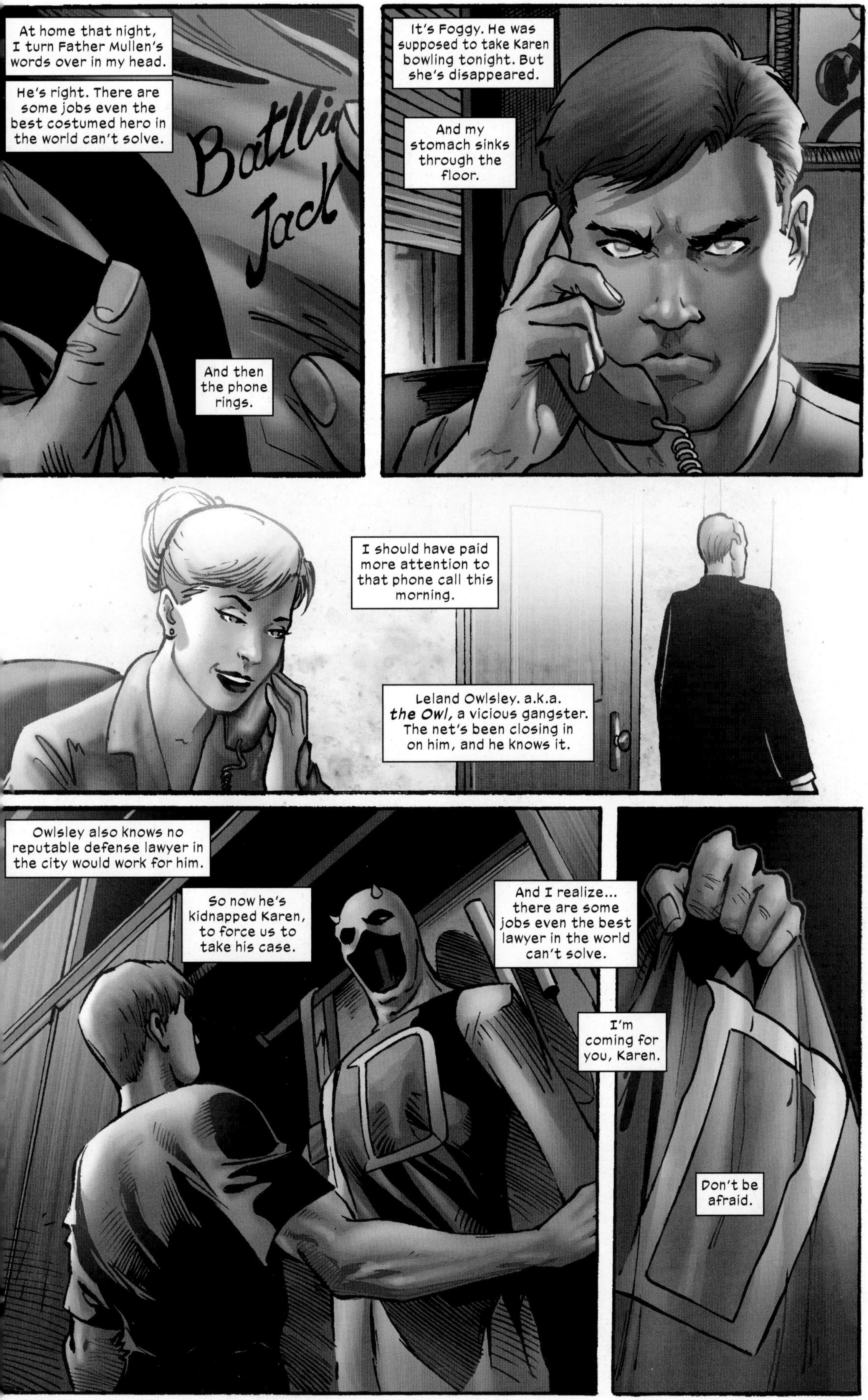

At home that night, I turn Father Mullen's words over in my head.
He's right. There are some jobs even the best costumed hero in the world can't solve.
Battlin' Jack
And then the phone rings.
It's Foggy. He was supposed to take Karen bowling tonight. But she's disappeared.
And my stomach sinks through the floor.
I should have paid more attention to that phone call this morning.
Leland Owlsley. a.k.a. *the Owl,* a vicious gangster. The net's been closing in on him, and he knows it.
Owlsley also knows no reputable defense lawyer in the city would work for him.
So now he's kidnapped Karen, to force us to take his case.
And I realize... there are some jobs even the best lawyer in the world can't solve.
I'm coming for you, Karen.
Don't be afraid.

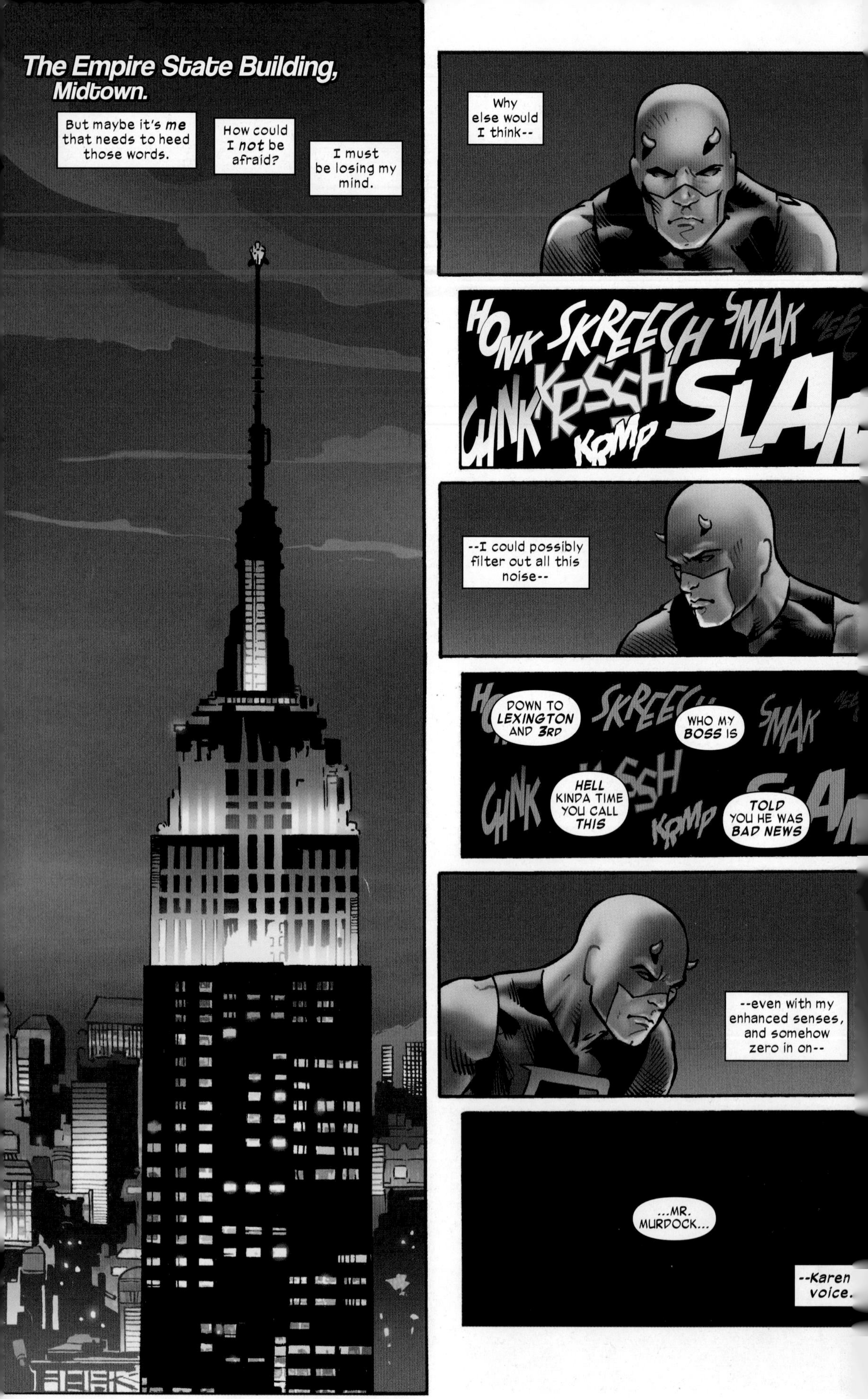
The Empire State Building, Midtown.
But maybe it's *me* that needs to heed those words.
How could I *not* be afraid?
I must be losing my mind.
Why else would I think--
HONK SKREECH SMAK
CHINK KRSSH KRMP SLAM
--I could possibly filter out all this noise--
DOWN TO LEXINGTON AND 3RD
WHO MY BOSS IS
HELL KINDA TIME YOU CALL THIS
TOLD YOU HE WAS BAD NEWS
--even with my enhanced senses, and somehow zero in on--
...MR. MURDOCK...
--Karen voice.

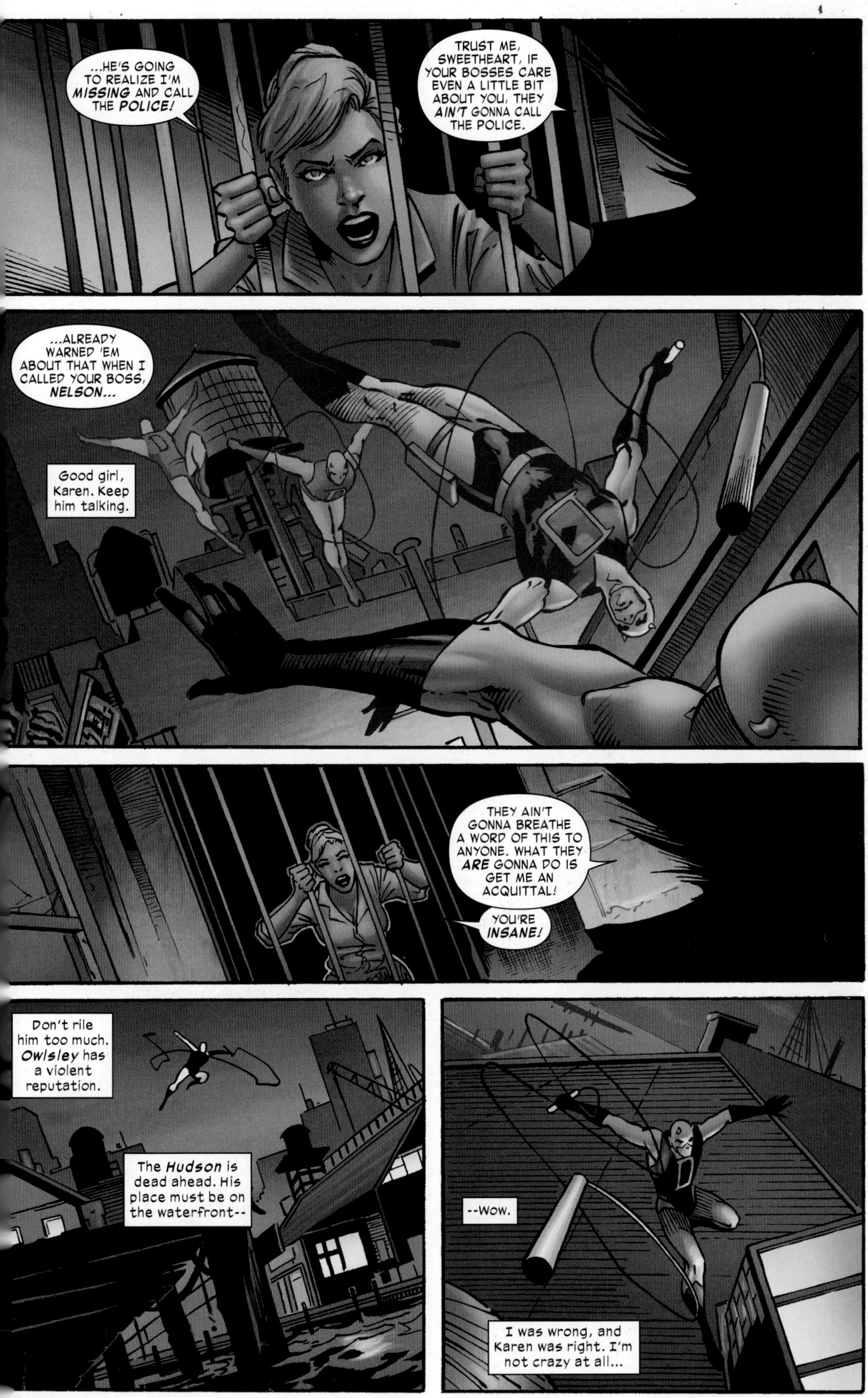
...HE'S GOING TO REALIZE I'M MISSING AND CALL THE POLICE!
TRUST ME, SWEETHEART, IF YOUR BOSSES CARE EVEN A LITTLE BIT ABOUT YOU, THEY AIN'T GONNA CALL THE POLICE.
...ALREADY WARNED 'EM ABOUT THAT WHEN I CALLED YOUR BOSS, NELSON...
Good girl, Karen. Keep him talking.
THEY AIN'T GONNA BREATHE A WORD OF THIS TO ANYONE. WHAT THEY ARE GONNA DO IS GET ME AN ACQUITTAL!
YOU'RE INSANE!
Don't rile him too much. Owlsley has a violent reputation.
The Hudson is dead ahead. His place must be on the waterfront--
--WOW.
I was wrong, and Karen was right. I'm not crazy at all...

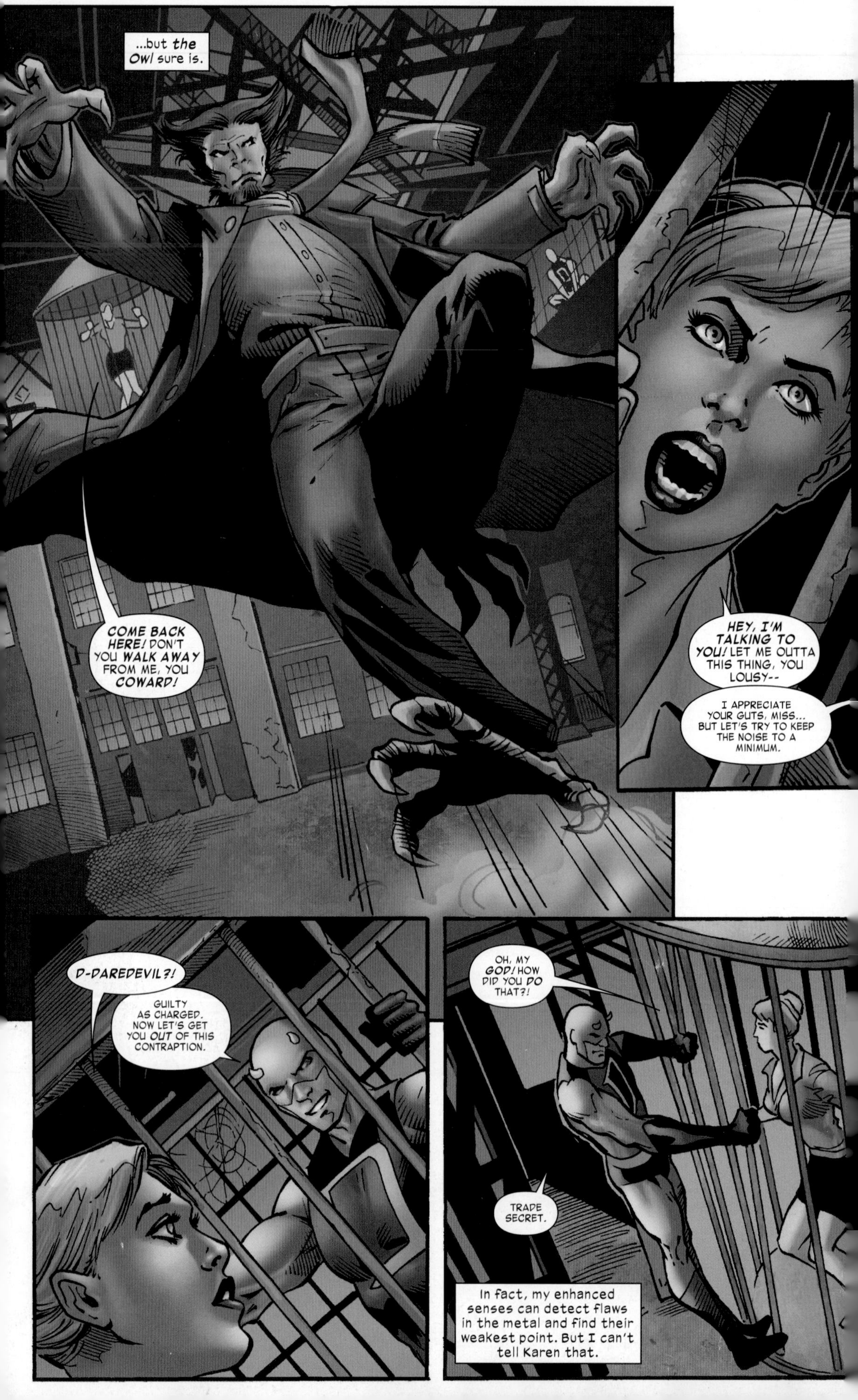
...but *the Owl* sure is.
HEY, I'M TALKING TO YOU! LET ME OUTTA THIS THING, YOU LOUSY--
COME BACK HERE! DON'T YOU WALK AWAY FROM ME, YOU COWARD!
I APPRECIATE YOUR GUTS, MISS... BUT LET'S TRY TO KEEP THE NOISE TO A MINIMUM.
D-DAREDEVIL?!
GUILTY AS CHARGED. NOW LET'S GET YOU OUT OF THIS CONTRAPTION.
OH, MY GOD! HOW DID YOU DO THAT?!
TRADE SECRET.
In fact, my enhanced senses can detect flaws in the metal and find their weakest point. But I can't tell Karen that.

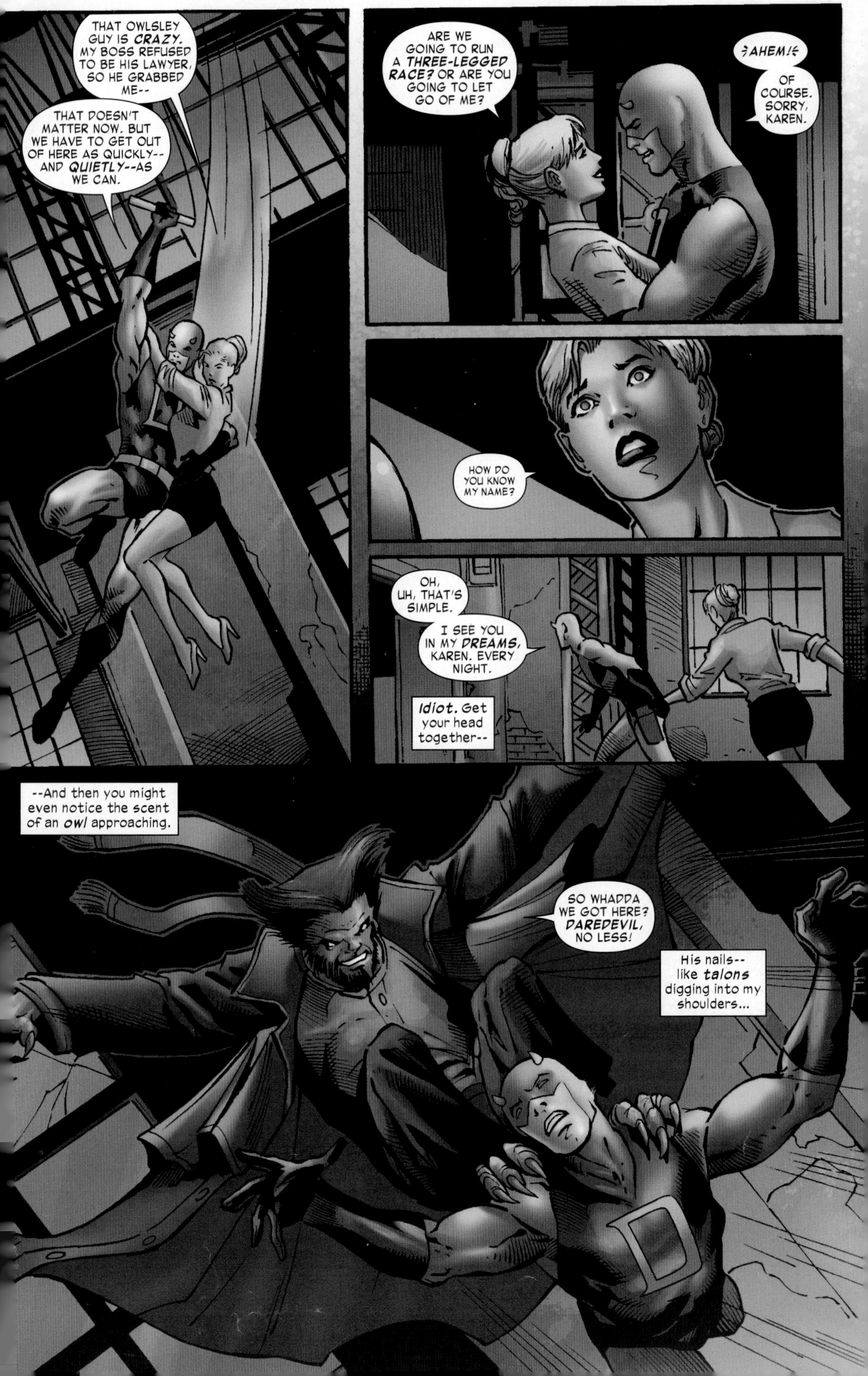
THAT OWLSLEY GUY IS CRAZY. MY BOSS REFUSED TO BE HIS LAWYER, SO HE GRABBED ME--
THAT DOESN'T MATTER NOW. BUT WE HAVE TO GET OUT OF HERE AS QUICKLY-- AND QUIETLY--AS WE CAN.
ARE WE GOING TO RUN A THREE-LEGGED RACE? OR ARE YOU GOING TO LET GO OF ME?
AHEM!
OF COURSE. SORRY, KAREN.
HOW DO YOU KNOW MY NAME?
OH, UH, THAT'S SIMPLE.
I SEE YOU IN MY DREAMS, KAREN. EVERY NIGHT.
Idiot. Get your head together--
--And then you might even notice the scent of an owl approaching.
SO WHADDA WE GOT HERE? DAREDEVIL, NO LESS!
His nails-- like talons digging into my shoulders...

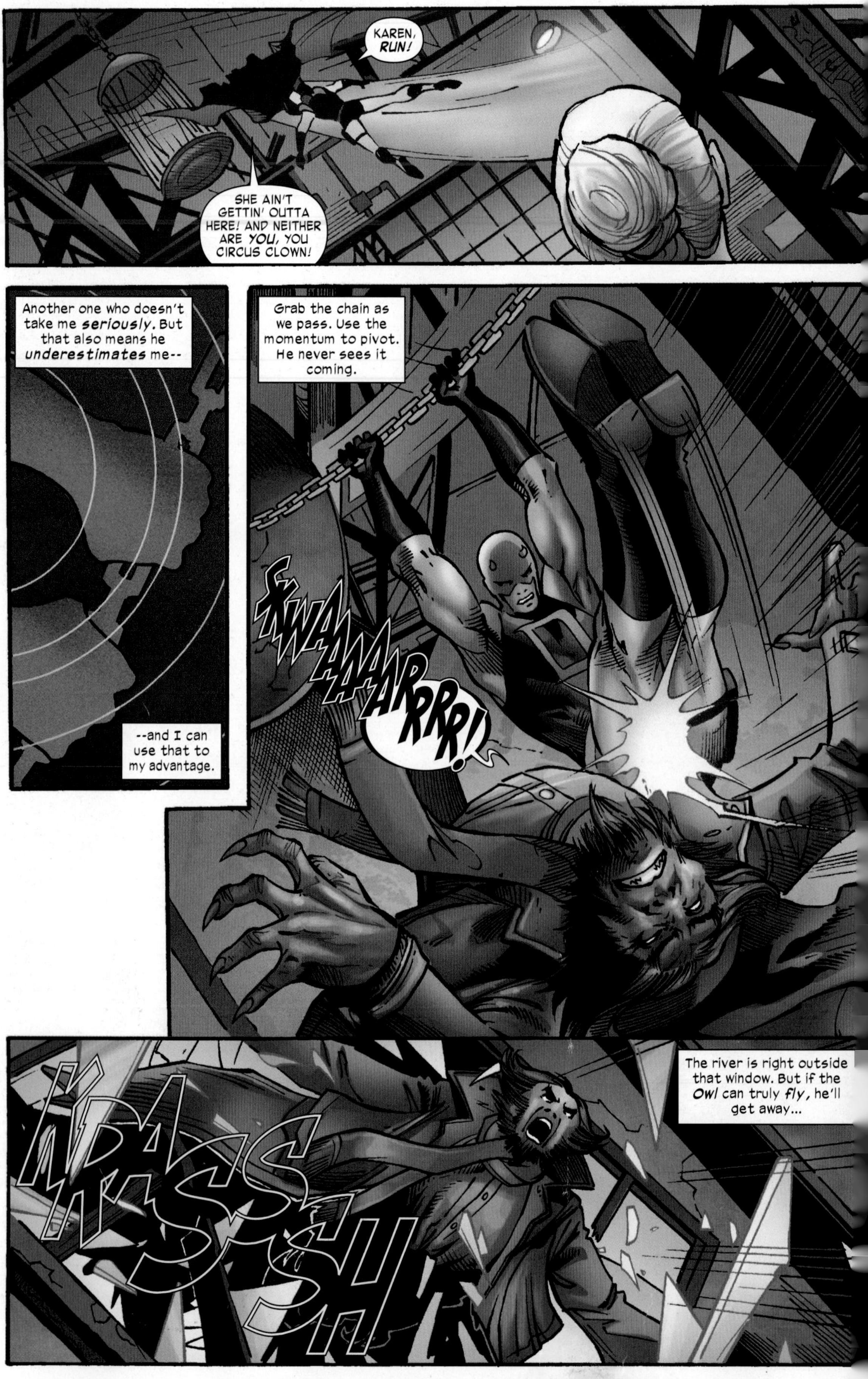
KAREN, RUN!
SHE AIN'T GETTIN' OUTTA HERE! AND NEITHER ARE YOU, YOU CIRCUS CLOWN!
Another one who doesn't take me seriously. But that also means he underestimates me--
--and I can use that to my advantage.
Grab the chain as we pass. Use the momentum to pivot. He never sees it coming.
FWAAAARRRR!
KRASSH
The river is right outside that window. But if the Owl can truly fly, he'll get away...

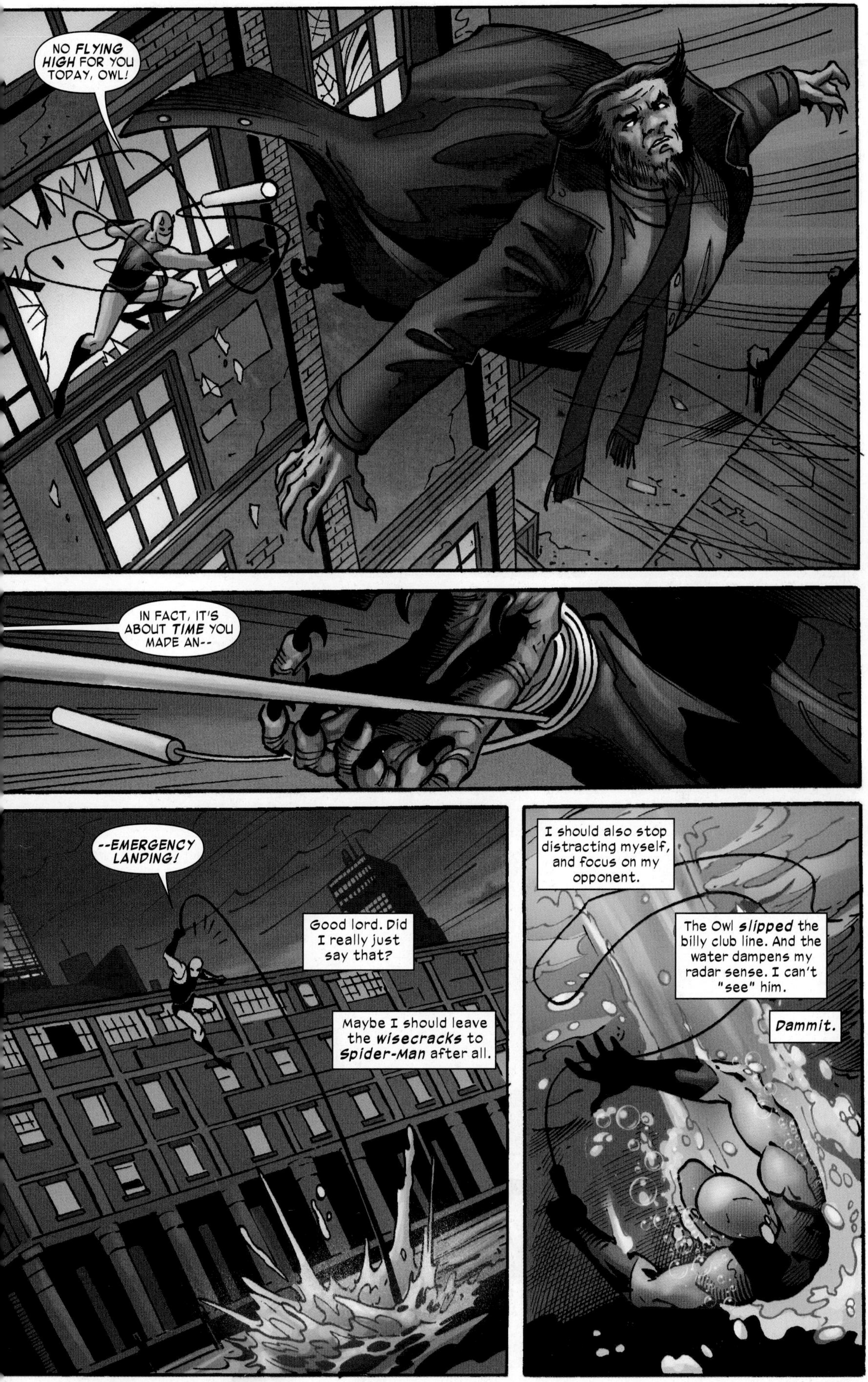
NO FLYING HIGH FOR YOU TODAY, OWL!
IN FACT, IT'S ABOUT TIME YOU MADE AN--
--EMERGENCY LANDING!
Good lord. Did I really just say that?
Maybe I should leave the wisecracks to Spider-Man after all.
I should also stop distracting myself, and focus on my opponent.
The Owl slipped the billy club line. And the water dampens my radar sense. I can't "see" him.
Dammit.

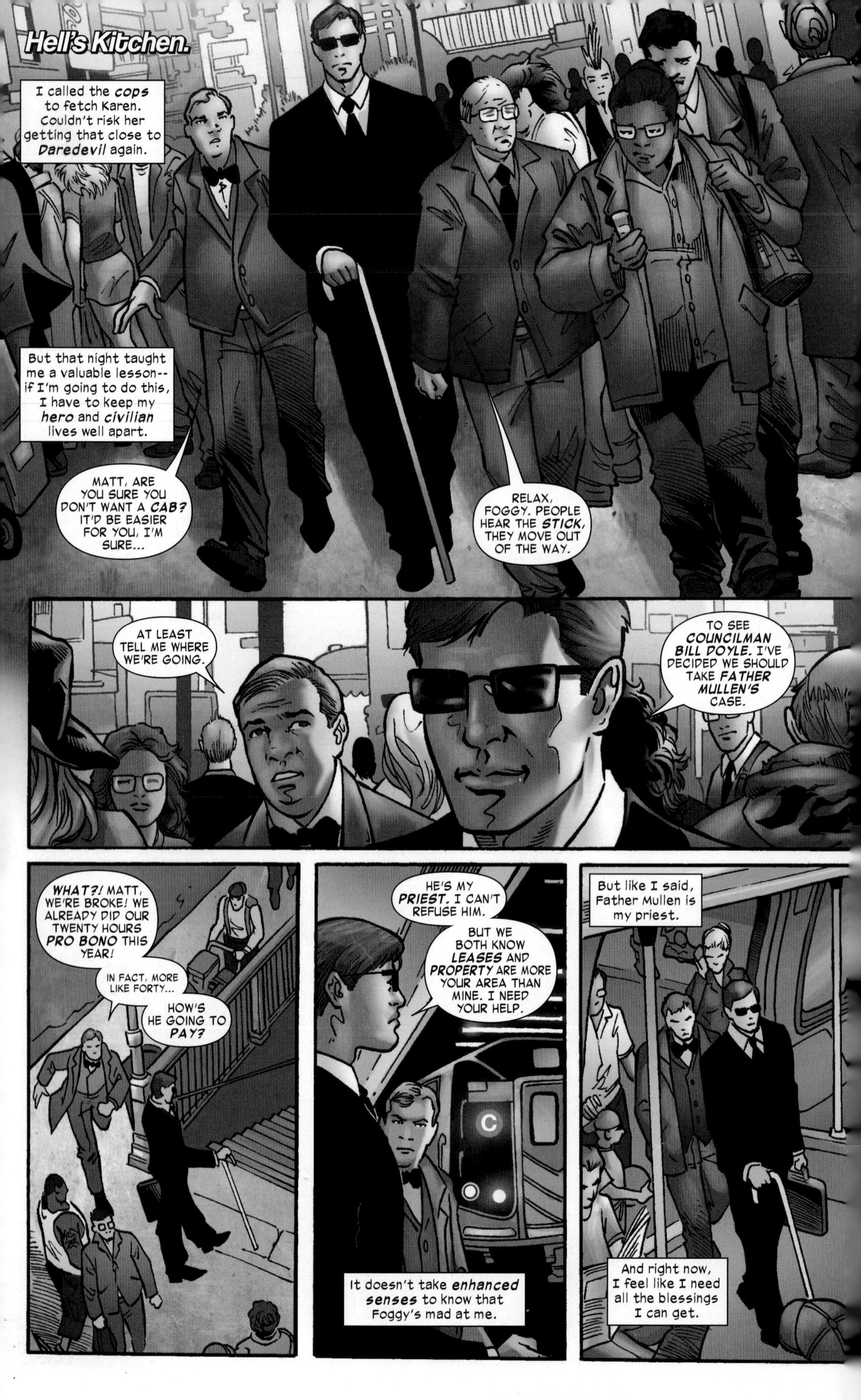

Hell's Kitchen.
I called the cops to fetch Karen. Couldn't risk her getting that close to Daredevil again.
But that night taught me a valuable lesson-- if I'm going to do this, I have to keep my hero and civilian lives well apart.
MATT, ARE YOU SURE YOU DON'T WANT A CAB? IT'D BE EASIER FOR YOU, I'M SURE...
RELAX, FOGGY. PEOPLE HEAR THE STICK, THEY MOVE OUT OF THE WAY.
AT LEAST TELL ME WHERE WE'RE GOING.
TO SEE COUNCILMAN BILL DOYLE. I'VE DECIDED WE SHOULD TAKE FATHER MULLEN'S CASE.
WHAT?! MATT, WE'RE BROKE! WE ALREADY DID OUR TWENTY HOURS PRO BONO THIS YEAR!
IN FACT, MORE LIKE FORTY...
HOW'S HE GOING TO PAY?
HE'S MY PRIEST. I CAN'T REFUSE HIM.
BUT WE BOTH KNOW LEASES AND PROPERTY ARE MORE YOUR AREA THAN MINE. I NEED YOUR HELP.
It doesn't take enhanced senses to know that Foggy's mad at me.
But like I said, Father Mullen is my priest.
And right now, I feel like I need all the blessings I can get.

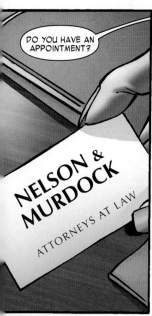

DO YOU HAVE AN APPOINTMENT?

NELSON & MURDOCK
ATTORNEYS AT LAW

Office of Councilman William Doyle, Hell's Kitchen.

UH, WELL...

THREE O'CLOCK. I CALLED AHEAD, AND I BELIEVE IT WAS YOU I SPOKE TO. REMEMBER?

I *know* it was her. Even allowing for phone distortion, there's no mistaking her tonal signature.

SURE, I GUESS. WAIT HERE.

Or that reedy *Brooklyn twang.*

DON'T MAKE THEM WAIT, DARLING. MY DOOR'S *ALWAYS* OPEN.

COME IN, FELLAS.

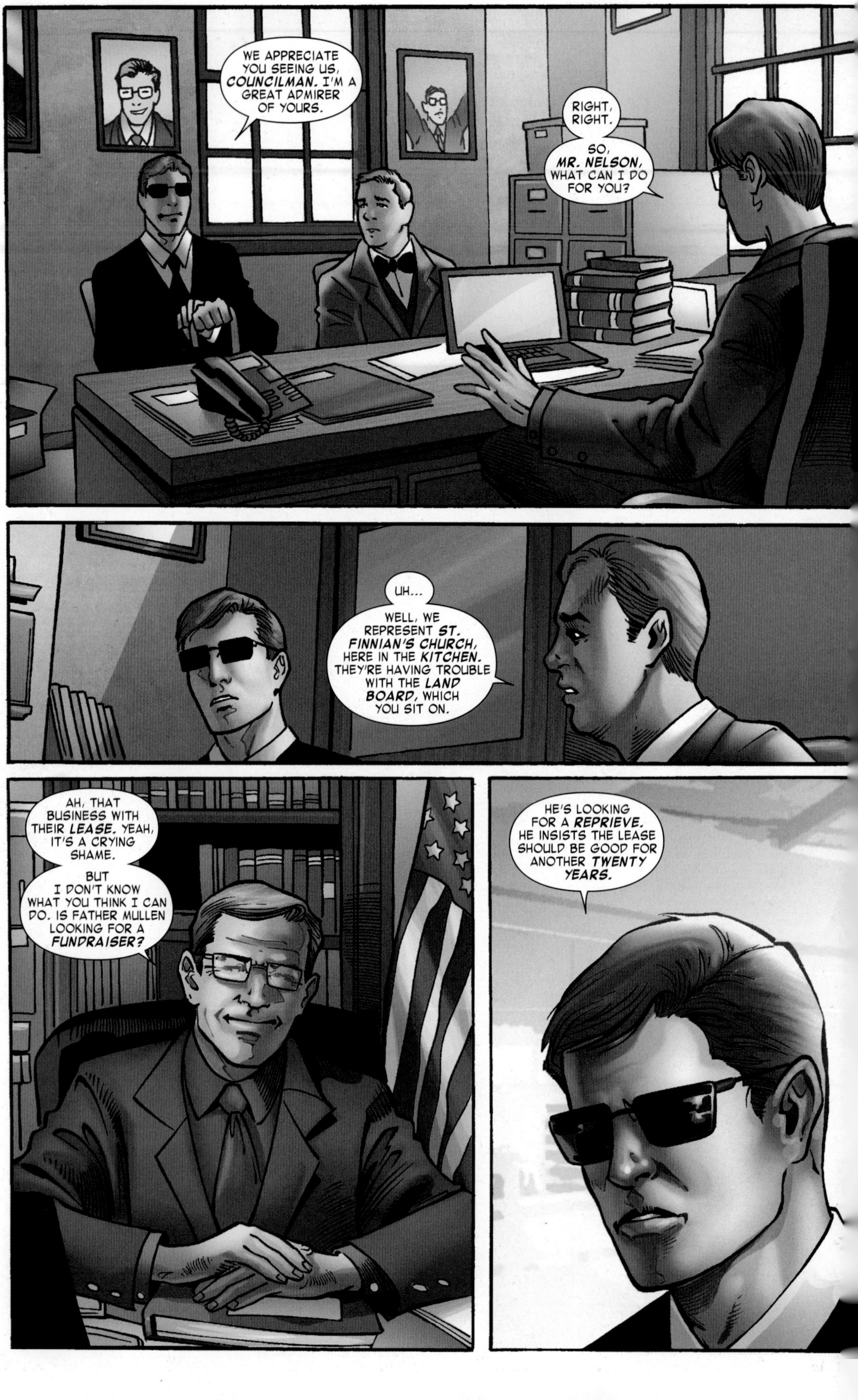
WE APPRECIATE YOU SEEING US, COUNCILMAN. I'M A GREAT ADMIRER OF YOURS.
RIGHT, RIGHT.
SO, MR. NELSON, WHAT CAN I DO FOR YOU?
UH...
WELL, WE REPRESENT ST. FINNIAN'S CHURCH, HERE IN THE KITCHEN. THEY'RE HAVING TROUBLE WITH THE LAND BOARD, WHICH YOU SIT ON.
AH, THAT BUSINESS WITH THEIR LEASE. YEAH, IT'S A CRYING SHAME.
BUT I DON'T KNOW WHAT YOU THINK I CAN DO. IS FATHER MULLEN LOOKING FOR A FUNDRAISER?
HE'S LOOKING FOR A REPRIEVE. HE INSISTS THE LEASE SHOULD BE GOOD FOR ANOTHER TWENTY YEARS.

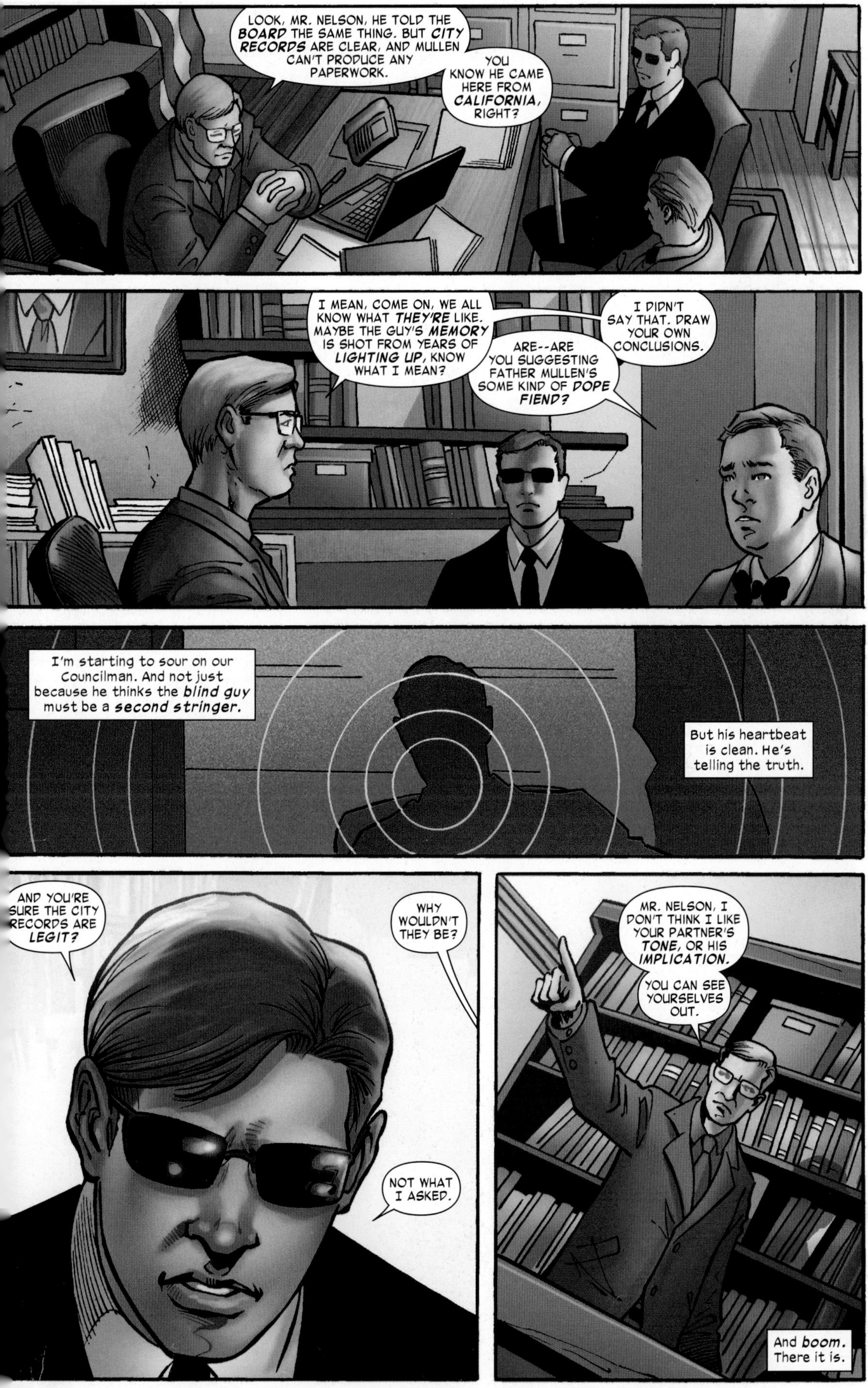

LOOK, MR. NELSON, HE TOLD THE BOARD THE SAME THING. BUT CITY RECORDS ARE CLEAR, AND MULLEN CAN'T PRODUCE ANY PAPERWORK.
YOU KNOW HE CAME HERE FROM CALIFORNIA, RIGHT?
I MEAN, COME ON, WE ALL KNOW WHAT THEY'RE LIKE. MAYBE THE GUY'S MEMORY IS SHOT FROM YEARS OF LIGHTING UP, KNOW WHAT I MEAN?
ARE--ARE YOU SUGGESTING FATHER MULLEN'S SOME KIND OF DOPE FIEND?
I DIDN'T SAY THAT. DRAW YOUR OWN CONCLUSIONS.
I'm starting to sour on our Councilman. And not just because he thinks the blind guy must be a second stringer.
But his heartbeat is clean. He's telling the truth.
AND YOU'RE SURE THE CITY RECORDS ARE LEGIT?
WHY WOULDN'T THEY BE?
NOT WHAT I ASKED.
MR. NELSON, I DON'T THINK I LIKE YOUR PARTNER'S TONE, OR HIS IMPLICATION.
YOU CAN SEE YOURSELVES OUT.
And boom. There it is.

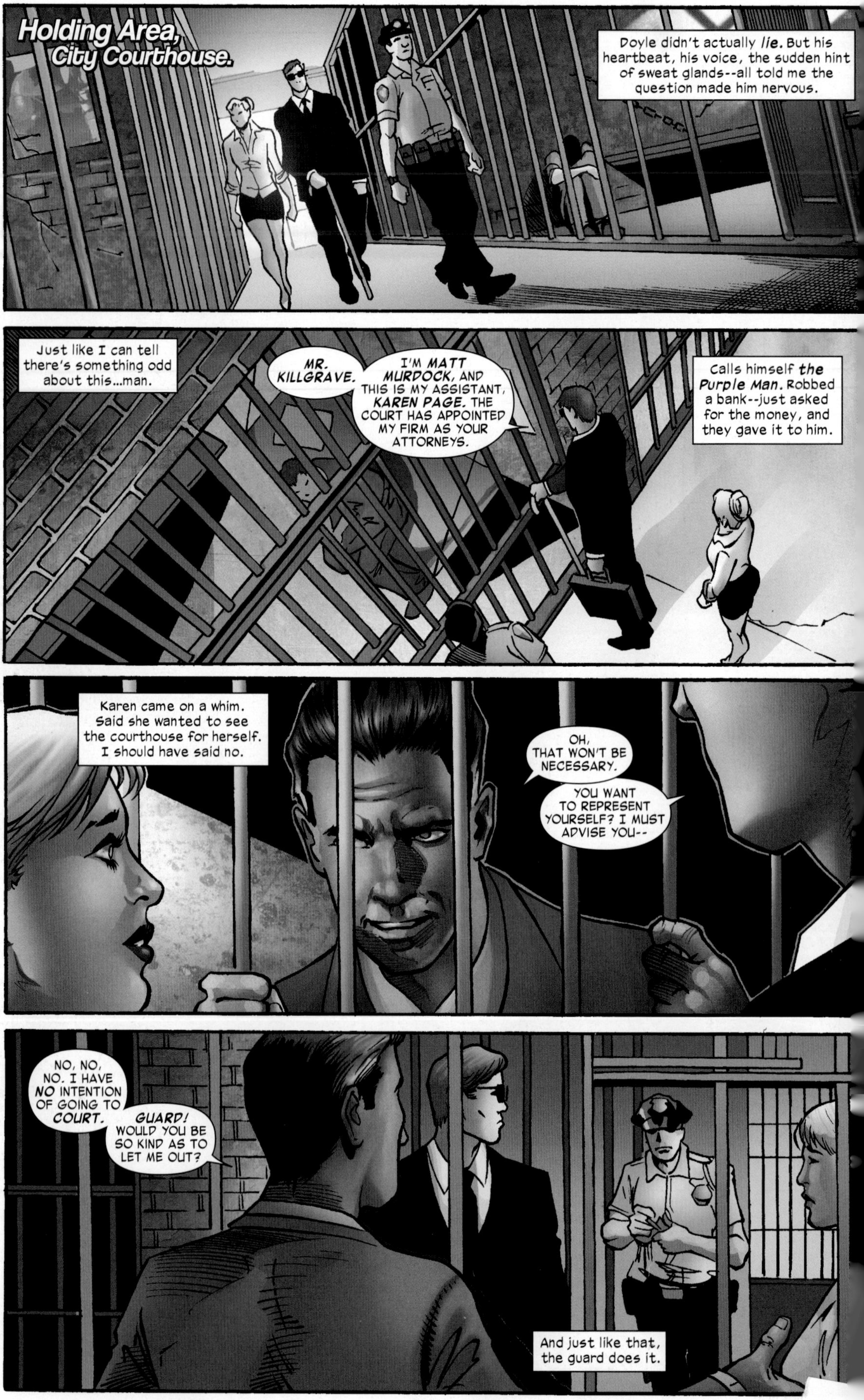

Holding Area, City Courthouse.
Doyle didn't actually *lie*. But his heartbeat, his voice, the sudden hint of sweat glands--all told me the question made him nervous.
Just like I can tell there's something odd about this...man.
MR. KILLGRAVE.
I'M MATT MURDOCK, AND THIS IS MY ASSISTANT, KAREN PAGE. THE COURT HAS APPOINTED MY FIRM AS YOUR ATTORNEYS.
Calls himself *the Purple Man*. Robbed a bank--just asked for the money, and they gave it to him.
Karen came on a whim. Said she wanted to see the courthouse for herself. I should have said no.
OH, THAT WON'T BE NECESSARY.
YOU WANT TO REPRESENT YOURSELF? I MUST ADVISE YOU--
NO, NO, NO. I HAVE NO INTENTION OF GOING TO COURT.
GUARD! WOULD YOU BE SO KIND AS TO LET ME OUT?
And just like that, the guard does it.

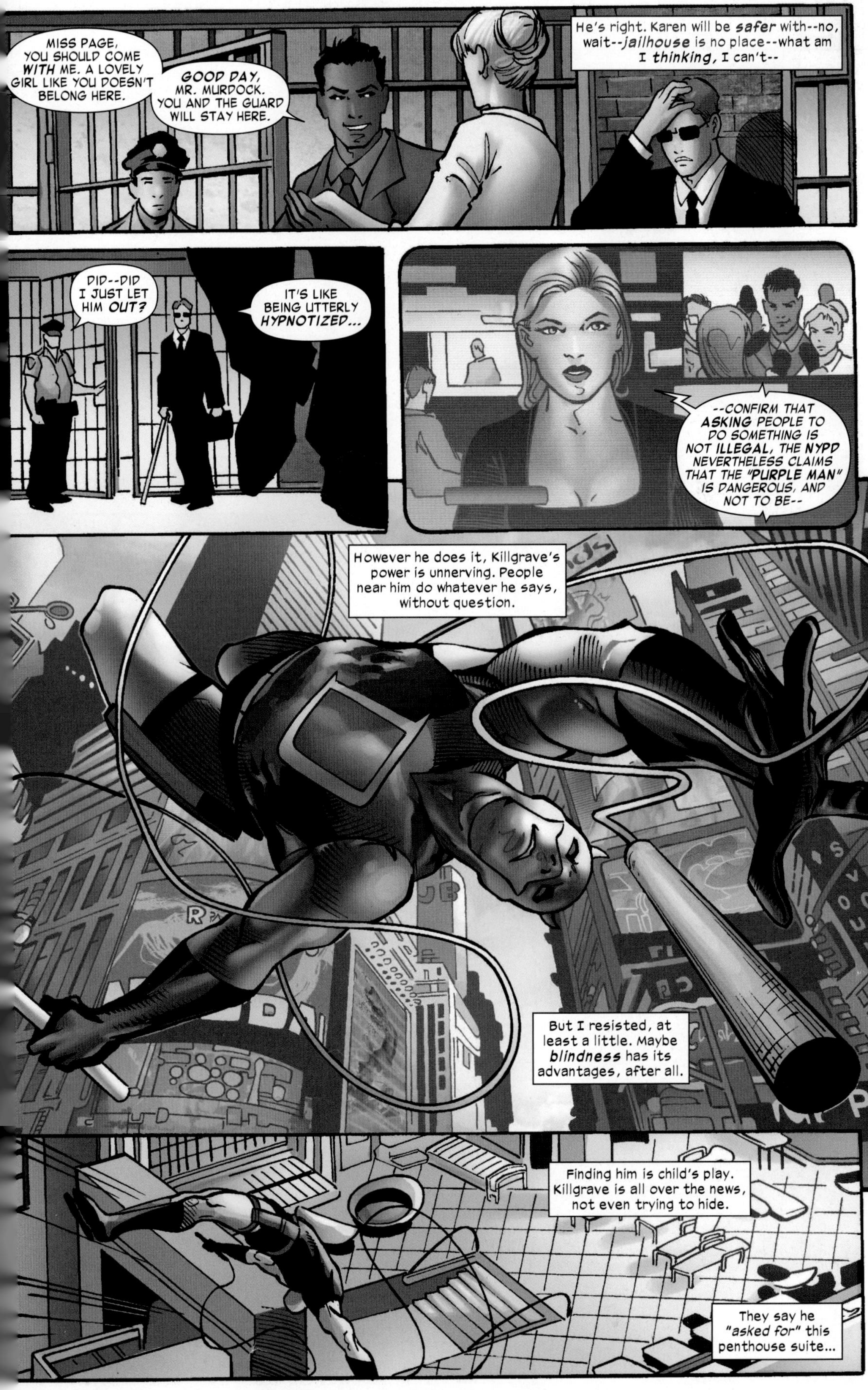
MISS PAGE, YOU SHOULD COME WITH ME. A LOVELY GIRL LIKE YOU DOESN'T BELONG HERE.
GOOD DAY, MR. MURDOCK. YOU AND THE GUARD WILL STAY HERE.
He's right. Karen will be safer with--no, wait--jailhouse is no place--what am I thinking, I can't--
DID--DID I JUST LET HIM OUT?
IT'S LIKE BEING UTTERLY HYPNOTIZED...
--CONFIRM THAT ASKING PEOPLE TO DO SOMETHING IS NOT ILLEGAL, THE NYPD NEVERTHELESS CLAIMS THAT THE "PURPLE MAN" IS DANGEROUS, AND NOT TO BE--
However he does it, Killgrave's power is unnerving. People near him do whatever he says, without question.
But I resisted, at least a little. Maybe blindness has its advantages, after all.
Finding him is child's play. Killgrave is all over the news, not even trying to hide.
They say he "asked for" this penthouse suite...

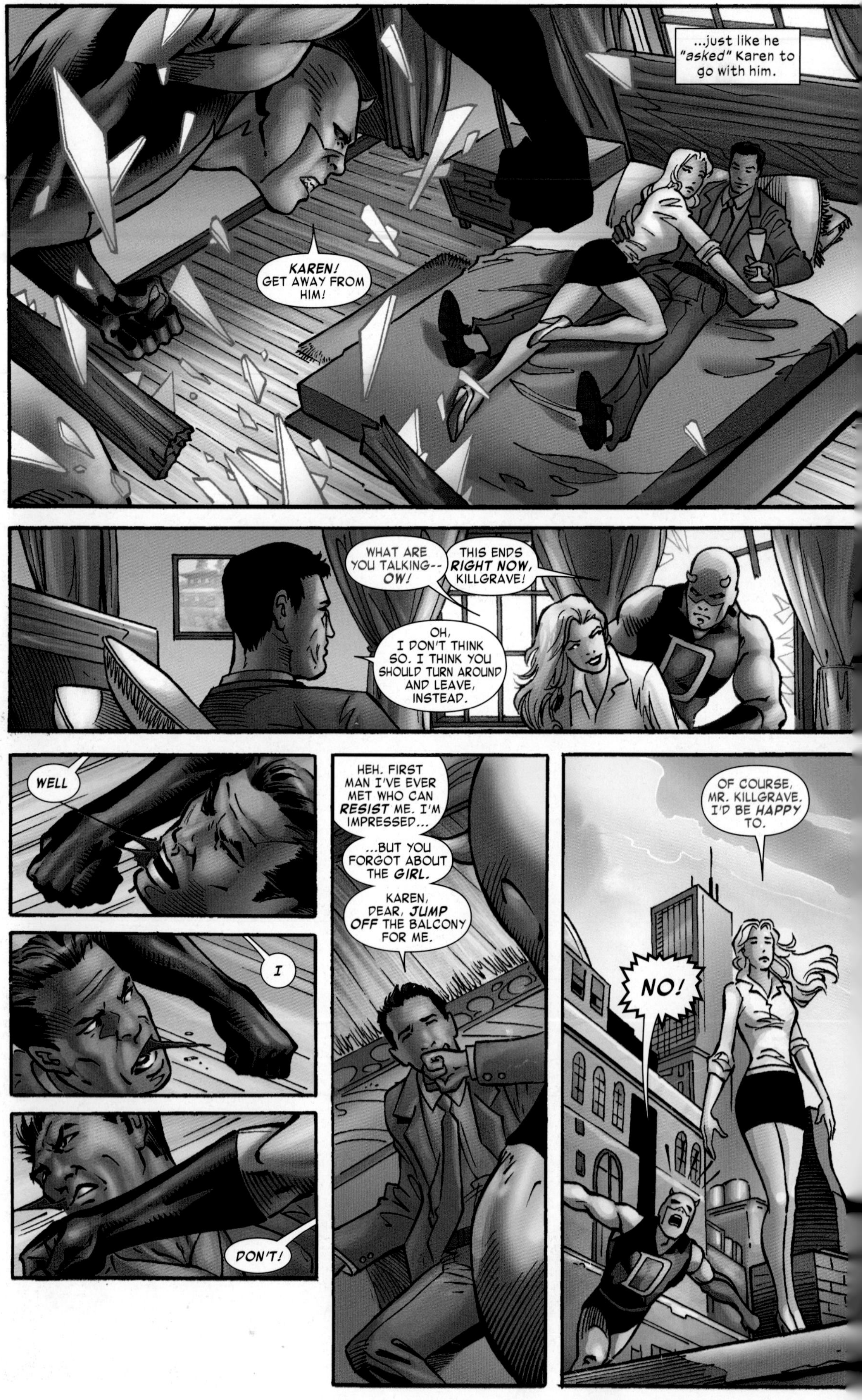
...just like he "asked" Karen to go with him.
KAREN! GET AWAY FROM HIM!
WHAT ARE YOU TALKING-- OW!
THIS ENDS RIGHT NOW, KILLGRAVE!
OH, I DON'T THINK SO. I THINK YOU SHOULD TURN AROUND AND LEAVE, INSTEAD.
WELL
I
DON'T!
HEH. FIRST MAN I'VE EVER MET WHO CAN RESIST ME. I'M IMPRESSED...
...BUT YOU FORGOT ABOUT THE GIRL.
KAREN, DEAR, JUMP OFF THE BALCONY FOR ME.
OF COURSE, MR. KILLGRAVE. I'D BE HAPPY TO.
NO!

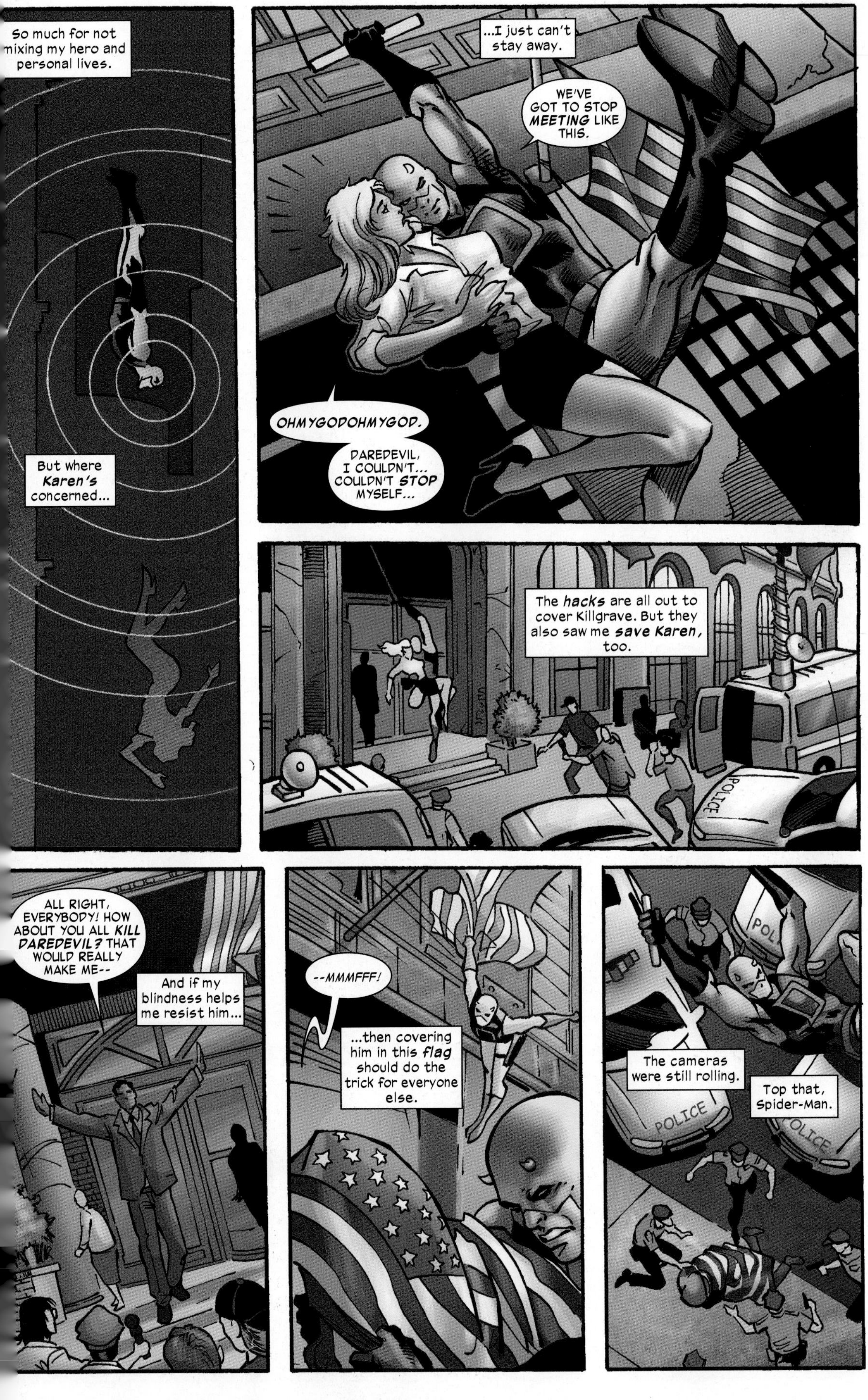
So much for not mixing my hero and personal lives.
But where Karen's concerned...
...I just can't stay away.
WE'VE GOT TO STOP MEETING LIKE THIS.
OHMYGODOHMYGOD.
DAREDEVIL, I COULDN'T... COULDN'T STOP MYSELF...
The hacks are all out to cover Killgrave. But they also saw me save Karen, too.
POLICE
ALL RIGHT, EVERYBODY! HOW ABOUT YOU ALL KILL DAREDEVIL? THAT WOULD REALLY MAKE ME--
And if my blindness helps me resist him...
--MMMFFF!
...then covering him in this flag should do the trick for everyone else.
POLICE
The cameras were still rolling.
POLICE
POLICE
Top that, Spider-Man.

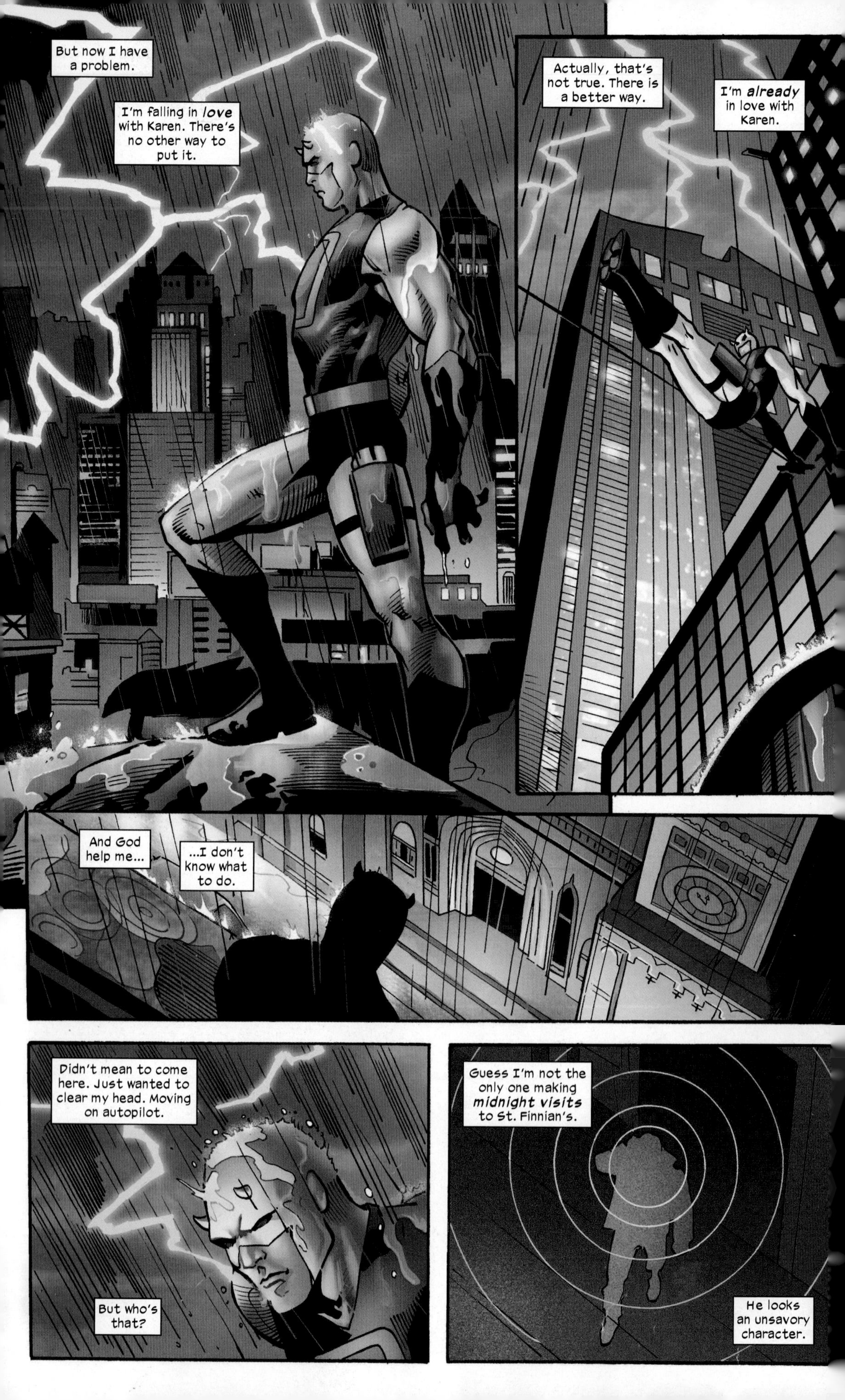
But now I have a problem.
I'm falling in *love* with Karen. There's no other way to put it.
Actually, that's not true. There is a better way.
I'm *already* in love with Karen.
And God help me...
...I don't know what to do.
Didn't mean to come here. Just wanted to clear my head. Moving on autopilot.
But who's that?
Guess I'm not the only one making *midnight visits* to St. Finnian's.
He looks an unsavory character.

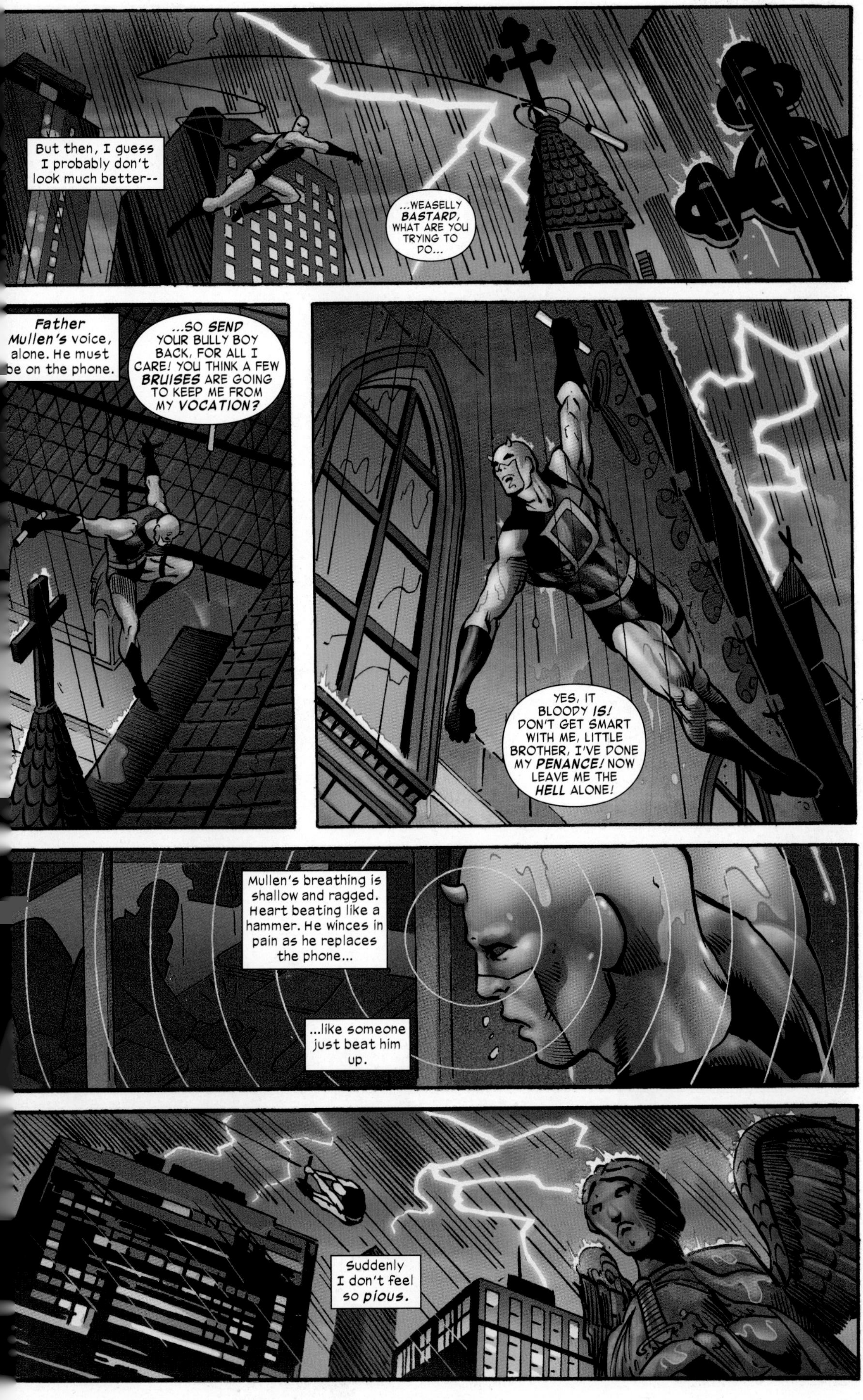

But then, I guess I probably don't look much better--
...WEASELLY BASTARD, WHAT ARE YOU TRYING TO DO...
Father Mullen's voice, alone. He must be on the phone.
...SO SEND YOUR BULLY BOY BACK, FOR ALL I CARE! YOU THINK A FEW BRUISES ARE GOING TO KEEP ME FROM MY VOCATION?
YES, IT BLOODY IS! DON'T GET SMART WITH ME, LITTLE BROTHER, I'VE DONE MY PENANCE! NOW LEAVE ME THE HELL ALONE!
Mullen's breathing is shallow and ragged. Heart beating like a hammer. He winces in pain as he replaces the phone...
...like someone just beat him up.
Suddenly I don't feel so pious.

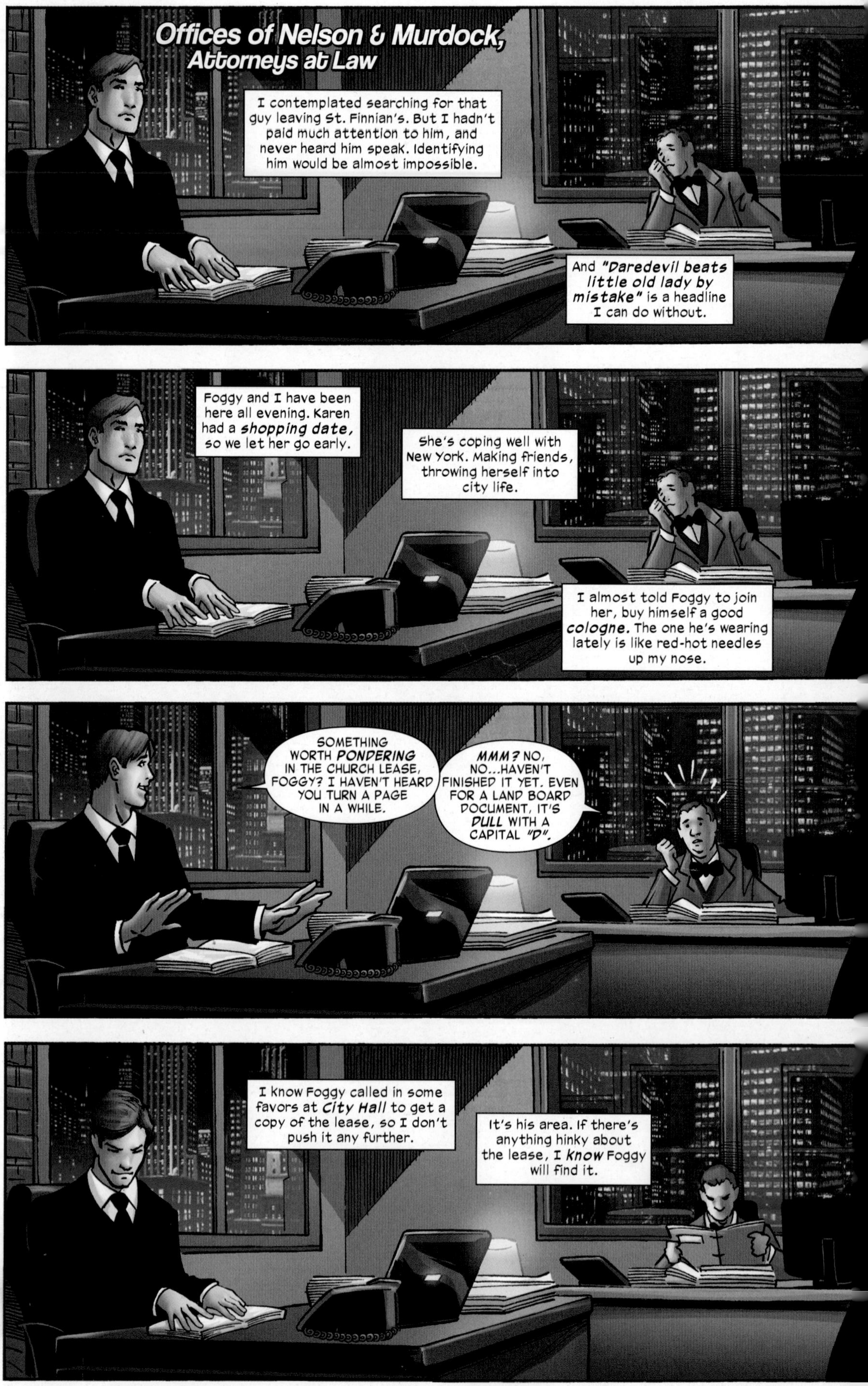
Offices of Nelson & Murdock, Attorneys at Law
I contemplated searching for that guy leaving St. Finnian's. But I hadn't paid much attention to him, and never heard him speak. Identifying him would be almost impossible.
And *"Daredevil beats little old lady by mistake"* is a headline I can do without.
Foggy and I have been here all evening. Karen had a *shopping date,* so we let her go early.
She's coping well with New York. Making friends, throwing herself into city life.
I almost told Foggy to join her, buy himself a good *cologne.* The one he's wearing lately is like red-hot needles up my nose.
SOMETHING WORTH *PONDERING* IN THE CHURCH LEASE, FOGGY? I HAVEN'T HEARD YOU TURN A PAGE IN A WHILE.
MMM? NO, NO...HAVEN'T FINISHED IT YET. EVEN FOR A LAND BOARD DOCUMENT, IT'S *DULL* WITH A CAPITAL *"D"*.
I know Foggy called in some favors at *City Hall* to get a copy of the lease, so I don't push it any further.
It's his area. If there's anything hinky about the lease, I *know* Foggy will find it.

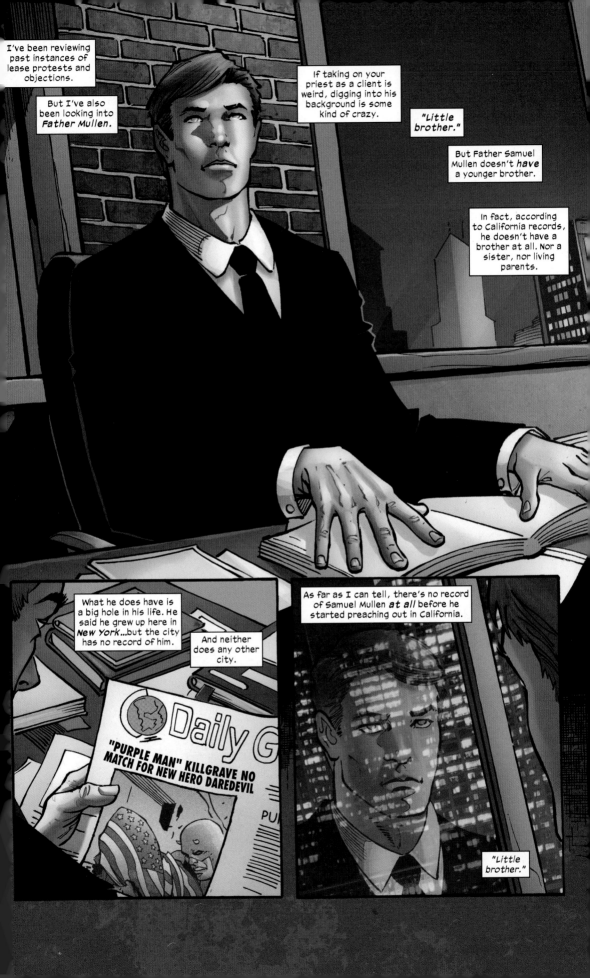

I've been reviewing past instances of lease protests and objections.

But I've also been looking into *Father Mullen.*

If taking on your priest as a client is weird, digging into his background is some kind of crazy.

"Little brother."

But Father Samuel Mullen doesn't *have* a younger brother.

In fact, according to California records, he doesn't have a brother at all. Nor a sister, nor living parents.

What he does have is a big hole in his life. He said he grew up here in *New York*...but the city has no record of him.

And neither does any other city.

As far as I can tell, there's no record of Samuel Mullen *at all* before he started preaching out in California.

"PURPLE MAN" KILLGRAVE NO MATCH FOR NEW HERO DAREDEVIL

Daily G

"Little brother."

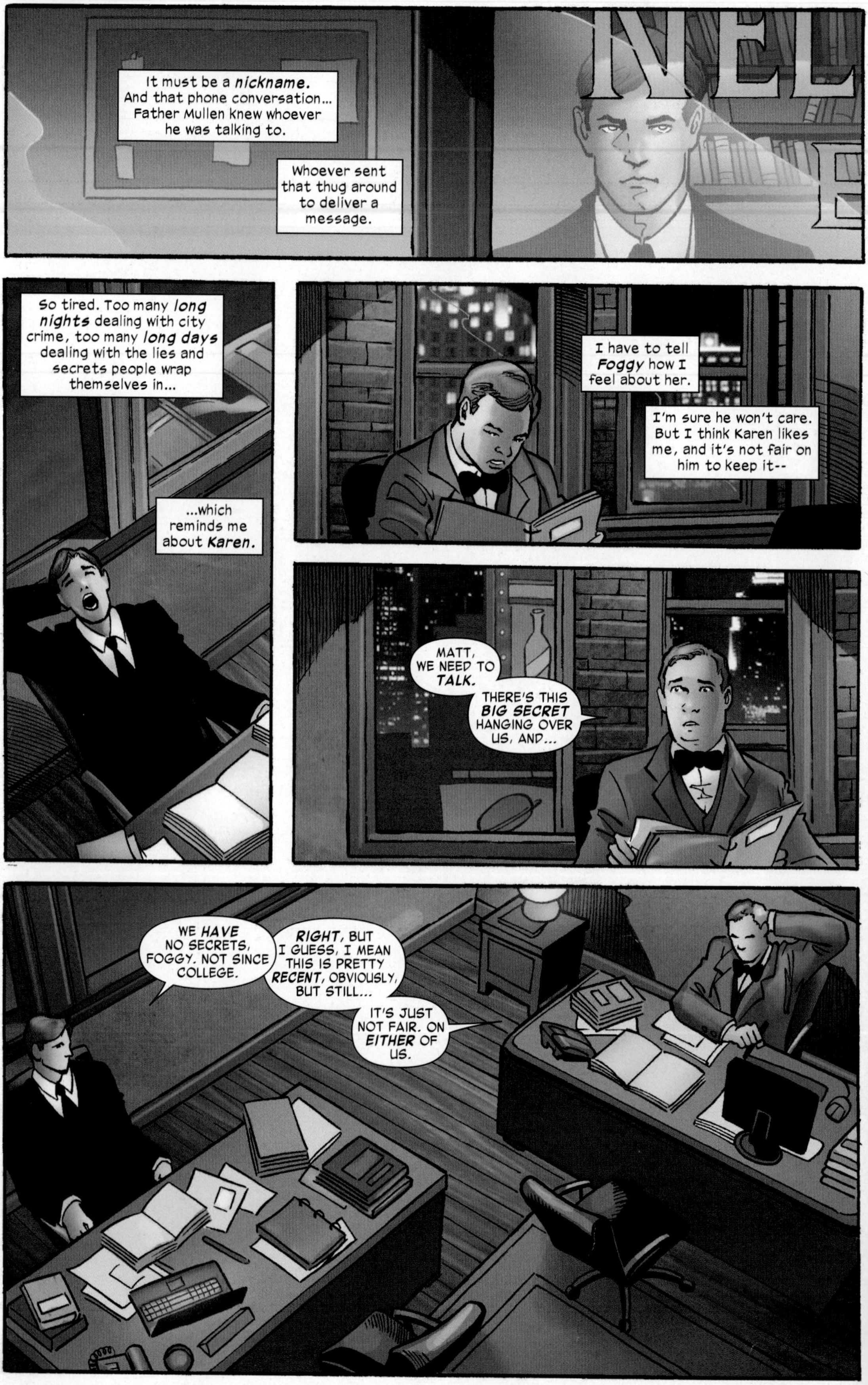
It must be a *nickname.* And that phone conversation... Father Mullen knew whoever he was talking to.
Whoever sent that thug around to deliver a message.
So tired. Too many *long nights* dealing with city crime, too many *long days* dealing with the lies and secrets people wrap themselves in...
...which reminds me about *Karen.*
I have to tell *Foggy* how I feel about her.
I'm sure he won't care. But I think Karen likes me, and it's not fair on him to keep it--
MATT, WE NEED TO *TALK.*
THERE'S THIS *BIG SECRET* HANGING OVER US, AND...
WE *HAVE* NO SECRETS, FOGGY. NOT SINCE COLLEGE.
RIGHT, BUT I GUESS, I MEAN THIS IS PRETTY *RECENT,* OBVIOUSLY, BUT STILL...
IT'S JUST NOT FAIR. ON *EITHER* OF US.

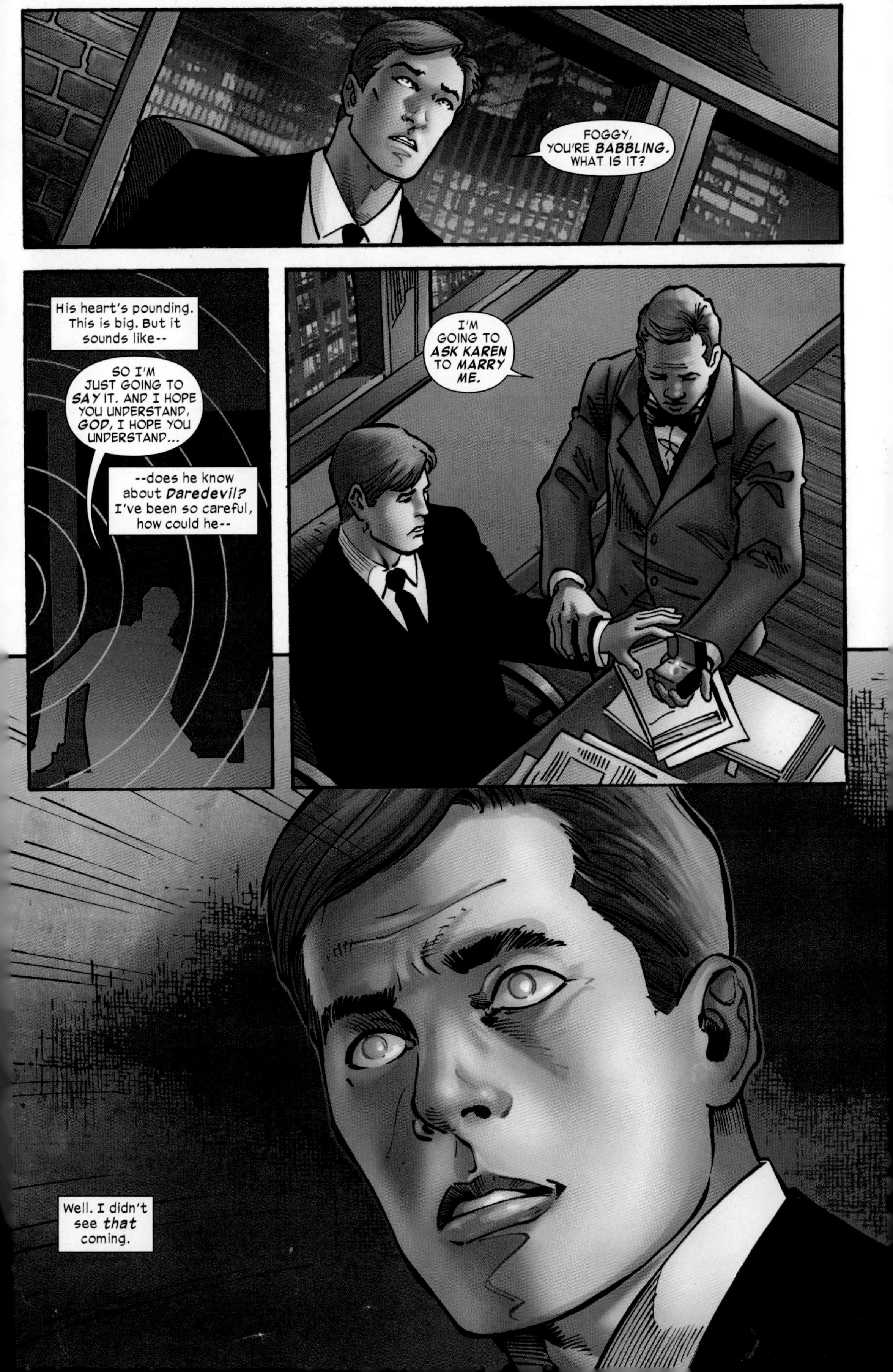
FOGGY, YOU'RE BABBLING. WHAT IS IT?
His heart's pounding. This is big. But it sounds like--
SO I'M JUST GOING TO SAY IT. AND I HOPE YOU UNDERSTAND, GOD, I HOPE YOU UNDERSTAND...
--does he know about Daredevil? I've been so careful, how could he--
I'M GOING TO ASK KAREN TO MARRY ME.
Well. I didn't see that coming.

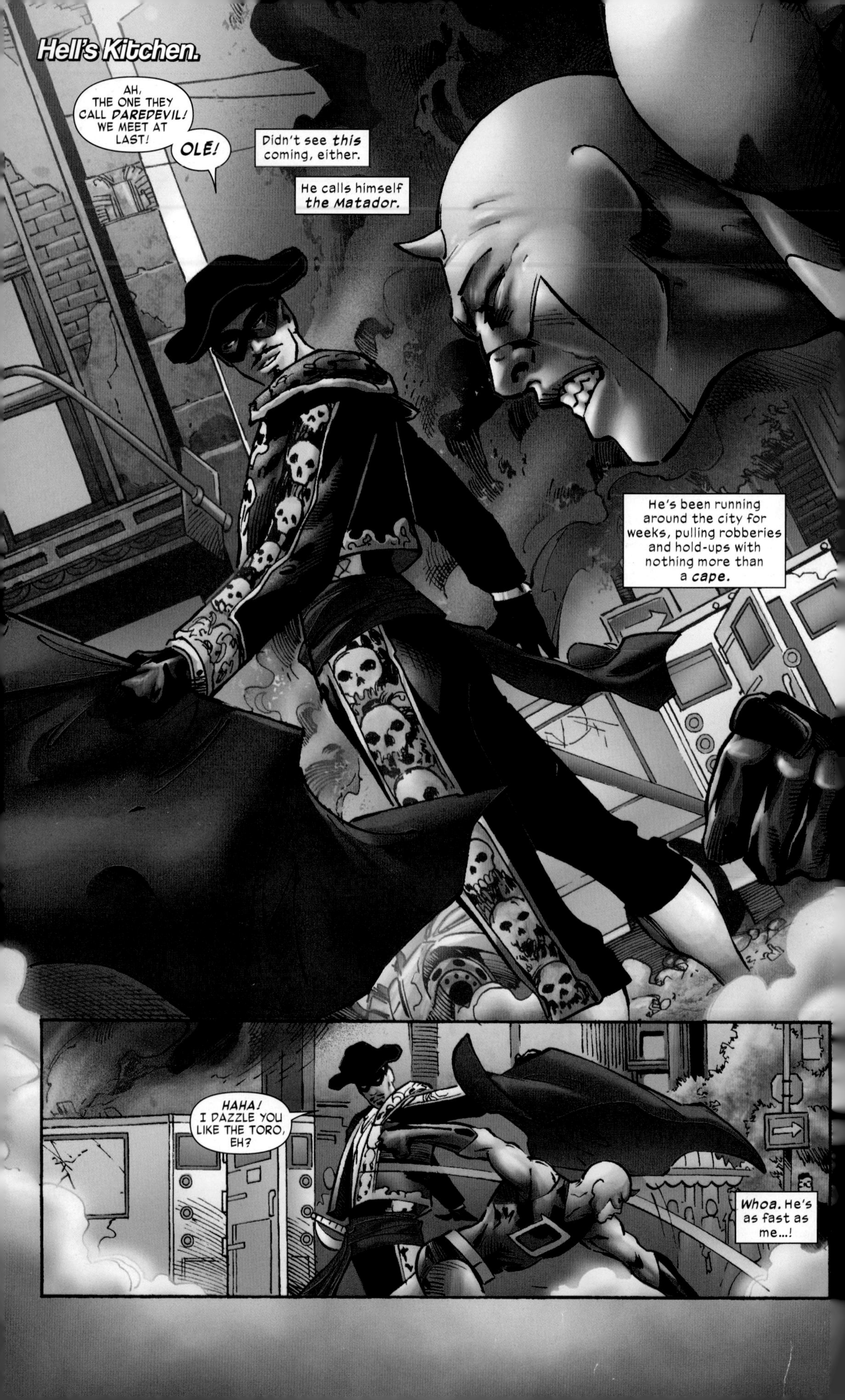
Hell's Kitchen.
AH, THE ONE THEY CALL DAREDEVIL! WE MEET AT LAST!
OLÉ!
Didn't see this coming, either.
He calls himself the Matador.
He's been running around the city for weeks, pulling robberies and hold-ups with nothing more than a cape.
HAHA! I DAZZLE YOU LIKE THE TORO, EH?
Whoa. He's as fast as me...!

I HAVE FOUGHT THE WORLD'S *FINEST* BULLS, SEÑOR SUPER HERO! HOW CAN *YOU* LAY A HAND ON ME?

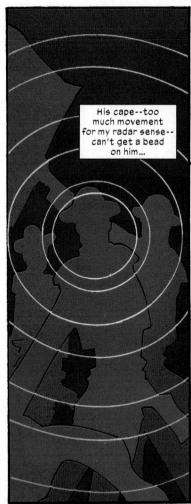

His cape--too much movement for my radar sense--can't get a bead on him...

THAT MANIAC... JUST *STANDING* THERE...IN THE MIDDLE OF THE ROAD...!

At least the *security guards* are safe. And despite the smoke, I can't hear or smell any fire from under the hood.

SO YOU *REFUSE* TO ATTACK AGAIN, EH? THEN I WILL *BRING* THE FIGHT TO YOU!

Should have seen that coming. *FOCUS*, Murdock!

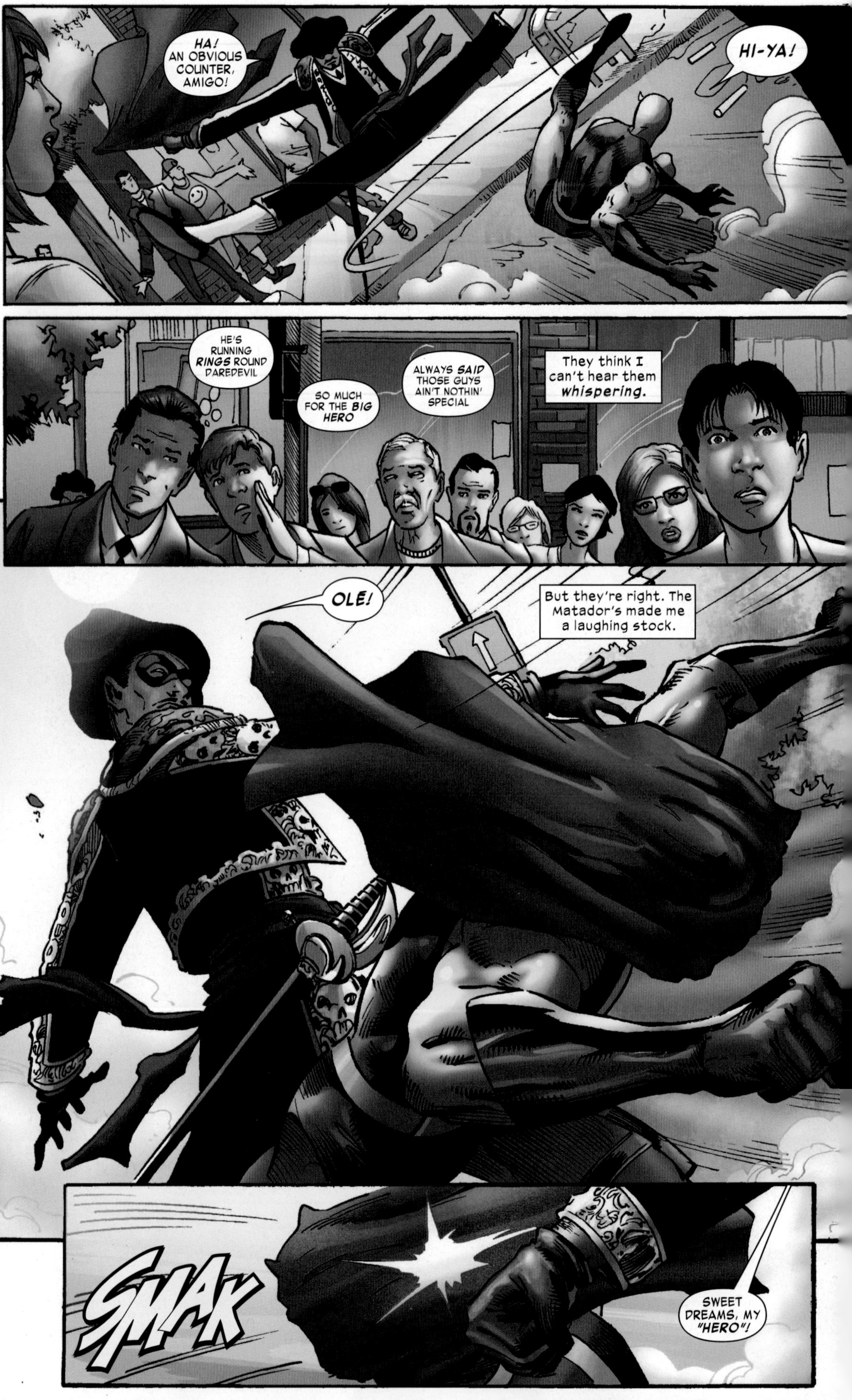
HA!
AN OBVIOUS
COUNTER,
AMIGO!
HI-YA!
HE'S
RUNNING
RINGS ROUND
DAREDEVIL
SO MUCH
FOR THE BIG
HERO
ALWAYS SAID
THOSE GUYS
AIN'T NOTHIN'
SPECIAL
They think I
can't hear them
whispering.
OLE!
But they're right. The
Matador's made me
a laughing stock.
SMAK
SWEET
DREAMS, MY
"HERO"!

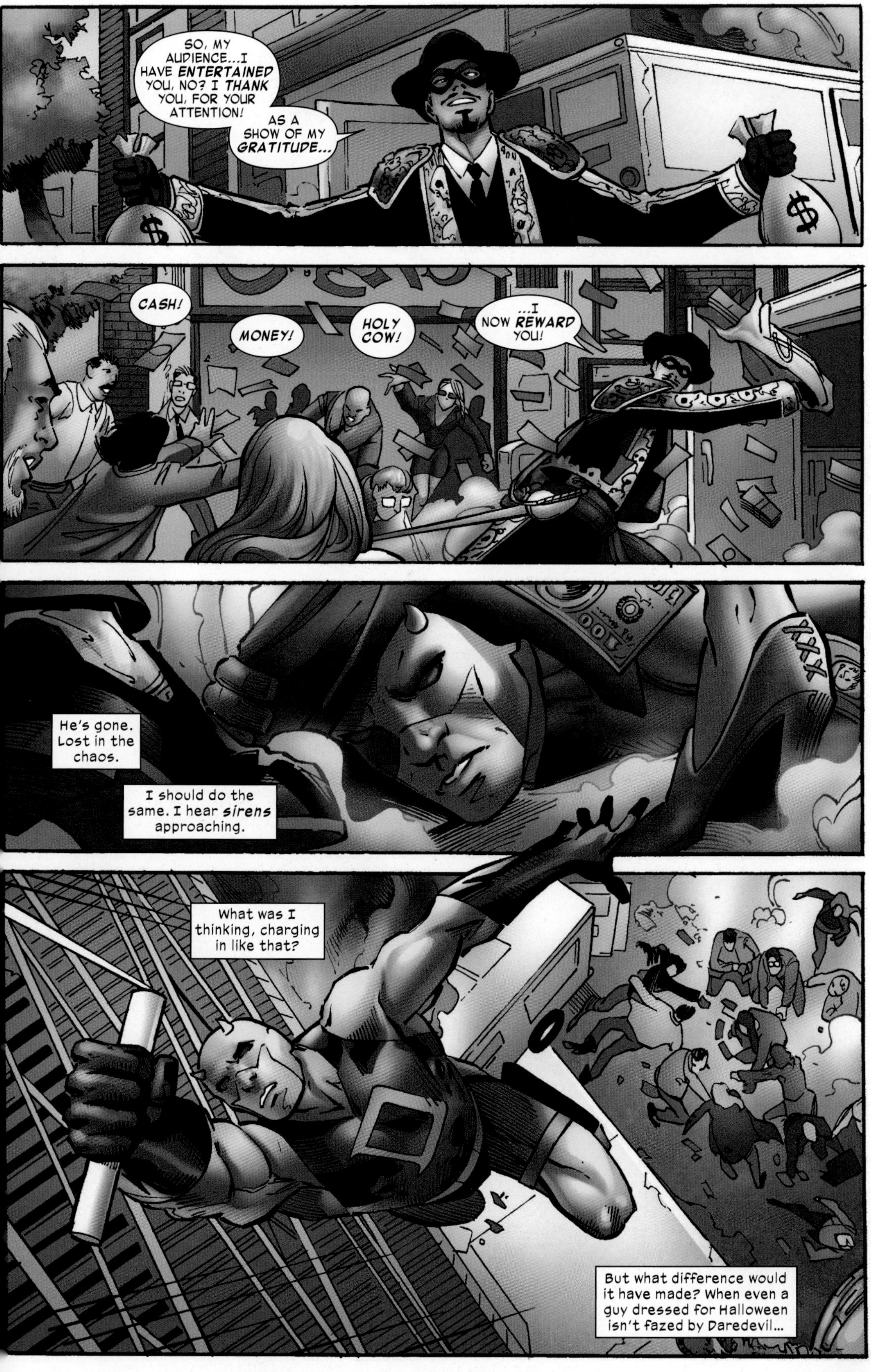
SO, MY AUDIENCE...I HAVE ENTERTAINED YOU, NO? I THANK YOU, FOR YOUR ATTENTION!
AS A SHOW OF MY GRATITUDE...
CASH!
MONEY!
HOLY COW!
...I NOW REWARD YOU!
He's gone. Lost in the chaos.
I should do the same. I hear sirens approaching.
What was I thinking, charging in like that?
But what difference would it have made? When even a guy dressed for Halloween isn't fazed by Daredevil...

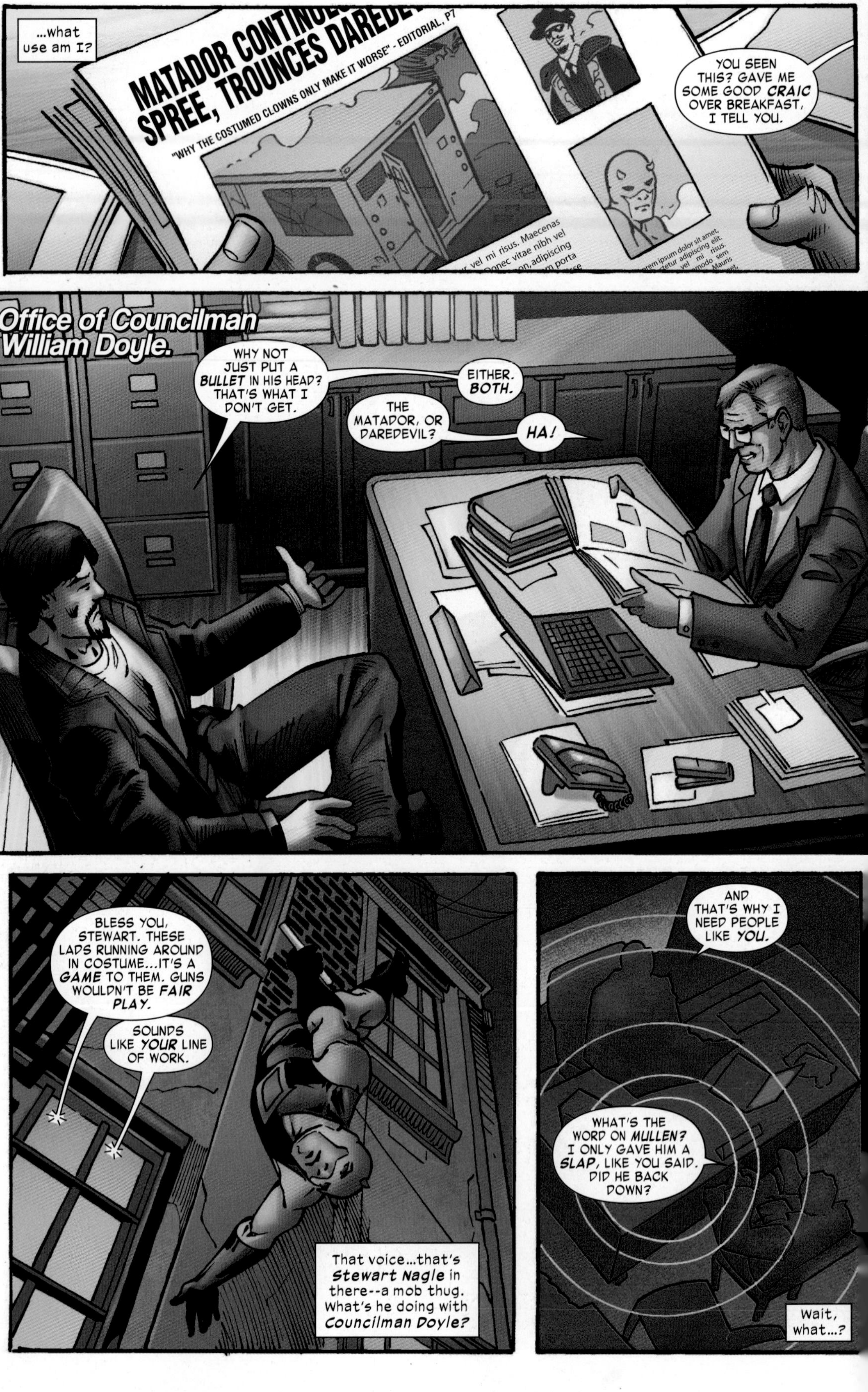

...what use am I?
MATADOR
SPREE, TROUNCES
"WHY THE COSTUMED CLOWNS ONLY MAKE IT WORSE" - EDITORIAL, P7
YOU SEEN THIS? GAVE ME SOME GOOD CRAIC OVER BREAKFAST, I TELL YOU.
Office of Councilman William Doyle.
WHY NOT JUST PUT A BULLET IN HIS HEAD? THAT'S WHAT I DON'T GET.
THE MATADOR, OR DAREDEVIL?
EITHER. BOTH.
HA!
BLESS YOU, STEWART. THESE LADS RUNNING AROUND IN COSTUME...IT'S A GAME TO THEM. GUNS WOULDN'T BE FAIR PLAY.
SOUNDS LIKE YOUR LINE OF WORK.
That voice...that's Stewart Nagle in there--a mob thug. What's he doing with Councilman Doyle?
AND THAT'S WHY I NEED PEOPLE LIKE YOU.
WHAT'S THE WORD ON MULLEN? I ONLY GAVE HIM A SLAP, LIKE YOU SAID. DID HE BACK DOWN?
Wait, what...?

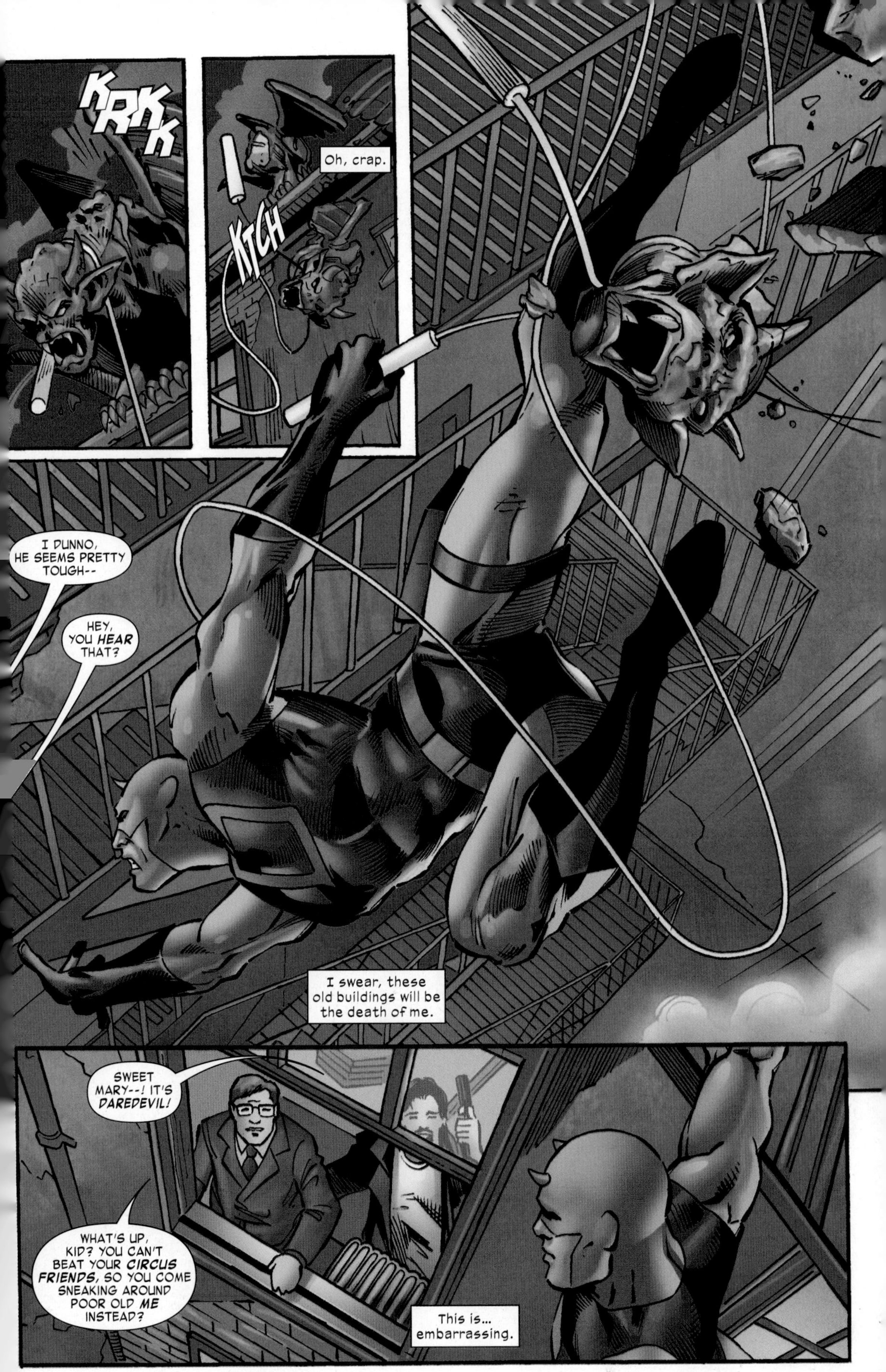
KRKK
Oh, crap.
KTCH
I DUNNO, HE SEEMS PRETTY TOUGH--
HEY, YOU HEAR THAT?
I swear, these old buildings will be the death of me.
SWEET MARY--! IT'S DAREDEVIL!
WHAT'S UP, KID? YOU CAN'T BEAT YOUR CIRCUS FRIENDS, SO YOU COME SNEAKING AROUND POOR OLD ME INSTEAD?
This is... embarrassing.

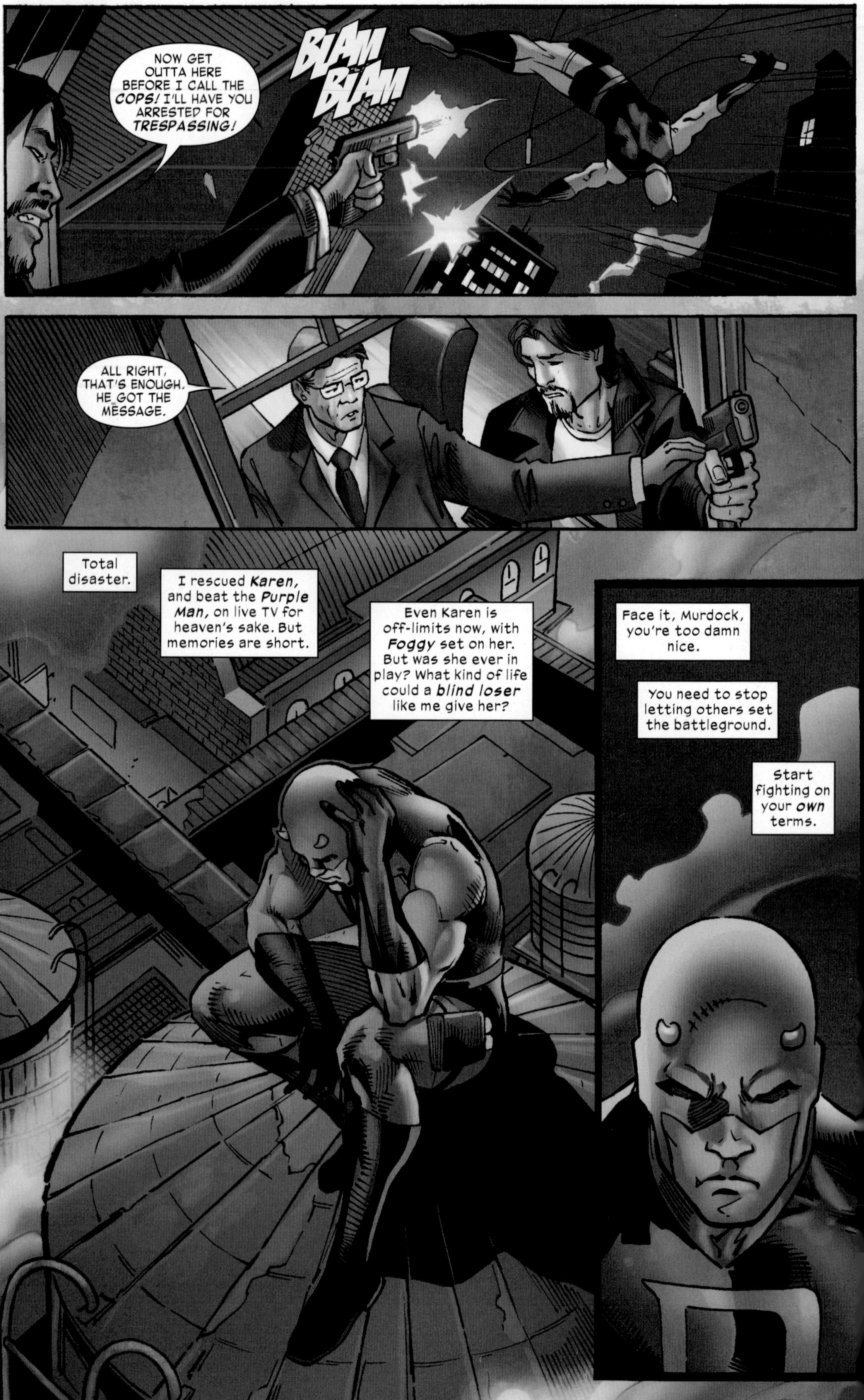

NOW GET OUTTA HERE BEFORE I CALL THE COPS! I'LL HAVE YOU ARRESTED FOR TRESPASSING!
BLAM BLAM
ALL RIGHT, THAT'S ENOUGH. HE GOT THE MESSAGE.
Total disaster.
I rescued Karen, and beat the Purple Man, on live TV for heaven's sake. But memories are short.
Even Karen is off-limits now, with Foggy set on her. But was she ever in play? What kind of life could a blind loser like me give her?
Face it, Murdock, you're too damn nice.
You need to stop letting others set the battleground.
Start fighting on your own terms.

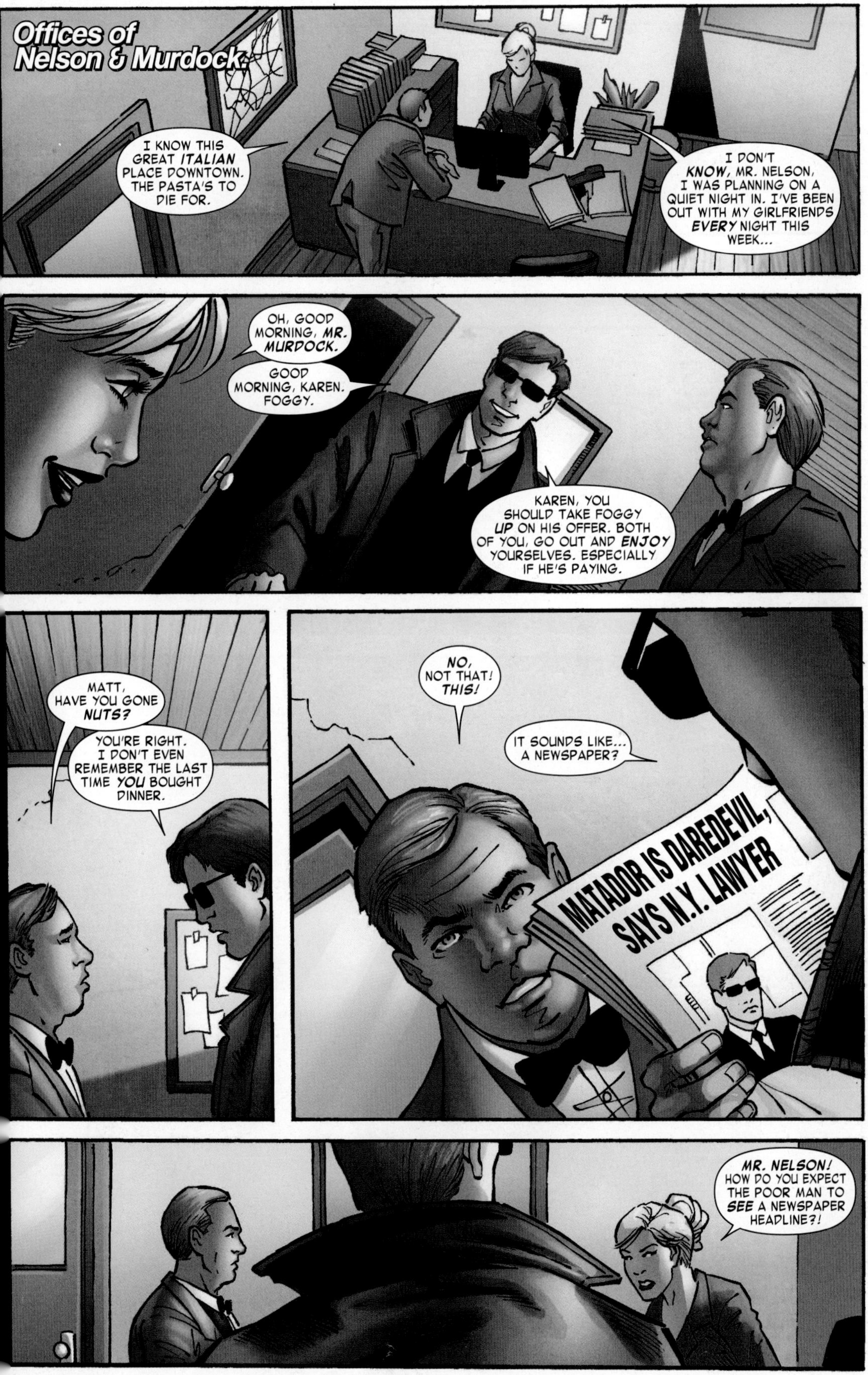
Offices of Nelson & Murdock.
I KNOW THIS GREAT ITALIAN PLACE DOWNTOWN. THE PASTA'S TO DIE FOR.
I DON'T KNOW, MR. NELSON, I WAS PLANNING ON A QUIET NIGHT IN. I'VE BEEN OUT WITH MY GIRLFRIENDS EVERY NIGHT THIS WEEK...
OH, GOOD MORNING, MR. MURDOCK.
GOOD MORNING, KAREN. FOGGY.
KAREN, YOU SHOULD TAKE FOGGY UP ON HIS OFFER. BOTH OF YOU, GO OUT AND ENJOY YOURSELVES. ESPECIALLY IF HE'S PAYING.
MATT, HAVE YOU GONE NUTS?
YOU'RE RIGHT. I DON'T EVEN REMEMBER THE LAST TIME YOU BOUGHT DINNER.
NO, NOT THAT! THIS!
IT SOUNDS LIKE... A NEWSPAPER?
MATADOR IS DAREDEVIL, SAYS N.Y. LAWYER
MR. NELSON! HOW DO YOU EXPECT THE POOR MAN TO SEE A NEWSPAPER HEADLINE?!

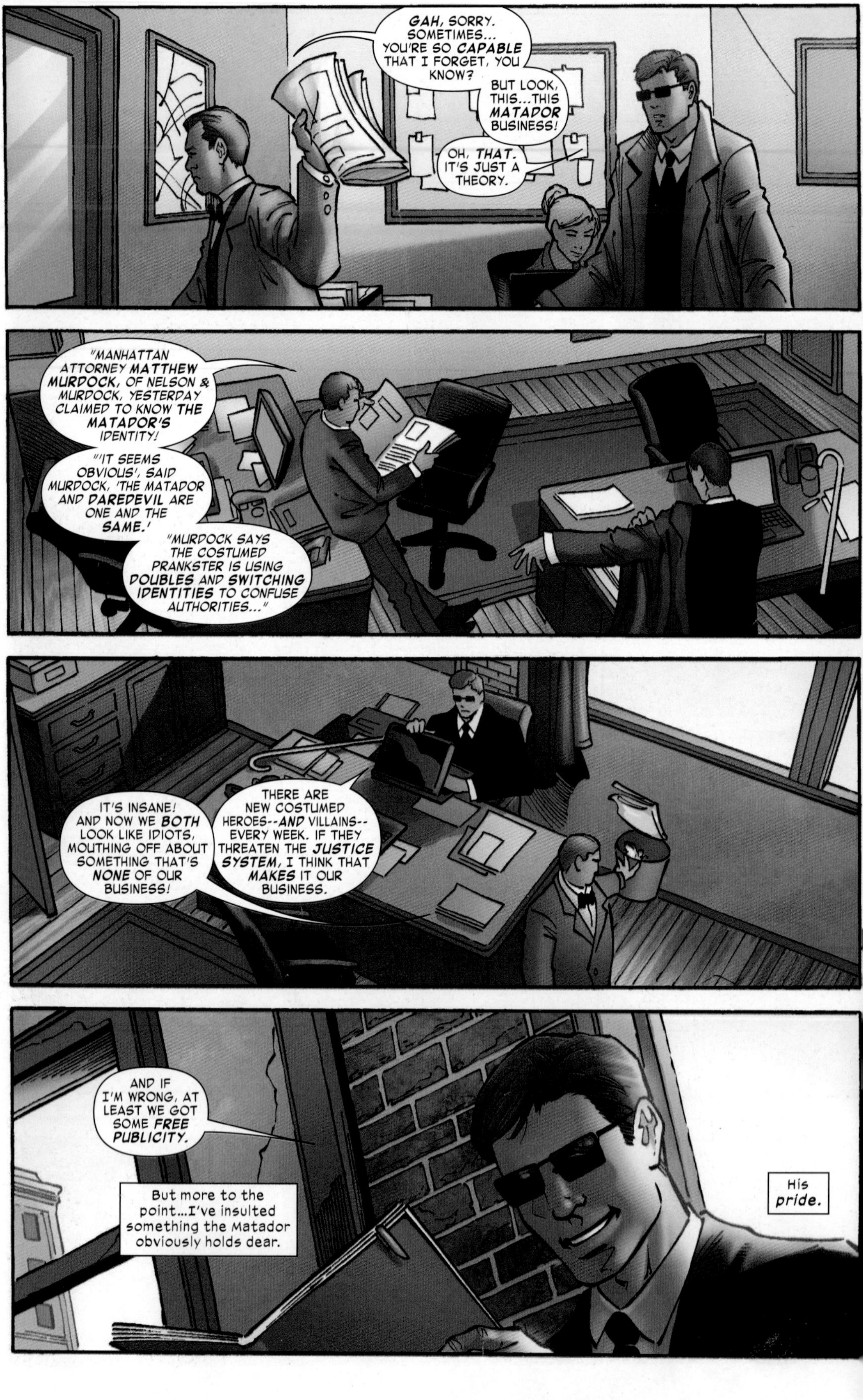
GAH, SORRY. SOMETIMES... YOU'RE SO CAPABLE THAT I FORGET, YOU KNOW?
BUT LOOK, THIS...THIS MATADOR BUSINESS!
OH, THAT. IT'S JUST A THEORY.
"MANHATTAN ATTORNEY MATTHEW MURDOCK, OF NELSON & MURDOCK, YESTERDAY CLAIMED TO KNOW THE MATADOR'S IDENTITY!
"'IT SEEMS OBVIOUS', SAID MURDOCK, 'THE MATADOR AND DAREDEVIL ARE ONE AND THE SAME.'
"MURDOCK SAYS THE COSTUMED PRANKSTER IS USING DOUBLES AND SWITCHING IDENTITIES TO CONFUSE AUTHORITIES..."
IT'S INSANE! AND NOW WE BOTH LOOK LIKE IDIOTS, MOUTHING OFF ABOUT SOMETHING THAT'S NONE OF OUR BUSINESS!
THERE ARE NEW COSTUMED HEROES--AND VILLAINS--EVERY WEEK. IF THEY THREATEN THE JUSTICE SYSTEM, I THINK THAT MAKES IT OUR BUSINESS.
AND IF I'M WRONG, AT LEAST WE GOT SOME FREE PUBLICITY.
But more to the point...I've insulted something the Matador obviously holds dear.
His pride.

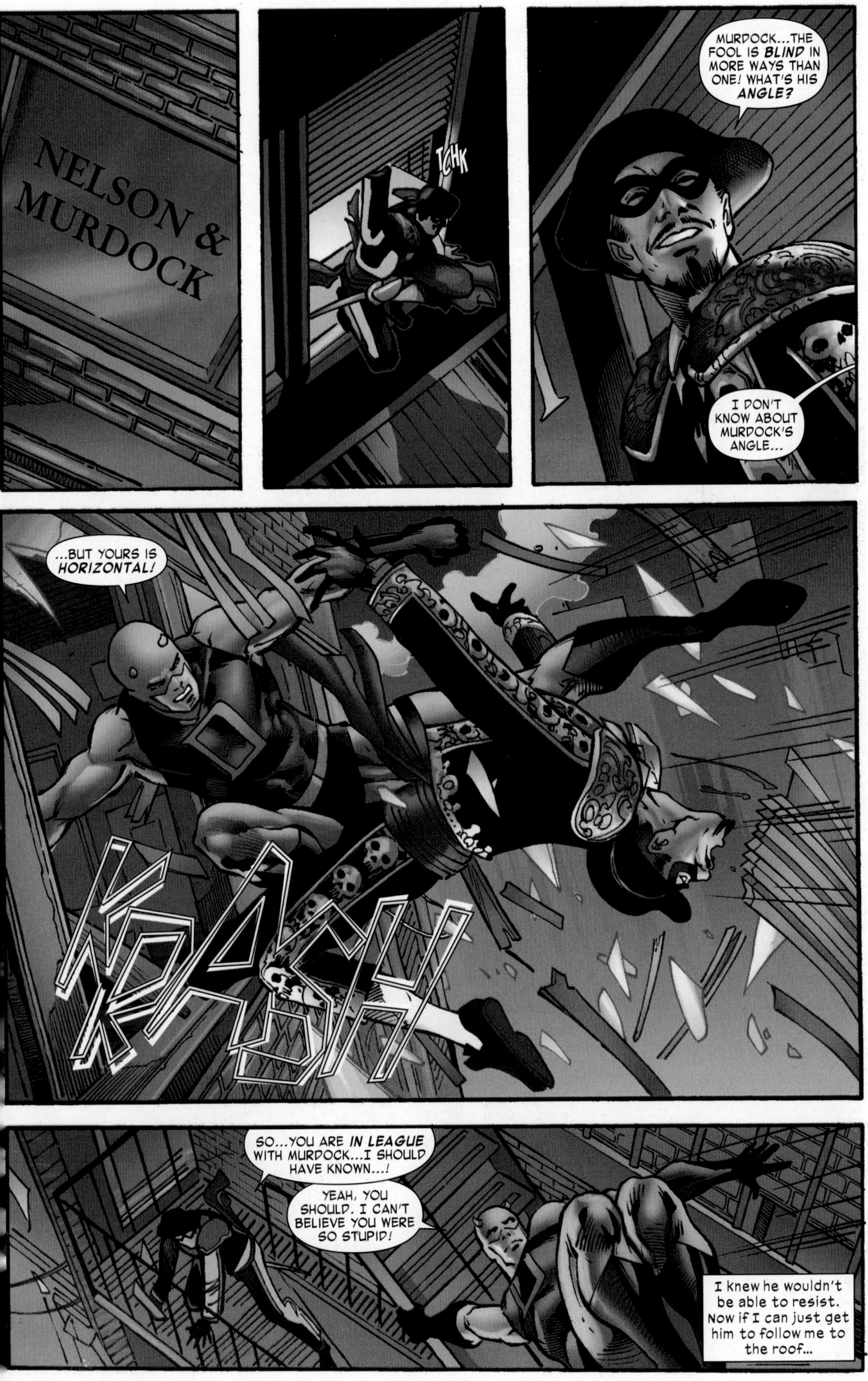
NELSON & MURDOCK
TCHK
MURDOCK...THE FOOL IS BLIND IN MORE WAYS THAN ONE! WHAT'S HIS ANGLE?
I DON'T KNOW ABOUT MURDOCK'S ANGLE...
...BUT YOURS IS HORIZONTAL!
KRASH
SO...YOU ARE IN LEAGUE WITH MURDOCK...I SHOULD HAVE KNOWN...!
YEAH, YOU SHOULD. I CAN'T BELIEVE YOU WERE SO STUPID!
I knew he wouldn't be able to resist. Now if I can just get him to follow me to the roof...

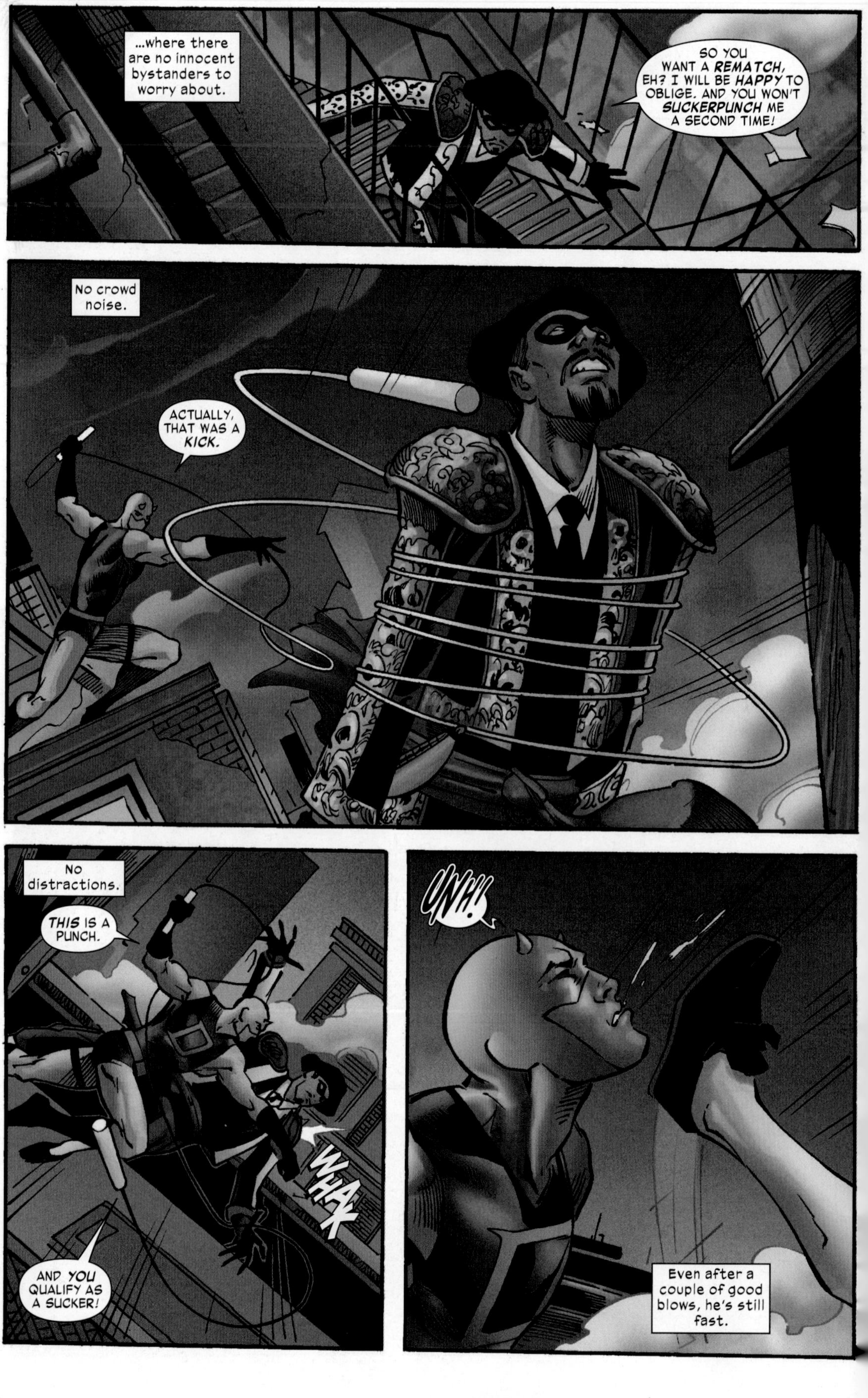
...where there are no innocent bystanders to worry about.
SO YOU WANT A REMATCH, EH? I WILL BE HAPPY TO OBLIGE. AND YOU WON'T SUCKERPUNCH ME A SECOND TIME!
No crowd noise.
ACTUALLY, THAT WAS A KICK.
No distractions.
THIS IS A PUNCH.
WHAK
AND YOU QUALIFY AS A SUCKER!
UNH!
Even after a couple of good blows, he's still fast.

HA! NOW YOU ARE AS BLIND AS YOUR LAWYER FRIEND!

OLÉ! TORO!

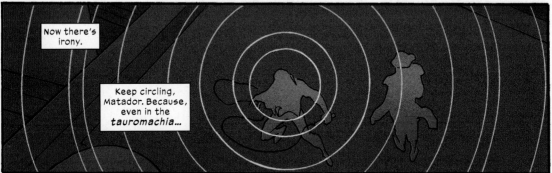

Now there's irony.

Keep circling, Matador. Because, even in the *tauromachia*...

...SOMETIMES, THE *BULL WINS!*

I checked the building was empty after Karen and Foggy left for dinner. I'll call the cops later...

...after taking care of some other business.

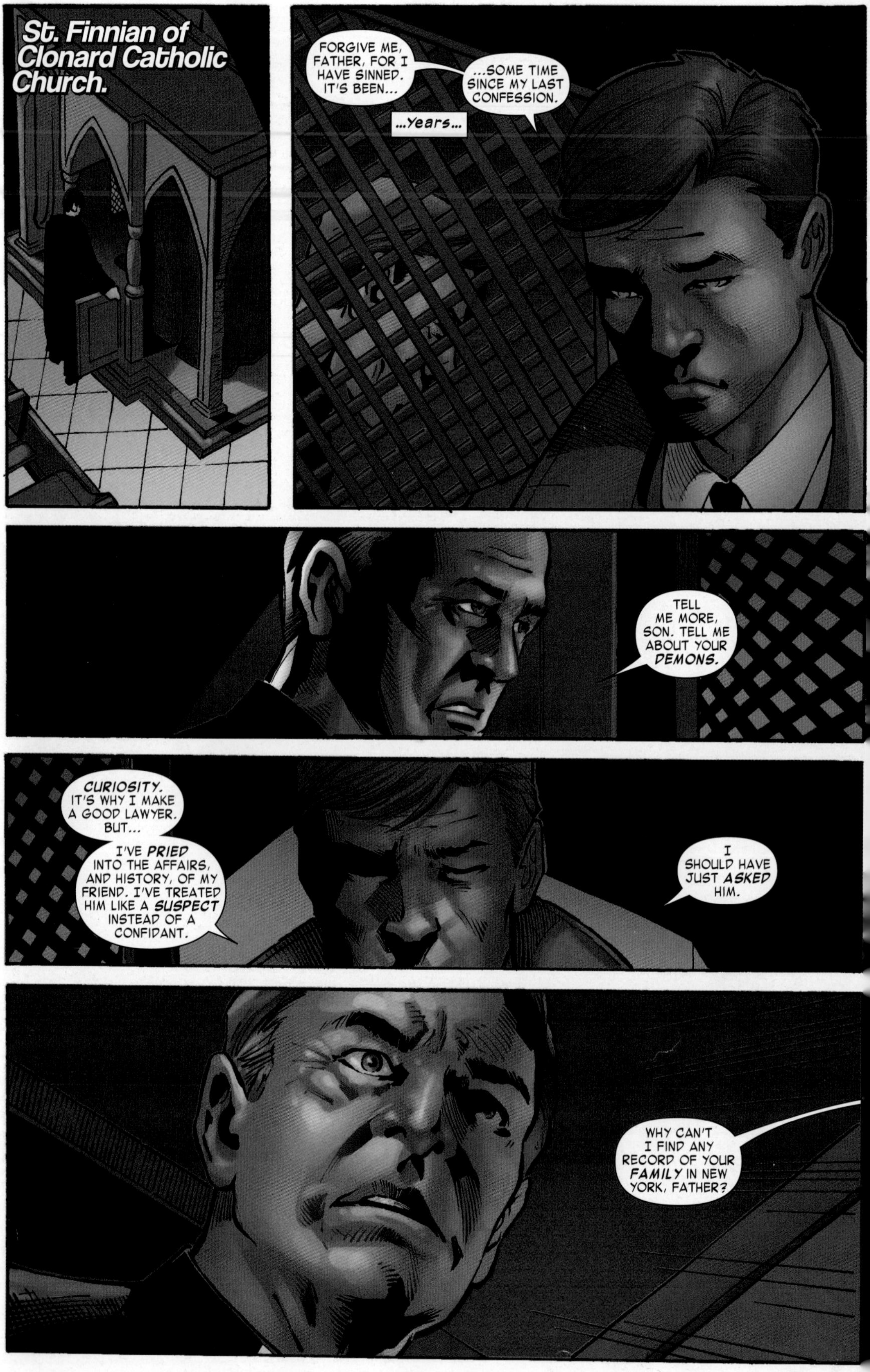
St. Finnian of Clonard Catholic Church.
FORGIVE ME, FATHER, FOR I HAVE SINNED. IT'S BEEN...
...SOME TIME SINCE MY LAST CONFESSION.
...Years...
TELL ME MORE, SON. TELL ME ABOUT YOUR DEMONS.
CURIOSITY. IT'S WHY I MAKE A GOOD LAWYER. BUT...
I'VE PRIED INTO THE AFFAIRS, AND HISTORY, OF MY FRIEND. I'VE TREATED HIM LIKE A SUSPECT INSTEAD OF A CONFIDANT.
I SHOULD HAVE JUST ASKED HIM.
WHY CAN'T I FIND ANY RECORD OF YOUR FAMILY IN NEW YORK, FATHER?

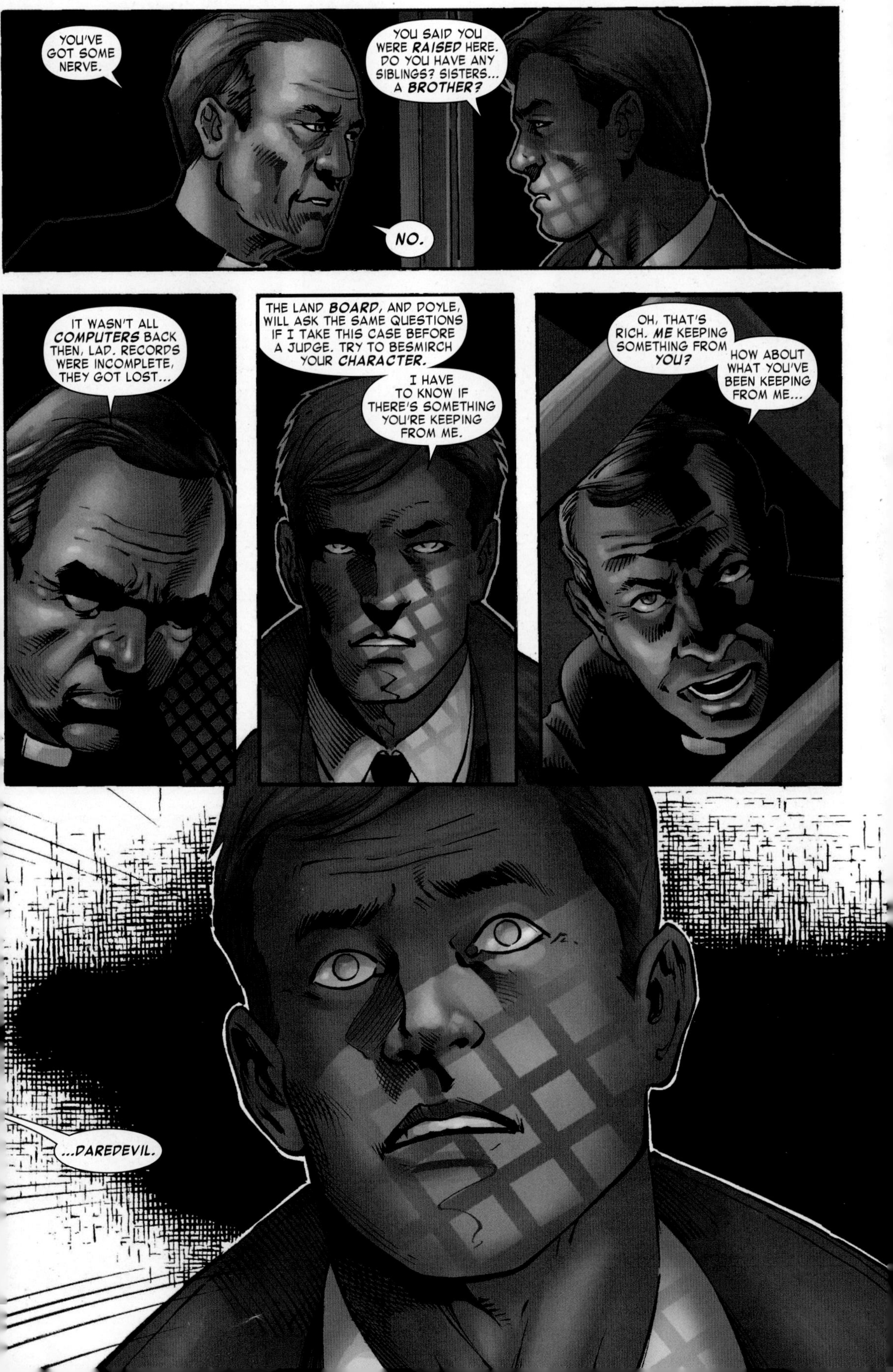

YOU'VE GOT SOME NERVE.
YOU SAID YOU WERE RAISED HERE. DO YOU HAVE ANY SIBLINGS? SISTERS... A BROTHER?
NO.
IT WASN'T ALL COMPUTERS BACK THEN, LAD. RECORDS WERE INCOMPLETE, THEY GOT LOST...
THE LAND BOARD, AND DOYLE, WILL ASK THE SAME QUESTIONS IF I TAKE THIS CASE BEFORE A JUDGE. TRY TO BESMIRCH YOUR CHARACTER.
I HAVE TO KNOW IF THERE'S SOMETHING YOU'RE KEEPING FROM ME.
OH, THAT'S RICH. ME KEEPING SOMETHING FROM YOU?
HOW ABOUT WHAT YOU'VE BEEN KEEPING FROM ME...
...DAREDEVIL.

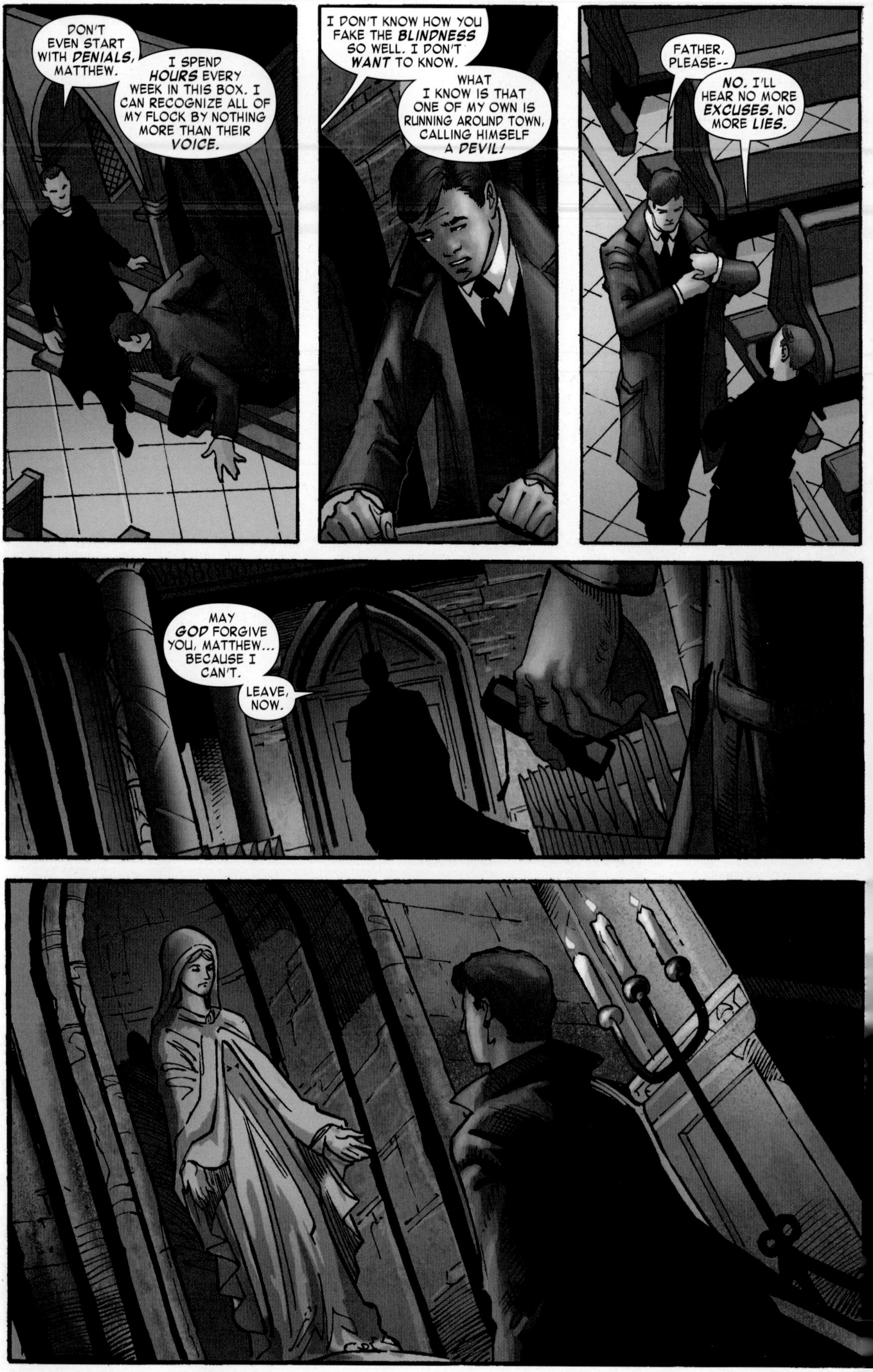
DON'T EVEN START WITH DENIALS, MATTHEW.
I SPEND HOURS EVERY WEEK IN THIS BOX. I CAN RECOGNIZE ALL OF MY FLOCK BY NOTHING MORE THAN THEIR VOICE.
I DON'T KNOW HOW YOU FAKE THE BLINDNESS SO WELL. I DON'T WANT TO KNOW.
WHAT I KNOW IS THAT ONE OF MY OWN IS RUNNING AROUND TOWN, CALLING HIMSELF A DEVIL!
FATHER, PLEASE--
NO. I'LL HEAR NO MORE EXCUSES. NO MORE LIES.
MAY GOD FORGIVE YOU, MATTHEW... BECAUSE I CAN'T.
LEAVE, NOW.

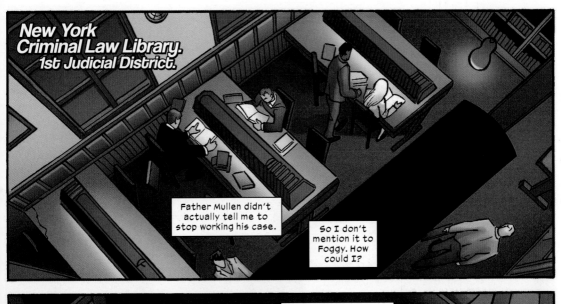

New York
Criminal Law Library.
1st Judicial District.

Father Mullen didn't actually tell me to stop working his case.

So I don't mention it to Foggy. How could I?

I don't mention that I've finally found a *Mullen* family in the records, Irish immigrants from years back.

But it doesn't fit. They had just one child-- *Maude*, a daughter. There's no record of her marrying, and she'd be at least seventy by now.

NOTHING BUT DEAD ENDS. *DAMMIT!*

WHAT'S THAT?

THE ORIGINAL *LEASE DOCUMENTS* ARE MISSING. IN FACT, I CAN'T FIND *ANY* LAND BOARD DOCUMENT FOR THE CHURCH, NOT EVEN GOING BACK *FIFTY YEARS*.

IT'S ABSURD! CITY LEASE AGREEMENTS DON'T JUST *VANISH* INTO THIN AIR!

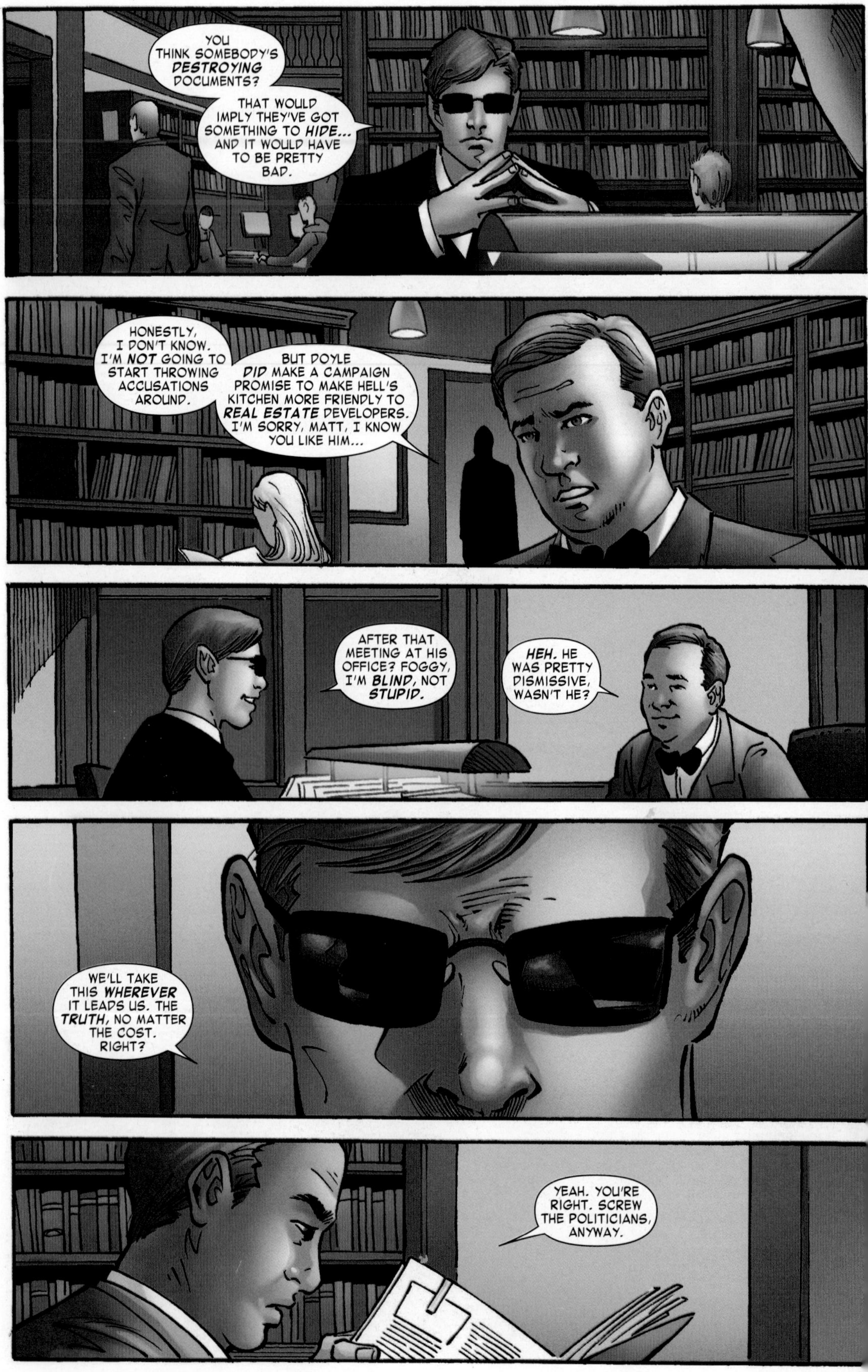
YOU THINK SOMEBODY'S DESTROYING DOCUMENTS?
THAT WOULD IMPLY THEY'VE GOT SOMETHING TO HIDE... AND IT WOULD HAVE TO BE PRETTY BAD.
HONESTLY, I DON'T KNOW. I'M NOT GOING TO START THROWING ACCUSATIONS AROUND.
BUT DOYLE DID MAKE A CAMPAIGN PROMISE TO MAKE HELL'S KITCHEN MORE FRIENDLY TO REAL ESTATE DEVELOPERS. I'M SORRY, MATT, I KNOW YOU LIKE HIM...
AFTER THAT MEETING AT HIS OFFICE? FOGGY, I'M BLIND, NOT STUPID.
HEH. HE WAS PRETTY DISMISSIVE, WASN'T HE?
WE'LL TAKE THIS WHEREVER IT LEADS US. THE TRUTH, NO MATTER THE COST. RIGHT?
YEAH. YOU'RE RIGHT. SCREW THE POLITICIANS, ANYWAY.

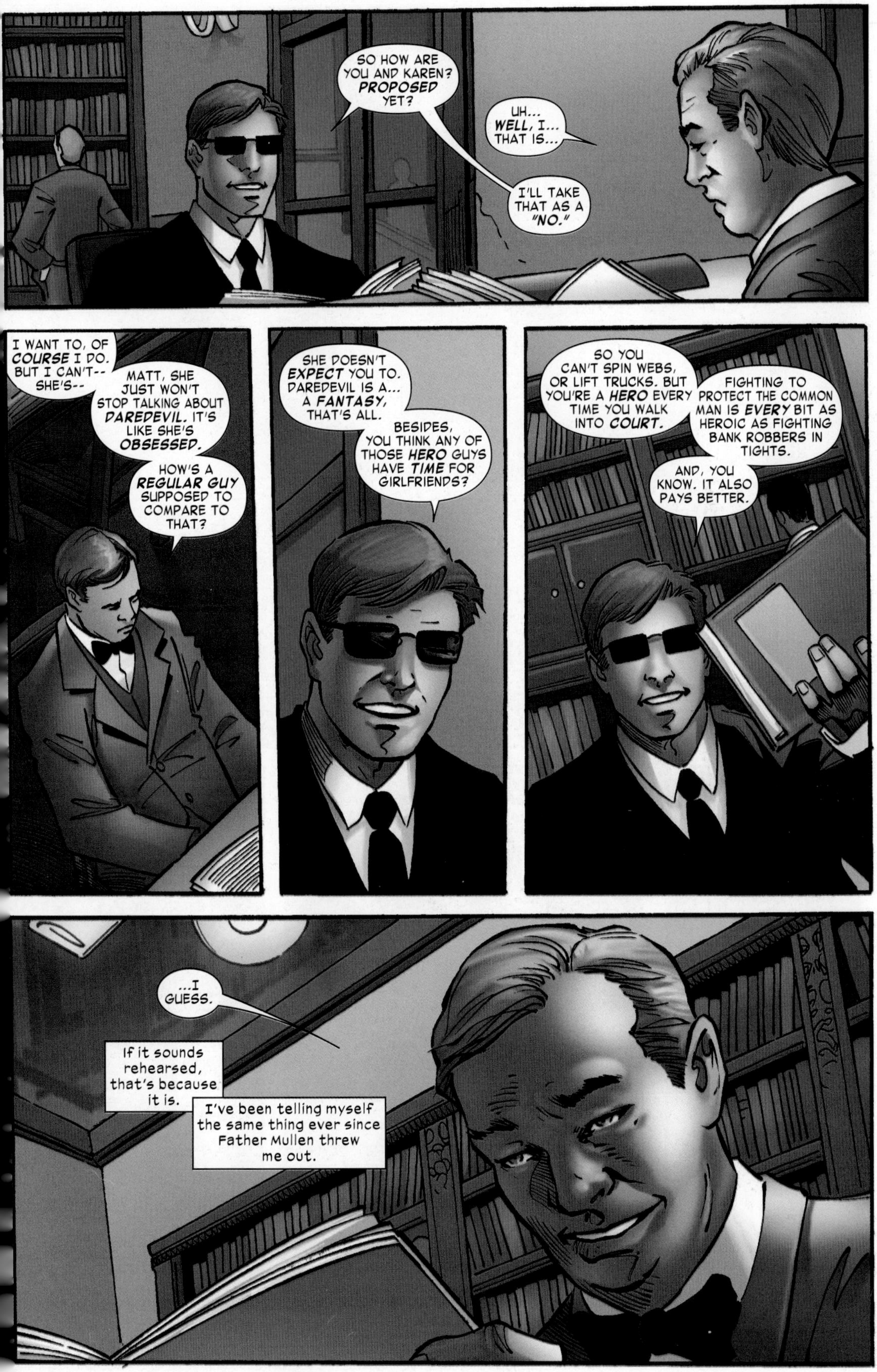

SO HOW ARE YOU AND KAREN? PROPOSED YET?
UH... WELL, I... THAT IS...
I'LL TAKE THAT AS A "NO."
I WANT TO, OF COURSE I DO. BUT I CAN'T-- SHE'S--
MATT, SHE JUST WON'T STOP TALKING ABOUT DAREDEVIL. IT'S LIKE SHE'S OBSESSED.
HOW'S A REGULAR GUY SUPPOSED TO COMPARE TO THAT?
SHE DOESN'T EXPECT YOU TO. DAREDEVIL IS A... A FANTASY, THAT'S ALL.
BESIDES, YOU THINK ANY OF THOSE HERO GUYS HAVE TIME FOR GIRLFRIENDS?
SO YOU CAN'T SPIN WEBS, OR LIFT TRUCKS. BUT YOU'RE A HERO EVERY TIME YOU WALK INTO COURT.
FIGHTING TO PROTECT THE COMMON MAN IS EVERY BIT AS HEROIC AS FIGHTING BANK ROBBERS IN TIGHTS.
AND, YOU KNOW. IT ALSO PAYS BETTER.
...I GUESS.
If it sounds rehearsed, that's because it is.
I've been telling myself the same thing ever since Father Mullen threw me out.

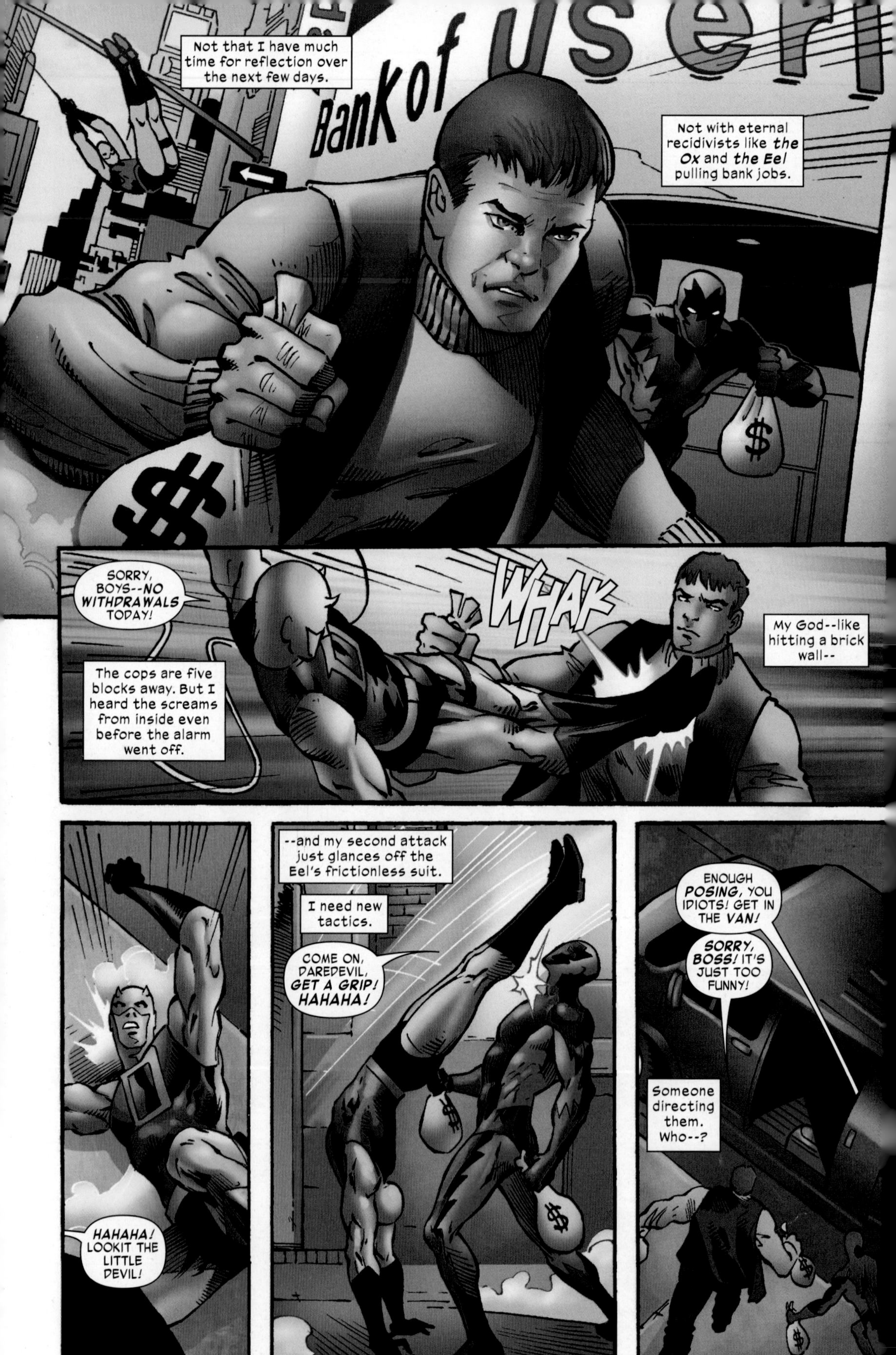

Not that I have much time for reflection over the next few days.
Bank of US
Not with eternal recidivists like *the Ox* and *the Eel* pulling bank jobs.
SORRY, BOYS--*NO WITHDRAWALS* TODAY!
WHAK
The cops are five blocks away. But I heard the screams from inside even before the alarm went off.
My God--like hitting a brick wall--
HAHAHA! LOOKIT THE LITTLE DEVIL!
--and my second attack just glances off the Eel's frictionless suit.
I need new tactics.
COME ON, DAREDEVIL, *GET A GRIP! HAHAHA!*
ENOUGH *POSING,* YOU IDIOTS! GET IN THE *VAN!*
SORRY, BOSS! IT'S JUST TOO FUNNY!
Someone directing them. Who--?

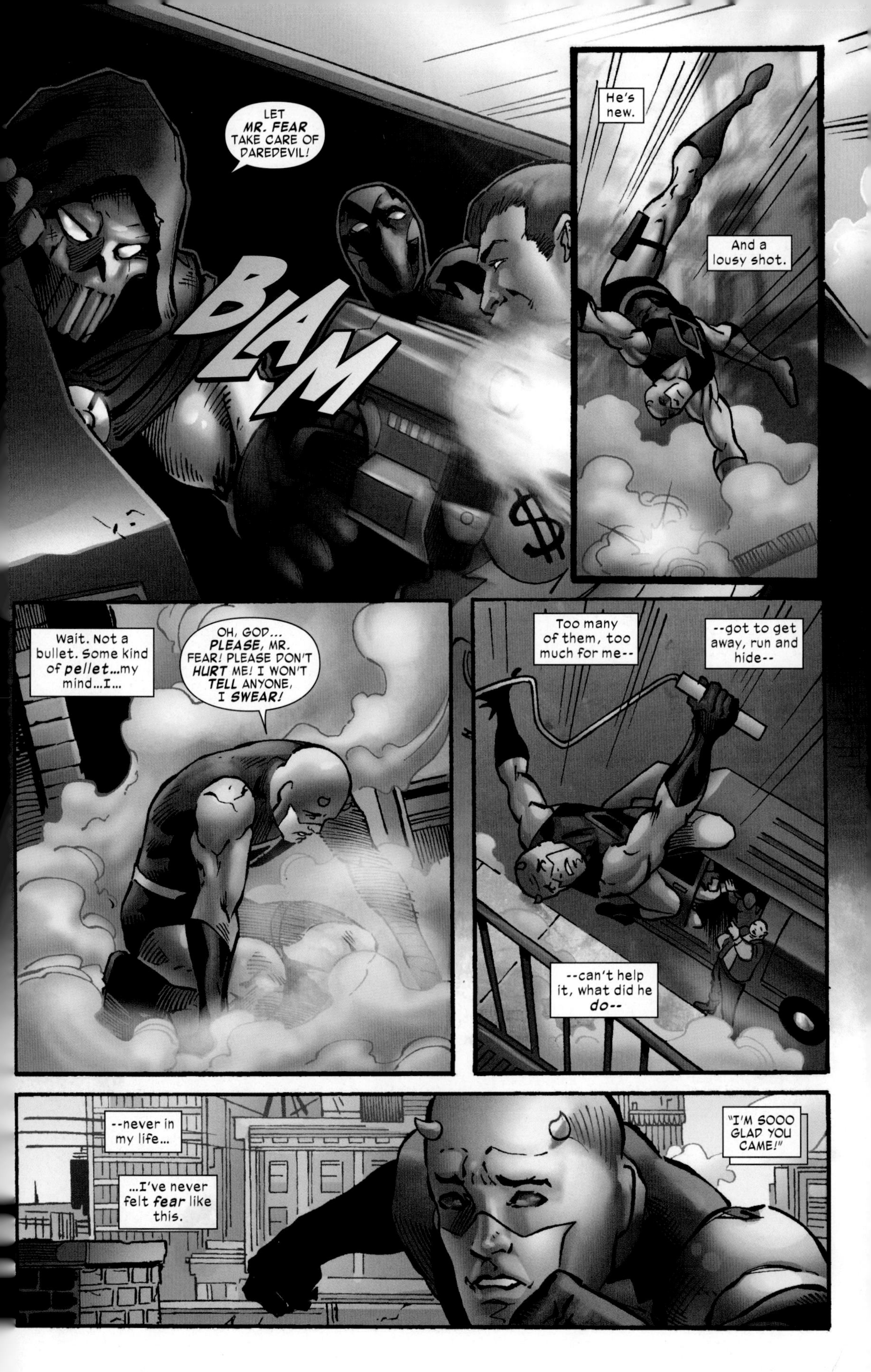
LET MR. FEAR TAKE CARE OF DAREDEVIL!
BLAM
He's new.
And a lousy shot.
Wait. Not a bullet. Some kind of pellet...my mind...I...
OH, GOD... PLEASE, MR. FEAR! PLEASE DON'T HURT ME! I WON'T TELL ANYONE, I SWEAR!
Too many of them, too much for me--
--got to get away, run and hide--
--can't help it, what did he do--
--never in my life...
...I've never felt fear like this.
"I'M SOOO GLAD YOU CAME!"

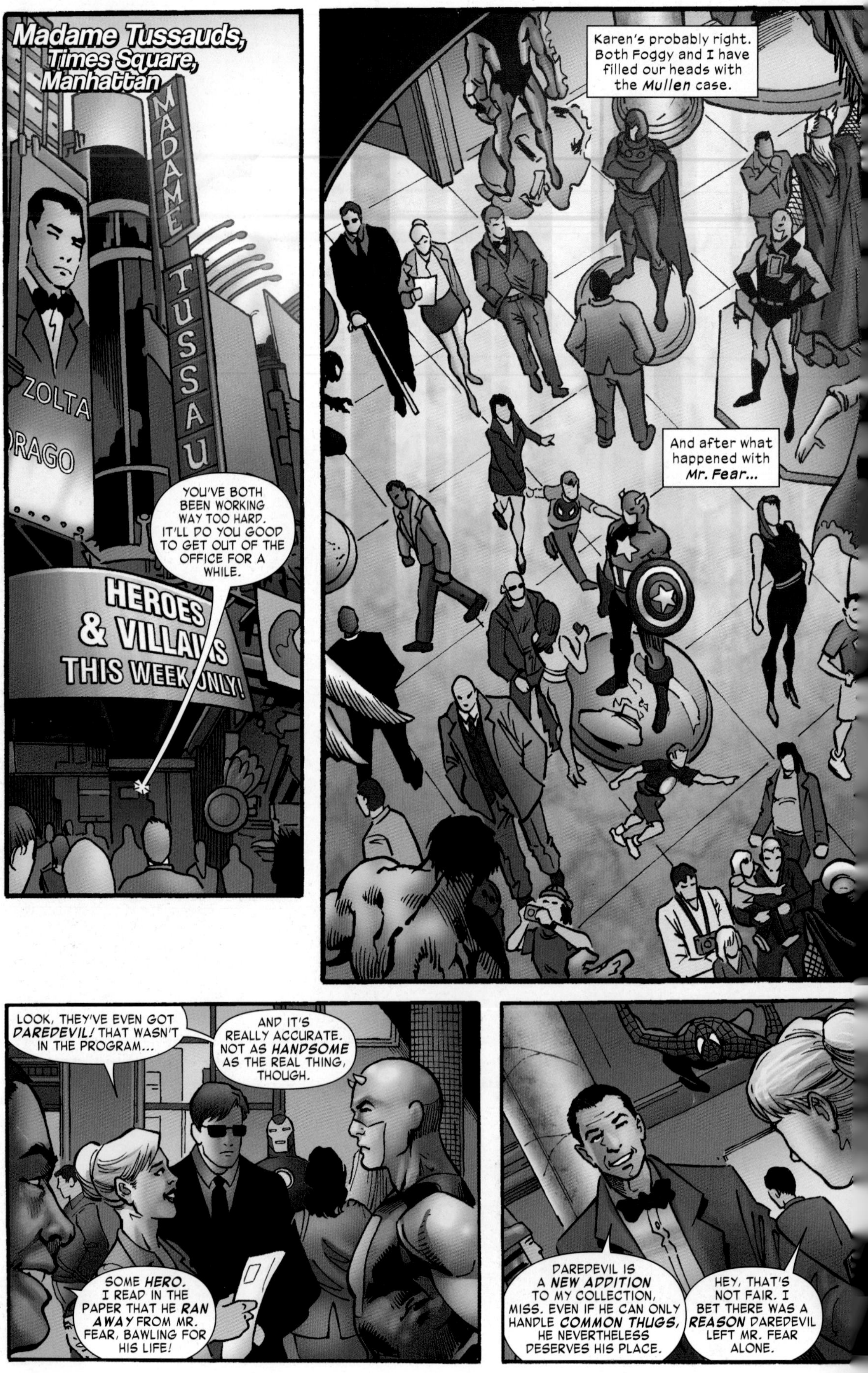
Madame Tussauds, Times Square, Manhattan
MADAME
TUSSAU
ZOLTA
YOU'VE BOTH BEEN WORKING WAY TOO HARD. IT'LL DO YOU GOOD TO GET OUT OF THE OFFICE FOR A WHILE.
HEROES & VILLAINS THIS WEEK ONLY!
Karen's probably right. Both Foggy and I have filled our heads with the *Mullen* case.
And after what happened with *Mr. Fear...*
LOOK, THEY'VE EVEN GOT *DAREDEVIL!* THAT WASN'T IN THE PROGRAM...
AND IT'S REALLY ACCURATE. NOT AS ***HANDSOME*** AS THE REAL THING, THOUGH.
SOME ***HERO.*** I READ IN THE PAPER THAT HE ***RAN AWAY*** FROM MR. FEAR, BAWLING FOR HIS LIFE!
DAREDEVIL IS A ***NEW ADDITION*** TO MY COLLECTION, MISS. EVEN IF HE CAN ONLY HANDLE ***COMMON THUGS,*** HE NEVERTHELESS DESERVES HIS PLACE.
HEY, THAT'S NOT FAIR. I BET THERE WAS A ***REASON*** DAREDEVIL LEFT MR. FEAR ALONE.

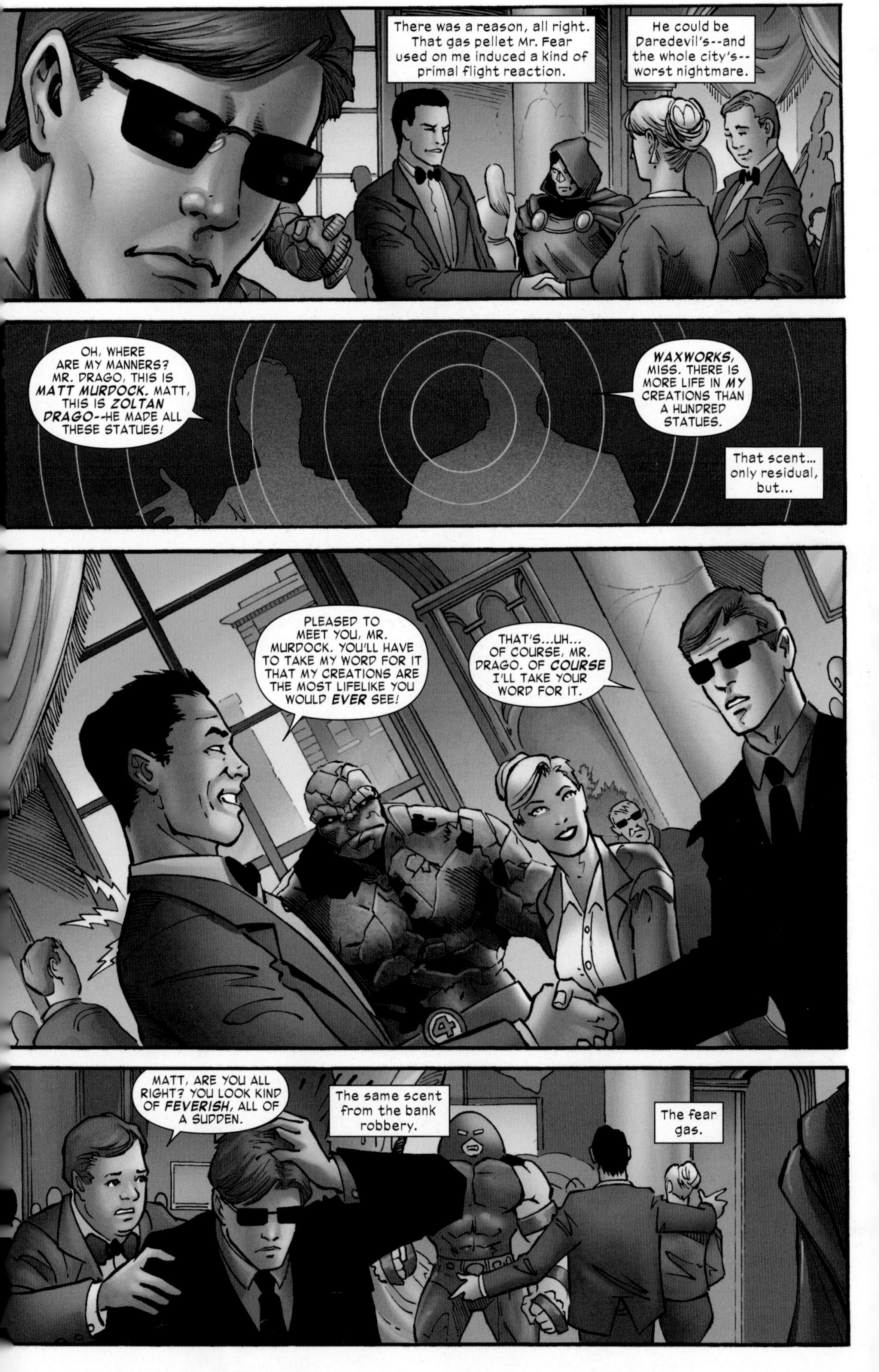
There was a reason, all right. That gas pellet Mr. Fear used on me induced a kind of primal flight reaction.
He could be Daredevil's--and the whole city's--worst nightmare.
OH, WHERE ARE MY MANNERS? MR. DRAGO, THIS IS MATT MURDOCK. MATT, THIS IS ZOLTAN DRAGO--HE MADE ALL THESE STATUES!
WAXWORKS, MISS. THERE IS MORE LIFE IN MY CREATIONS THAN A HUNDRED STATUES.
That scent... only residual, but...
PLEASED TO MEET YOU, MR. MURDOCK. YOU'LL HAVE TO TAKE MY WORD FOR IT THAT MY CREATIONS ARE THE MOST LIFELIKE YOU WOULD EVER SEE!
THAT'S...UH... OF COURSE, MR. DRAGO. OF COURSE I'LL TAKE YOUR WORD FOR IT.
MATT, ARE YOU ALL RIGHT? YOU LOOK KIND OF FEVERISH, ALL OF A SUDDEN.
The same scent from the bank robbery.
The fear gas.

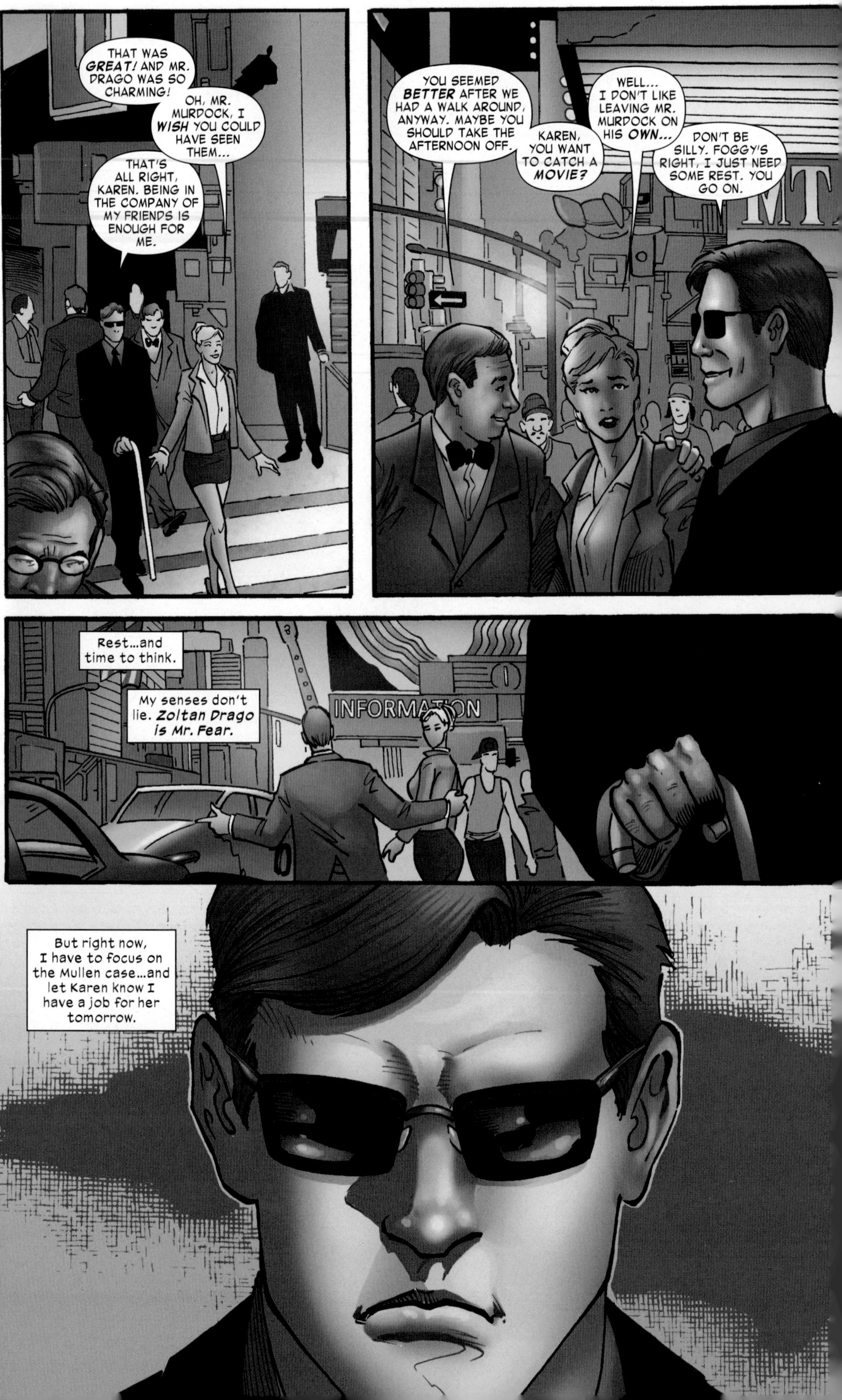

THAT WAS *GREAT!* AND MR. DRAGO WAS SO CHARMING!
OH, MR. MURDOCK, I *WISH* YOU COULD HAVE SEEN THEM...
THAT'S ALL RIGHT, KAREN. BEING IN THE COMPANY OF MY FRIENDS IS ENOUGH FOR ME.
YOU SEEMED *BETTER* AFTER WE HAD A WALK AROUND, ANYWAY. MAYBE YOU SHOULD TAKE THE AFTERNOON OFF.
KAREN, YOU WANT TO CATCH A *MOVIE?*
WELL... I DON'T LIKE LEAVING MR. MURDOCK ON HIS *OWN...*
DON'T BE SILLY. FOGGY'S RIGHT, I JUST NEED SOME REST. YOU GO ON.
Rest...and time to think.
INFORMATION
My senses don't lie. *Zoltan Drago is Mr. Fear.*
But right now, I have to focus on the Mullen case...and let Karen know I have a job for her tomorrow.

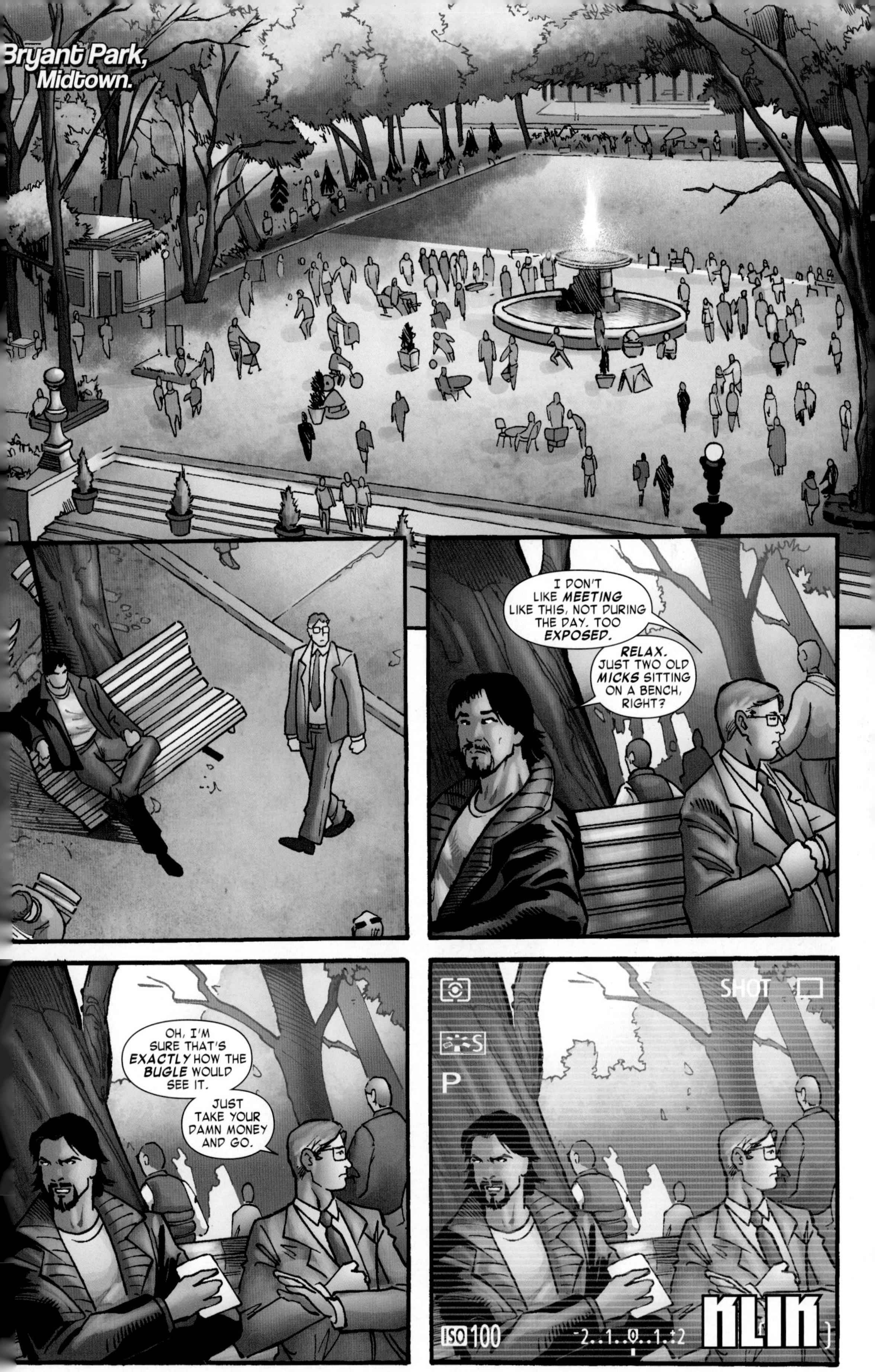
Bryant Park, Midtown.
I DON'T LIKE MEETING LIKE THIS, NOT DURING THE DAY. TOO EXPOSED.
RELAX. JUST TWO OLD MICKS SITTING ON A BENCH, RIGHT?
OH, I'M SURE THAT'S EXACTLY HOW THE BUGLE WOULD SEE IT.
JUST TAKE YOUR DAMN MONEY AND GO.
SHOT
P
ISO 100
-2..1..0..1..2
KLIK

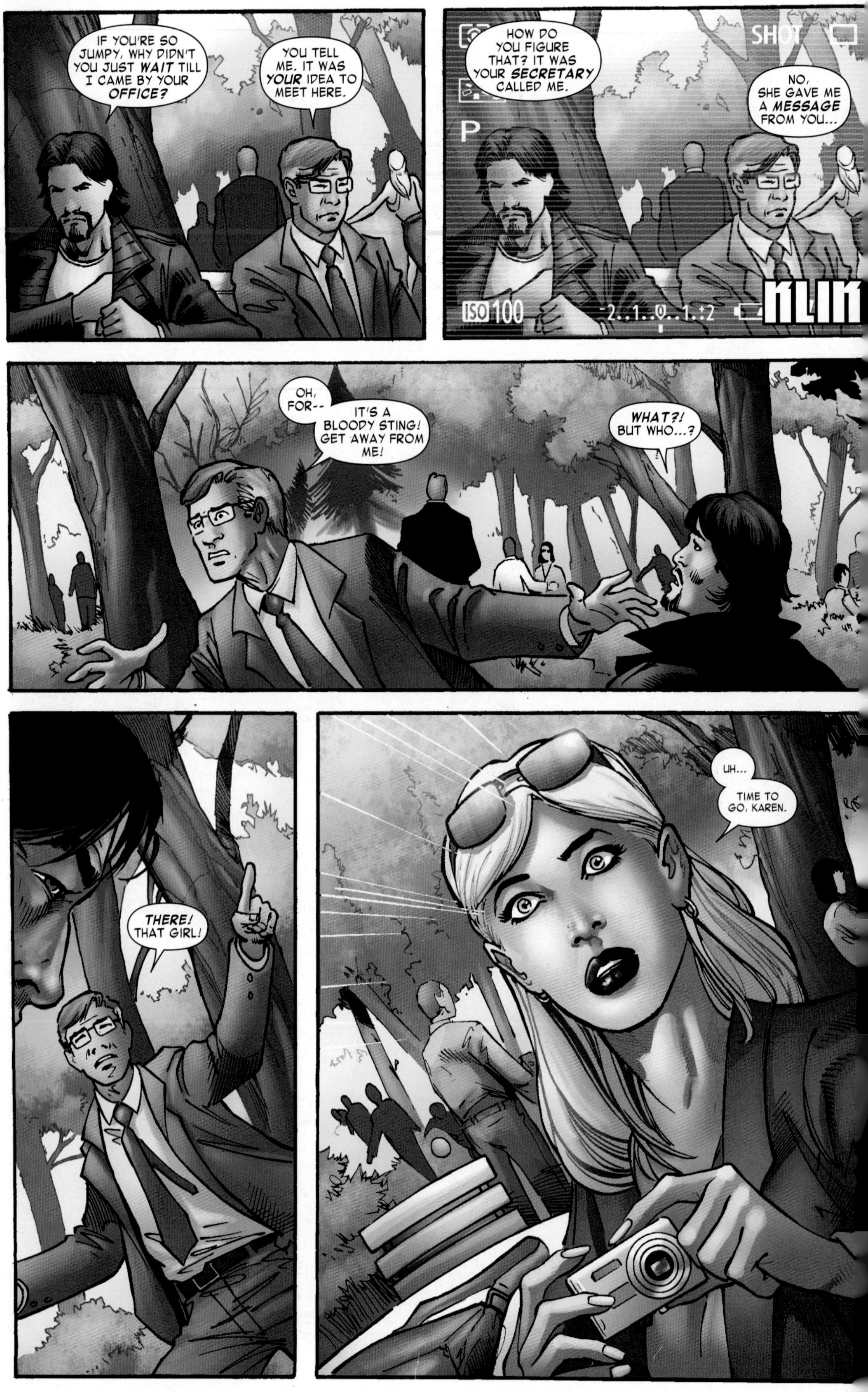

IF YOU'RE SO JUMPY, WHY DIDN'T YOU JUST WAIT TILL I CAME BY YOUR OFFICE?
YOU TELL ME. IT WAS YOUR IDEA TO MEET HERE.
SHOT
HOW DO YOU FIGURE THAT? IT WAS YOUR SECRETARY CALLED ME.
NO, SHE GAVE ME A MESSAGE FROM YOU...
P
ISO 100
KLIK
OH, FOR--
IT'S A BLOODY STING! GET AWAY FROM ME!
WHAT?! BUT WHO...?
THERE! THAT GIRL!
UH...
TIME TO GO, KAREN.

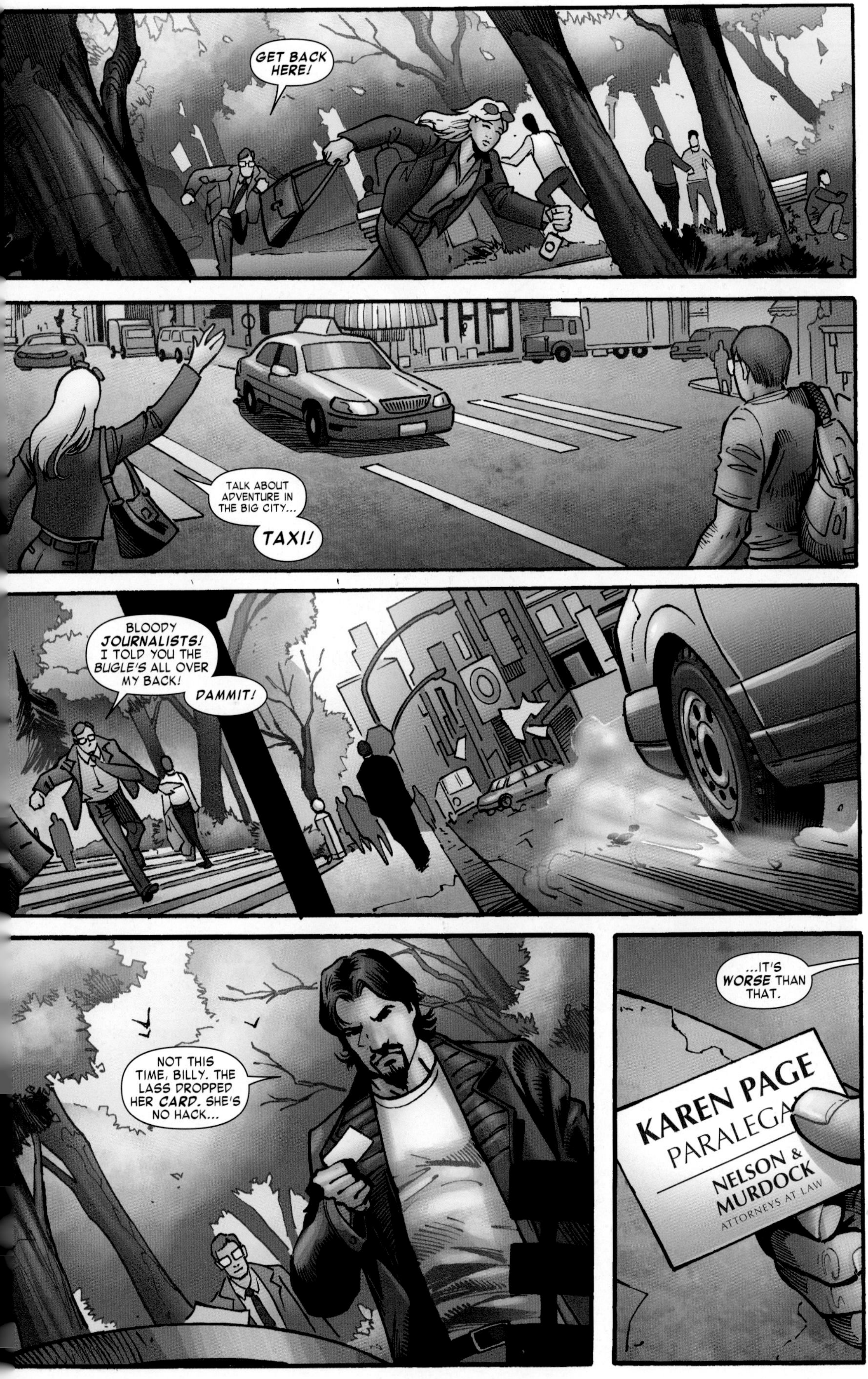
GET BACK HERE!
TALK ABOUT ADVENTURE IN THE BIG CITY...
TAXI!
BLOODY JOURNALISTS! I TOLD YOU THE BUGLE'S ALL OVER MY BACK!
DAMMIT!
NOT THIS TIME, BILLY. THE LASS DROPPED HER CARD. SHE'S NO HACK...
...IT'S WORSE THAN THAT.
KAREN PAGE
PARALEGA
NELSON & MURDOCK
ATTORNEYS AT LAW

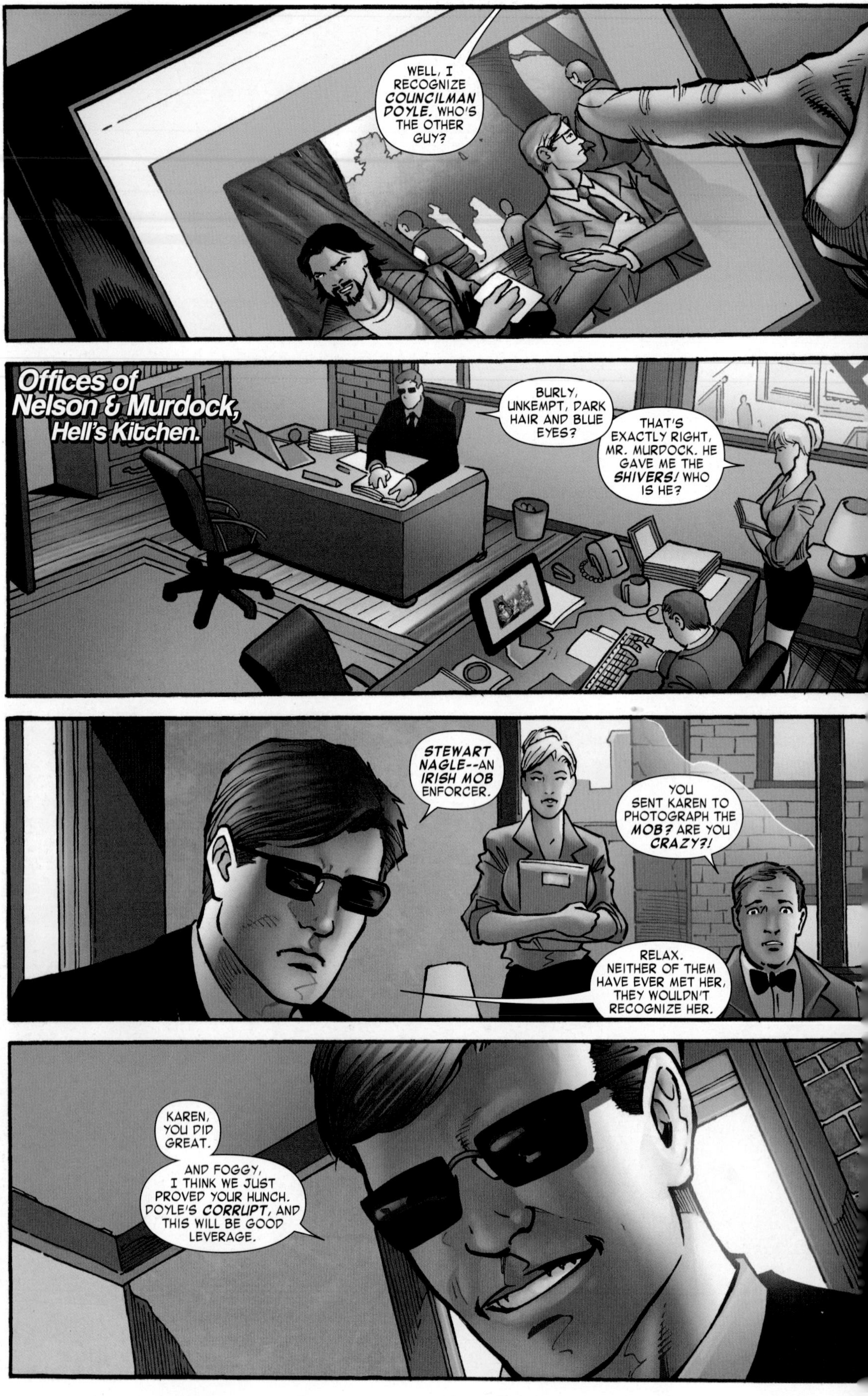

WELL, I RECOGNIZE COUNCILMAN DOYLE. WHO'S THE OTHER GUY?
Offices of Nelson & Murdock, Hell's Kitchen.
BURLY, UNKEMPT, DARK HAIR AND BLUE EYES?
THAT'S EXACTLY RIGHT, MR. MURDOCK. HE GAVE ME THE SHIVERS! WHO IS HE?
STEWART NAGLE--AN IRISH MOB ENFORCER.
YOU SENT KAREN TO PHOTOGRAPH THE MOB? ARE YOU CRAZY?!
RELAX. NEITHER OF THEM HAVE EVER MET HER, THEY WOULDN'T RECOGNIZE HER.
KAREN, YOU DID GREAT.
AND FOGGY, I THINK WE JUST PROVED YOUR HUNCH. DOYLE'S CORRUPT, AND THIS WILL BE GOOD LEVERAGE.

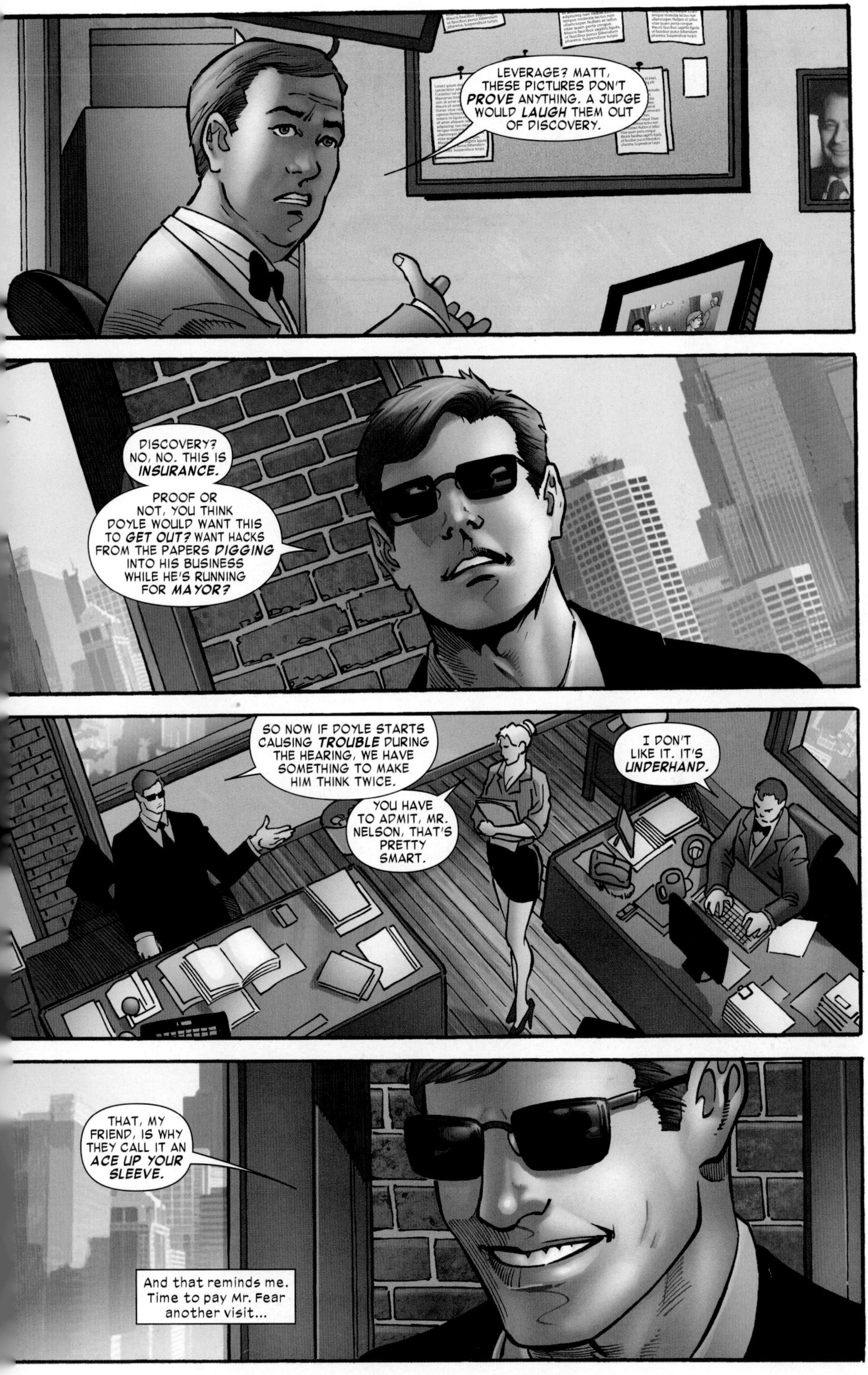
LEVERAGE? MATT, THESE PICTURES DON'T PROVE ANYTHING. A JUDGE WOULD LAUGH THEM OUT OF DISCOVERY.
DISCOVERY? NO, NO. THIS IS INSURANCE.
PROOF OR NOT, YOU THINK DOYLE WOULD WANT THIS TO GET OUT? WANT HACKS FROM THE PAPERS DIGGING INTO HIS BUSINESS WHILE HE'S RUNNING FOR MAYOR?
SO NOW IF DOYLE STARTS CAUSING TROUBLE DURING THE HEARING, WE HAVE SOMETHING TO MAKE HIM THINK TWICE.
YOU HAVE TO ADMIT, MR. NELSON, THAT'S PRETTY SMART.
I DON'T LIKE IT. IT'S UNDERHAND.
THAT, MY FRIEND, IS WHY THEY CALL IT AN ACE UP YOUR SLEEVE.
And that reminds me. Time to pay Mr. Fear another visit...

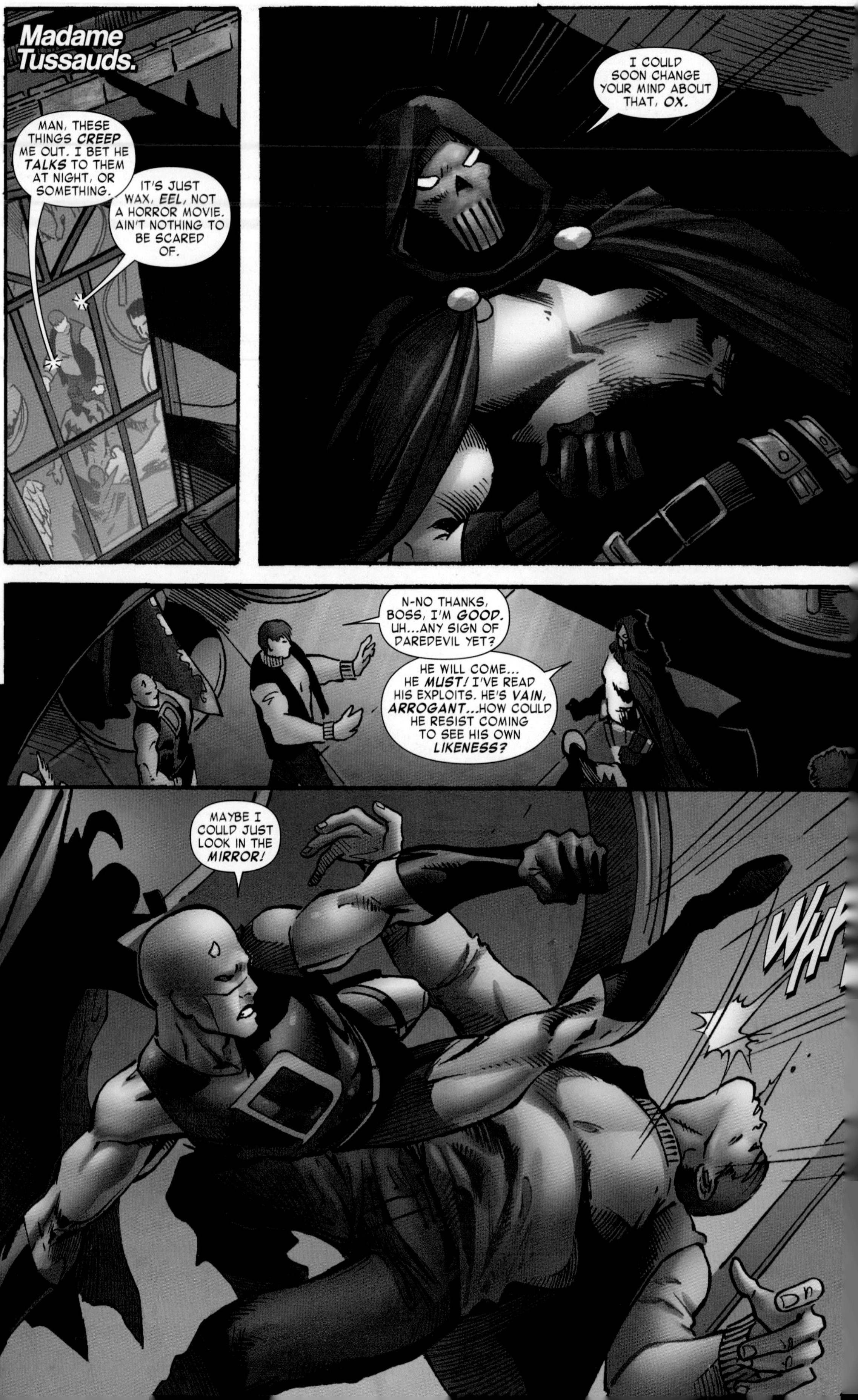

Madame Tussauds.
MAN, THESE THINGS CREEP ME OUT. I BET HE TALKS TO THEM AT NIGHT, OR SOMETHING.
IT'S JUST WAX, EEL, NOT A HORROR MOVIE. AIN'T NOTHING TO BE SCARED OF.
I COULD SOON CHANGE YOUR MIND ABOUT THAT, OX.
N-NO THANKS, BOSS, I'M GOOD. UH...ANY SIGN OF DAREDEVIL YET?
HE WILL COME... HE MUST! I'VE READ HIS EXPLOITS. HE'S VAIN, ARROGANT...HOW COULD HE RESIST COMING TO SEE HIS OWN LIKENESS?
MAYBE I COULD JUST LOOK IN THE MIRROR!

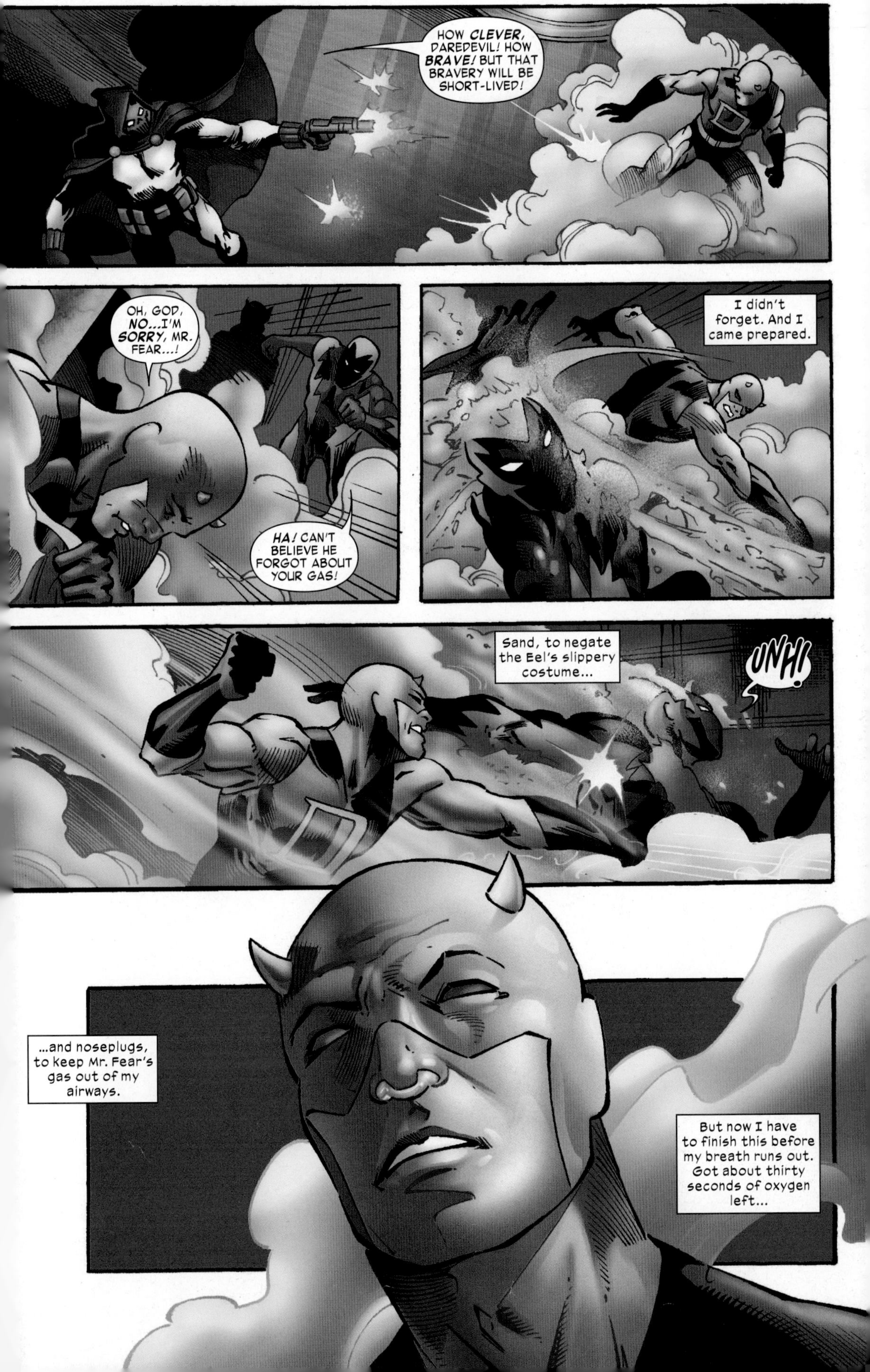

HOW CLEVER, DAREDEVIL! HOW BRAVE! BUT THAT BRAVERY WILL BE SHORT-LIVED!
OH, GOD, NO...I'M SORRY, MR. FEAR...!
HA! CAN'T BELIEVE HE FORGOT ABOUT YOUR GAS!
I didn't forget. And I came prepared.
Sand, to negate the Eel's slippery costume...
UNH!
...and noseplugs, to keep Mr. Fear's gas out of my airways.
But now I have to finish this before my breath runs out. Got about thirty seconds of oxygen left...

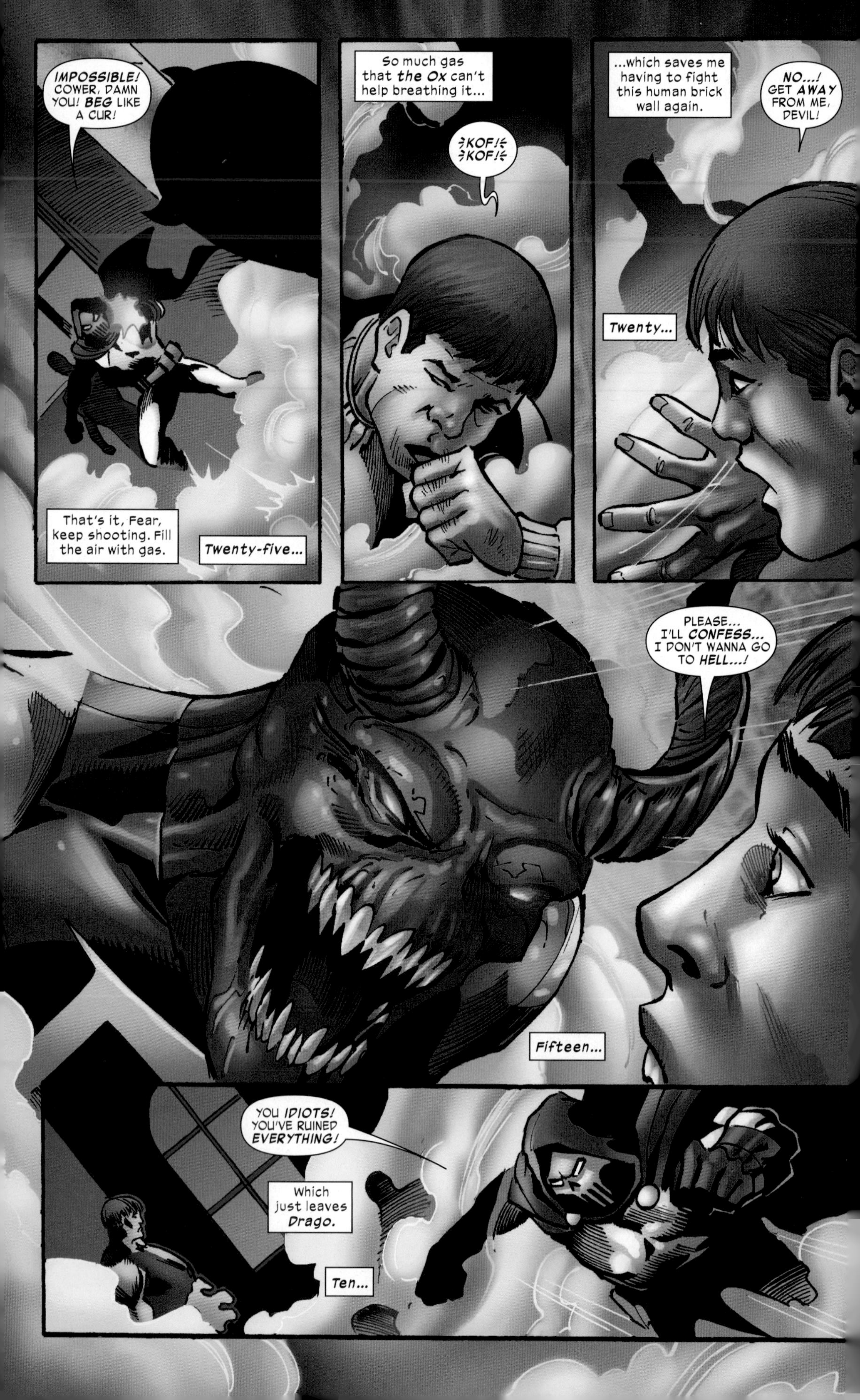

IMPOSSIBLE! COWER, DAMN YOU! BEG LIKE A CUR!
That's it, Fear, keep shooting. Fill the air with gas.
Twenty-five...
So much gas that the Ox can't help breathing it...
KOF! KOF!
...which saves me having to fight this human brick wall again.
NO...! GET AWAY FROM ME, DEVIL!
Twenty...
PLEASE... I'LL CONFESS... I DON'T WANNA GO TO HELL...!
Fifteen...
YOU IDIOTS! YOU'VE RUINED EVERYTHING!
Which just leaves Drago.
Ten...

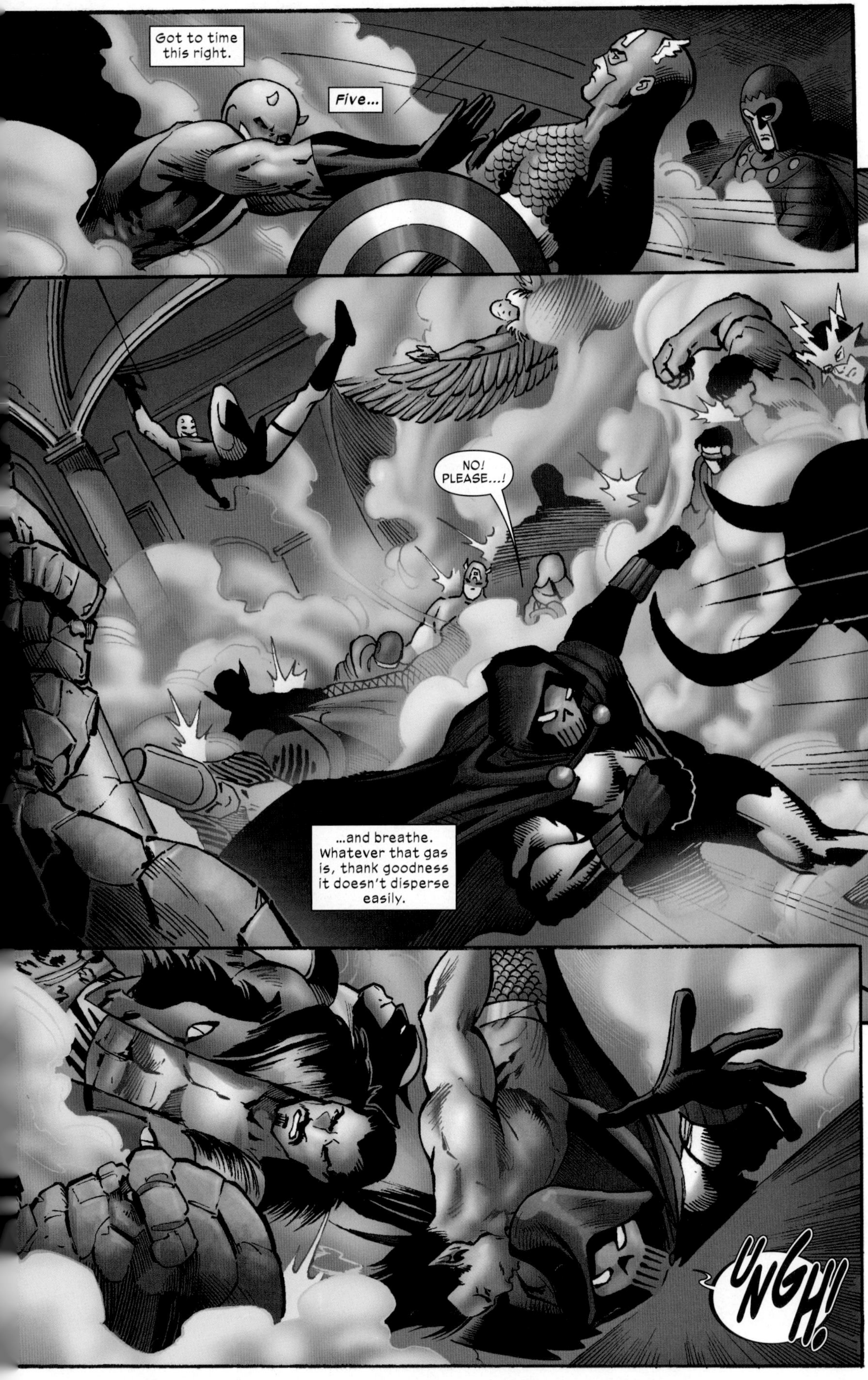
Got to time this right.
Five...
NO! PLEASE...!
...and breathe. Whatever that gas is, thank goodness it doesn't disperse easily.
UNGH!!

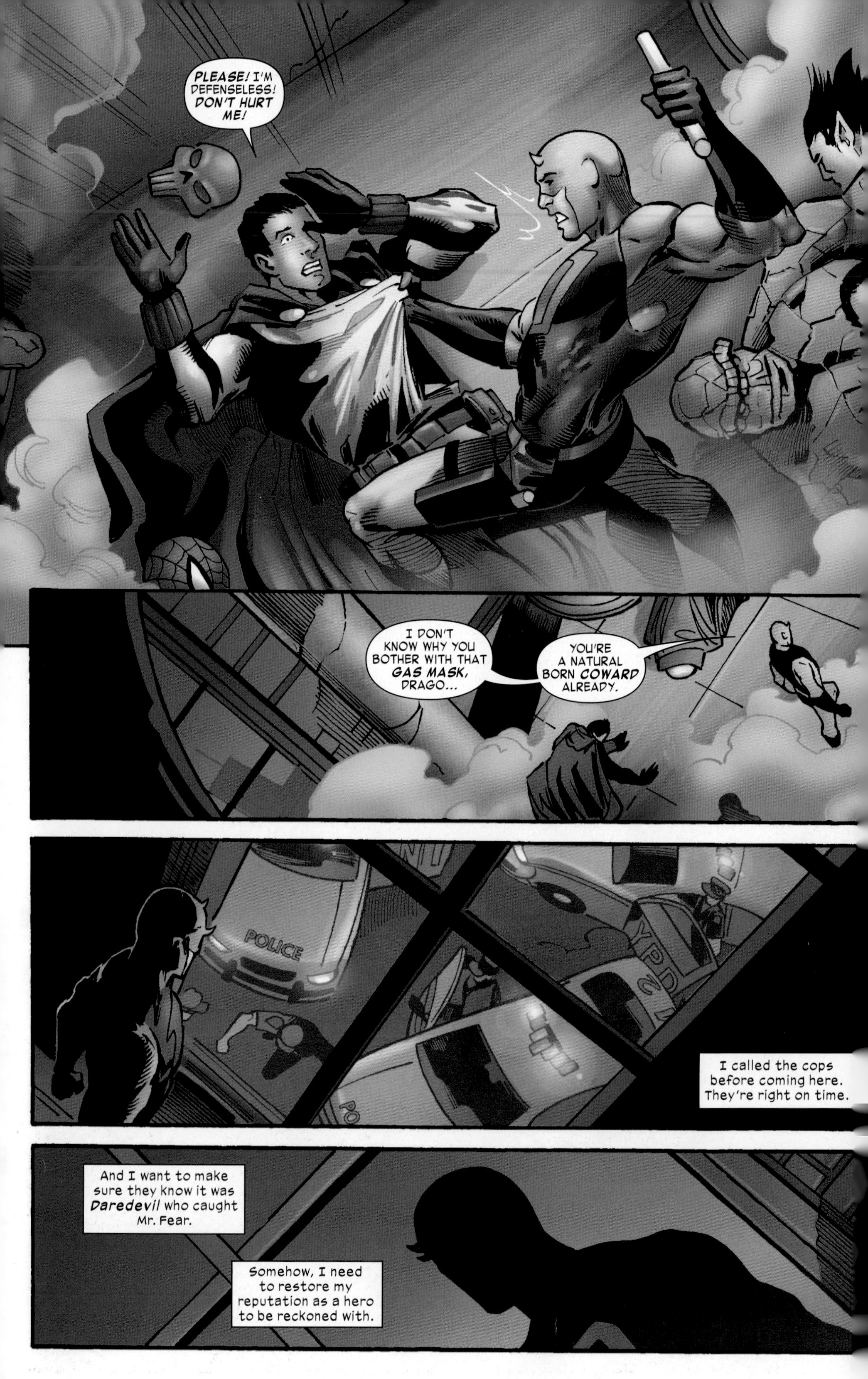
PLEASE! I'M DEFENSELESS! DON'T HURT ME!
I DON'T KNOW WHY YOU BOTHER WITH THAT GAS MASK, DRAGO...
YOU'RE A NATURAL BORN COWARD ALREADY.
POLICE
I called the cops before coming here. They're right on time.
And I want to make sure they know it was Daredevil who caught Mr. Fear.
Somehow, I need to restore my reputation as a hero to be reckoned with.

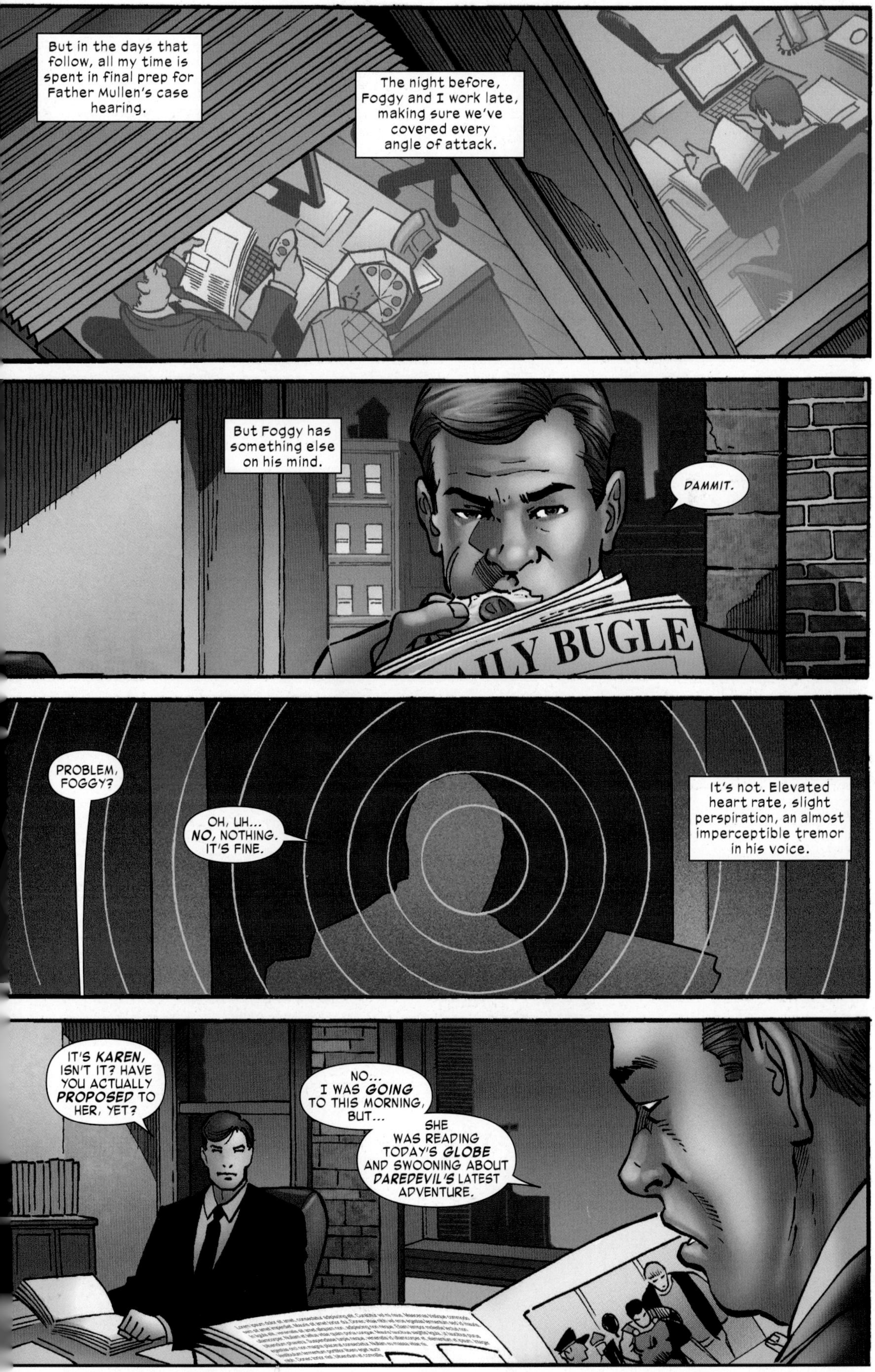
But in the days that follow, all my time is spent in final prep for Father Mullen's case hearing.
The night before, Foggy and I work late, making sure we've covered every angle of attack.
But Foggy has something else on his mind.
DAMMIT.
ILY BUGLE
PROBLEM, FOGGY?
OH, UH... NO, NOTHING. IT'S FINE.
It's not. Elevated heart rate, slight perspiration, an almost imperceptible tremor in his voice.
IT'S KAREN, ISN'T IT? HAVE YOU ACTUALLY PROPOSED TO HER, YET?
NO... I WAS GOING TO THIS MORNING, BUT...
SHE WAS READING TODAY'S GLOBE AND SWOONING ABOUT DAREDEVIL'S LATEST ADVENTURE.

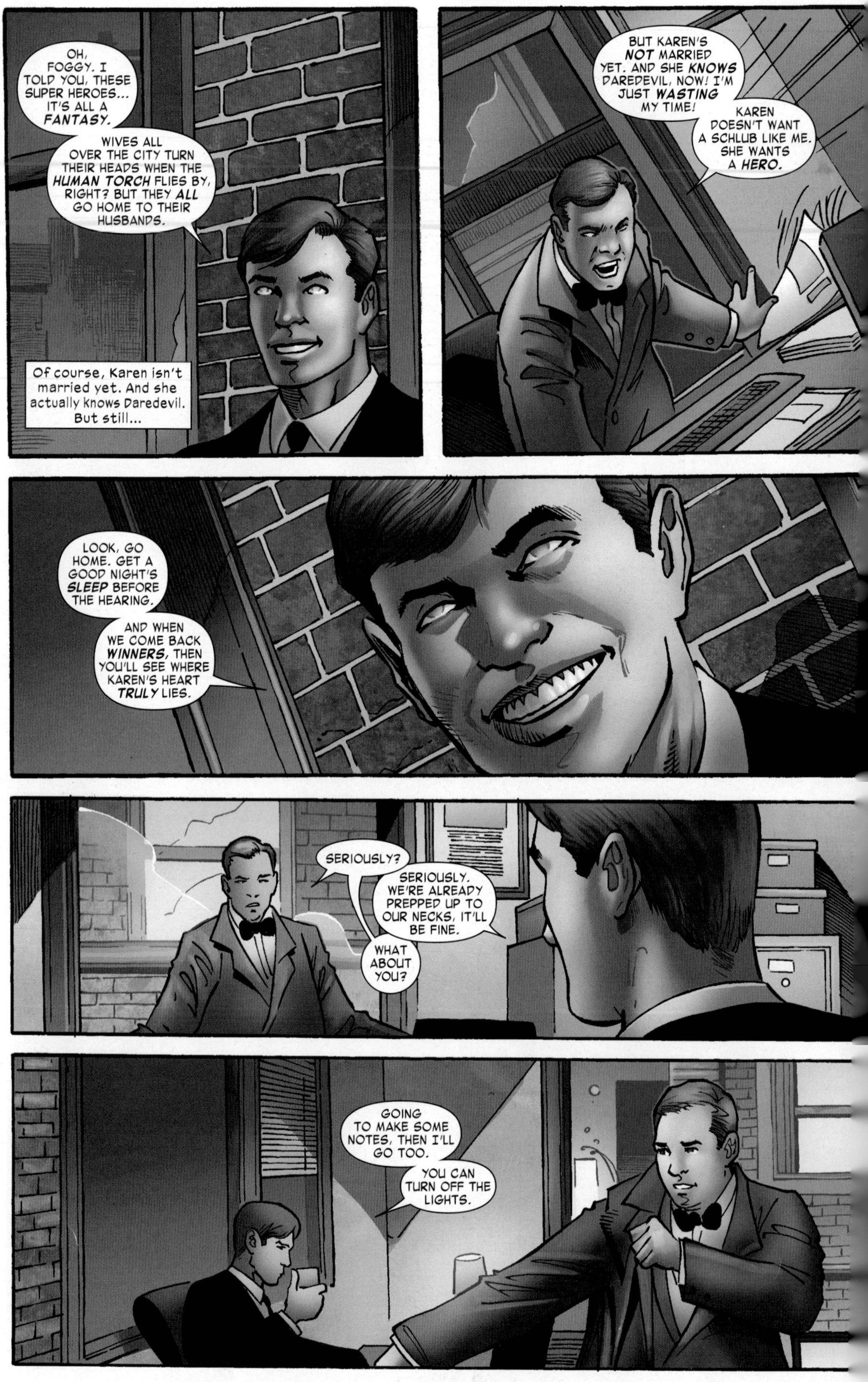
OH, FOGGY. I TOLD YOU, THESE SUPER HEROES... IT'S ALL A FANTASY.
WIVES ALL OVER THE CITY TURN THEIR HEADS WHEN THE HUMAN TORCH FLIES BY, RIGHT? BUT THEY ALL GO HOME TO THEIR HUSBANDS.
Of course, Karen isn't married yet. And she actually knows Daredevil. But still...
BUT KAREN'S NOT MARRIED YET. AND SHE KNOWS DAREDEVIL, NOW! I'M JUST WASTING MY TIME!
KAREN DOESN'T WANT A SCHLUB LIKE ME. SHE WANTS A HERO.
LOOK, GO HOME. GET A GOOD NIGHT'S SLEEP BEFORE THE HEARING.
AND WHEN WE COME BACK WINNERS, THEN YOU'LL SEE WHERE KAREN'S HEART TRULY LIES.
SERIOUSLY?
SERIOUSLY. WE'RE ALREADY PREPPED UP TO OUR NECKS, IT'LL BE FINE.
WHAT ABOUT YOU?
GOING TO MAKE SOME NOTES, THEN I'LL GO TOO.
YOU CAN TURN OFF THE LIGHTS.

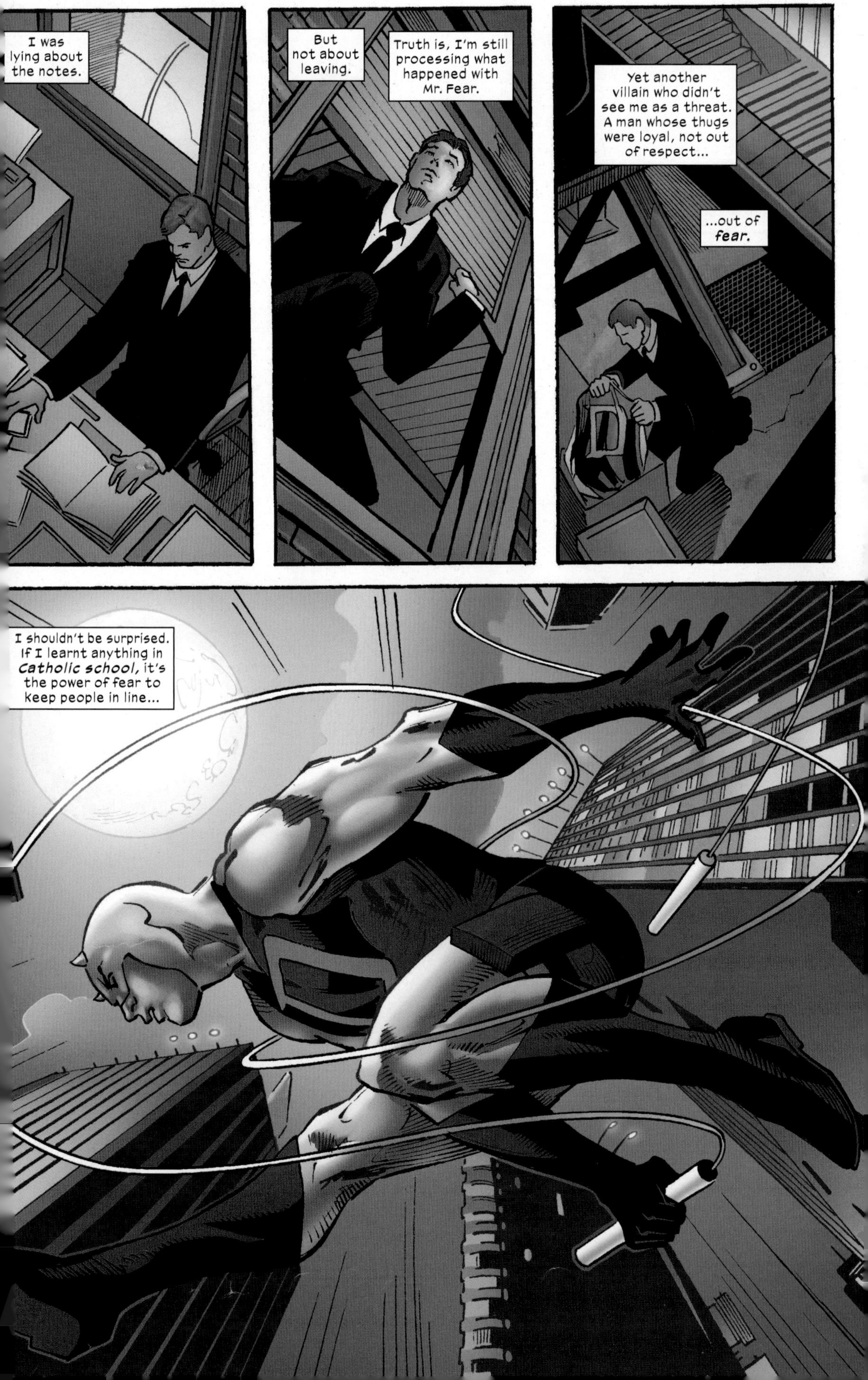
I was lying about the notes.
But not about leaving.
Truth is, I'm still processing what happened with Mr. Fear.
Yet another villain who didn't see me as a threat. A man whose thugs were loyal, not out of respect...
...out of *fear.*
I shouldn't be surprised. If I learnt anything in *Catholic school,* it's the power of fear to keep people in line...

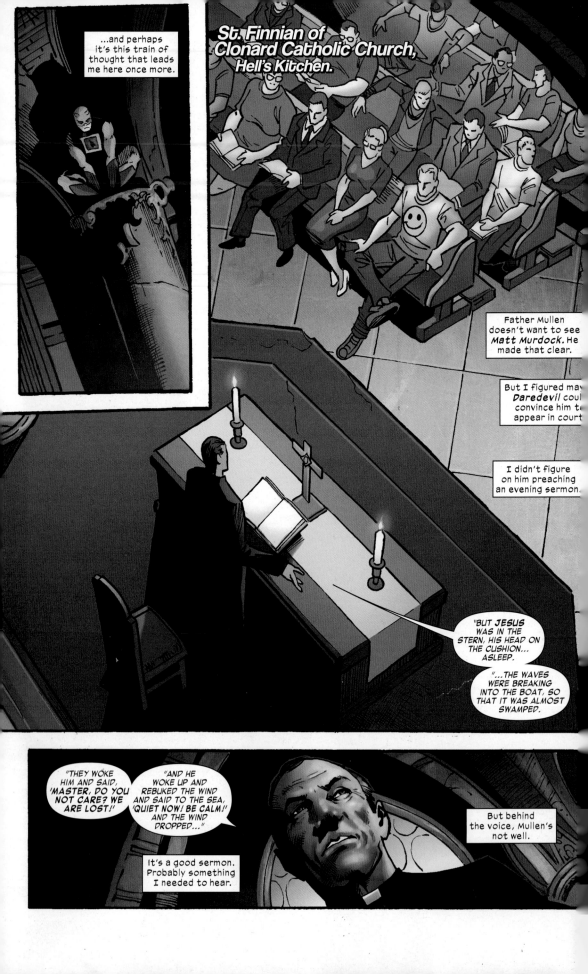

...and perhaps it's this train of thought that leads me here once more.

St. Finnian of Clonard Catholic Church, Hell's Kitchen.

Father Mullen doesn't want to see *Matt Murdock*. He made that clear.

But I figured may *Daredevil* coul convince him t appear in court

I didn't figure on him preaching an evening sermon.

"BUT *JESUS* WAS IN THE STERN, HIS HEAD ON THE CUSHION... ASLEEP.

"...THE WAVES WERE BREAKING INTO THE BOAT, SO THAT IT WAS ALMOST SWAMPED.

"THEY WOKE HIM AND SAID, 'MASTER, DO YOU NOT CARE? WE ARE LOST!'

"AND HE WOKE UP AND REBUKED THE WIND AND SAID TO THE SEA, 'QUIET NOW! BE CALM!' AND THE WIND DROPPED..."

It's a good sermon. Probably something I needed to hear.

But behind the voice, Mullen's not well.

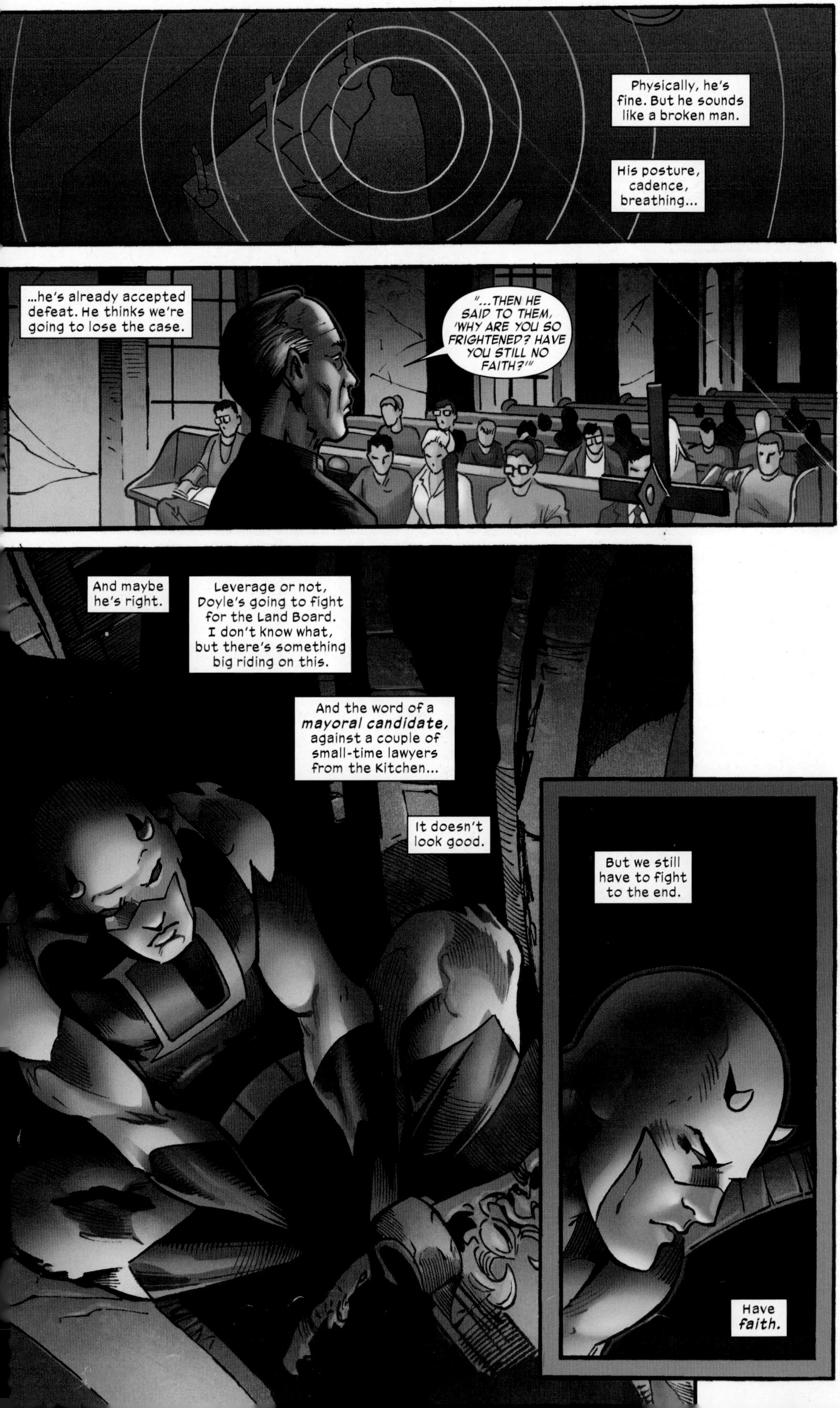
Physically, he's fine. But he sounds like a broken man.
His posture, cadence, breathing...
...he's already accepted defeat. He thinks we're going to lose the case.
"...THEN HE SAID TO THEM, 'WHY ARE YOU SO FRIGHTENED? HAVE YOU STILL NO FAITH?'"
And maybe he's right.
Leverage or not, Doyle's going to fight for the Land Board. I don't know what, but there's something big riding on this.
And the word of a *mayoral candidate,* against a couple of small-time lawyers from the Kitchen...
It doesn't look good.
But we still have to fight to the end.
Have *faith.*

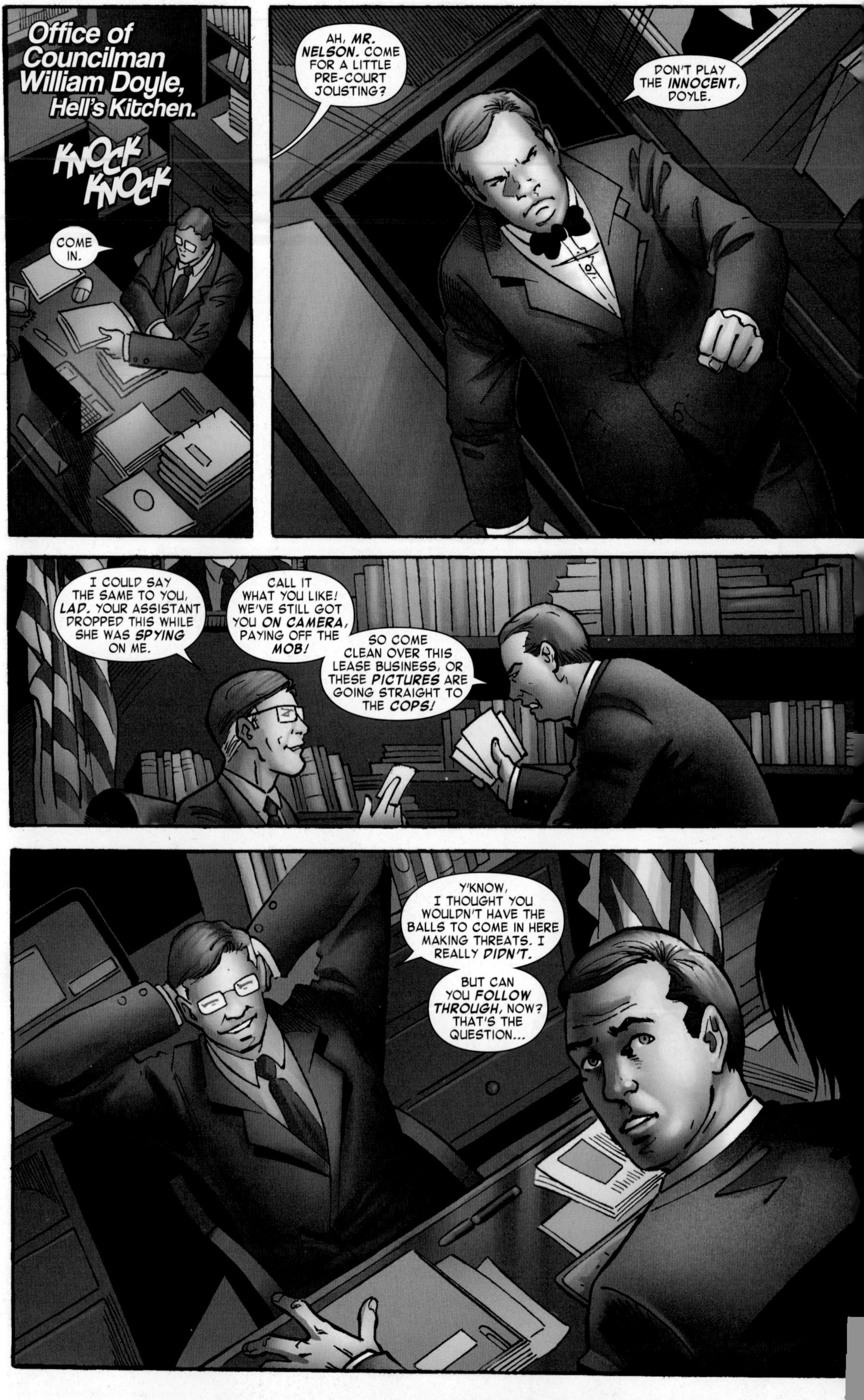

Office of Councilman William Doyle, Hell's Kitchen.
KNOCK KNOCK
COME IN.
AH, MR. NELSON. COME FOR A LITTLE PRE-COURT JOUSTING?
DON'T PLAY THE INNOCENT, DOYLE.
I COULD SAY THE SAME TO YOU, LAD. YOUR ASSISTANT DROPPED THIS WHILE SHE WAS SPYING ON ME.
CALL IT WHAT YOU LIKE! WE'VE STILL GOT YOU ON CAMERA, PAYING OFF THE MOB!
SO COME CLEAN OVER THIS LEASE BUSINESS, OR THESE PICTURES ARE GOING STRAIGHT TO THE COPS!
Y'KNOW, I THOUGHT YOU WOULDN'T HAVE THE BALLS TO COME IN HERE MAKING THREATS. I REALLY DIDN'T.
BUT CAN YOU FOLLOW THROUGH, NOW? THAT'S THE QUESTION...

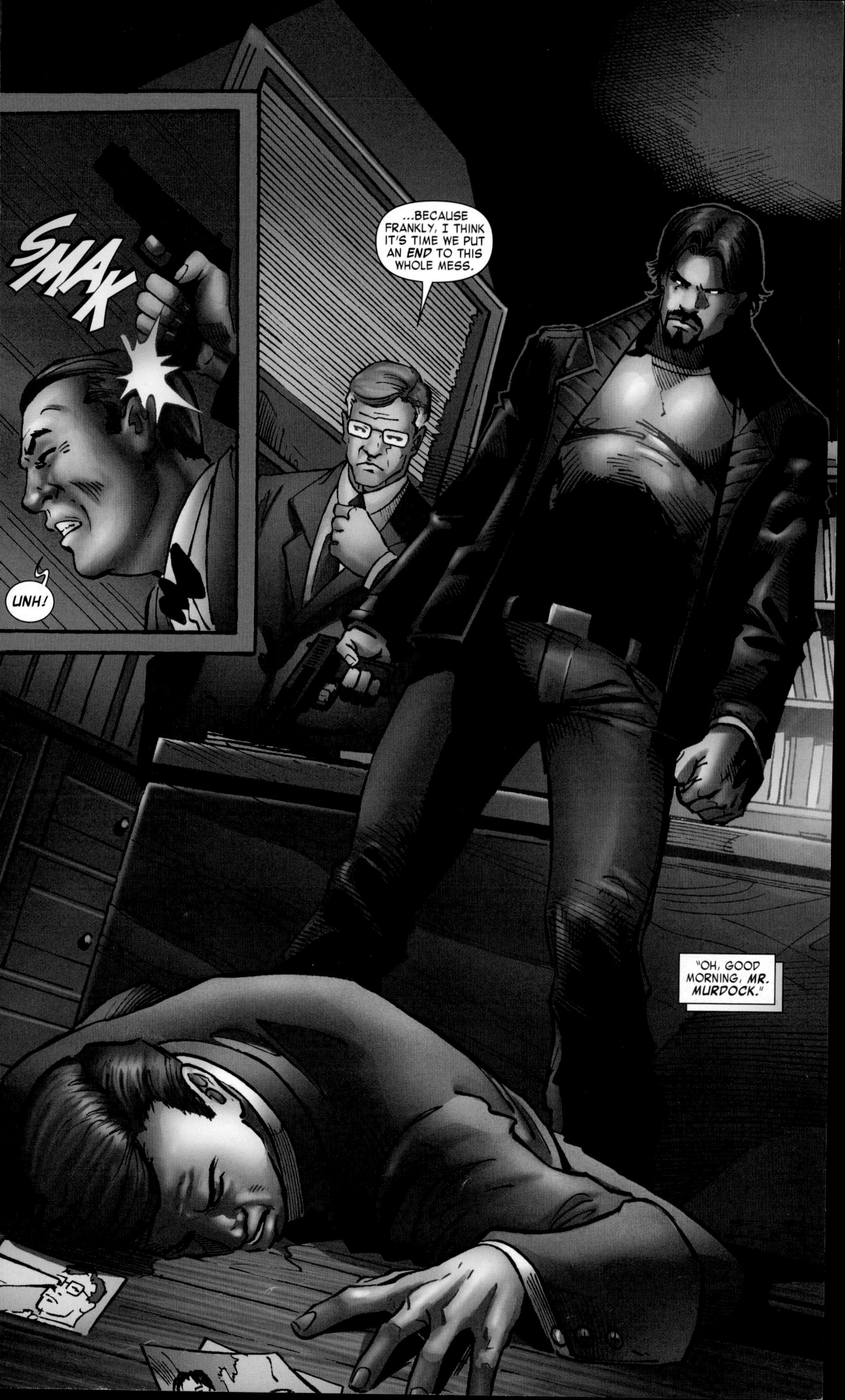
SMAK
UNH!
...BECAUSE FRANKLY, I THINK IT'S TIME WE PUT AN END TO THIS WHOLE MESS.
"OH, GOOD MORNING, MR. MURDOCK."

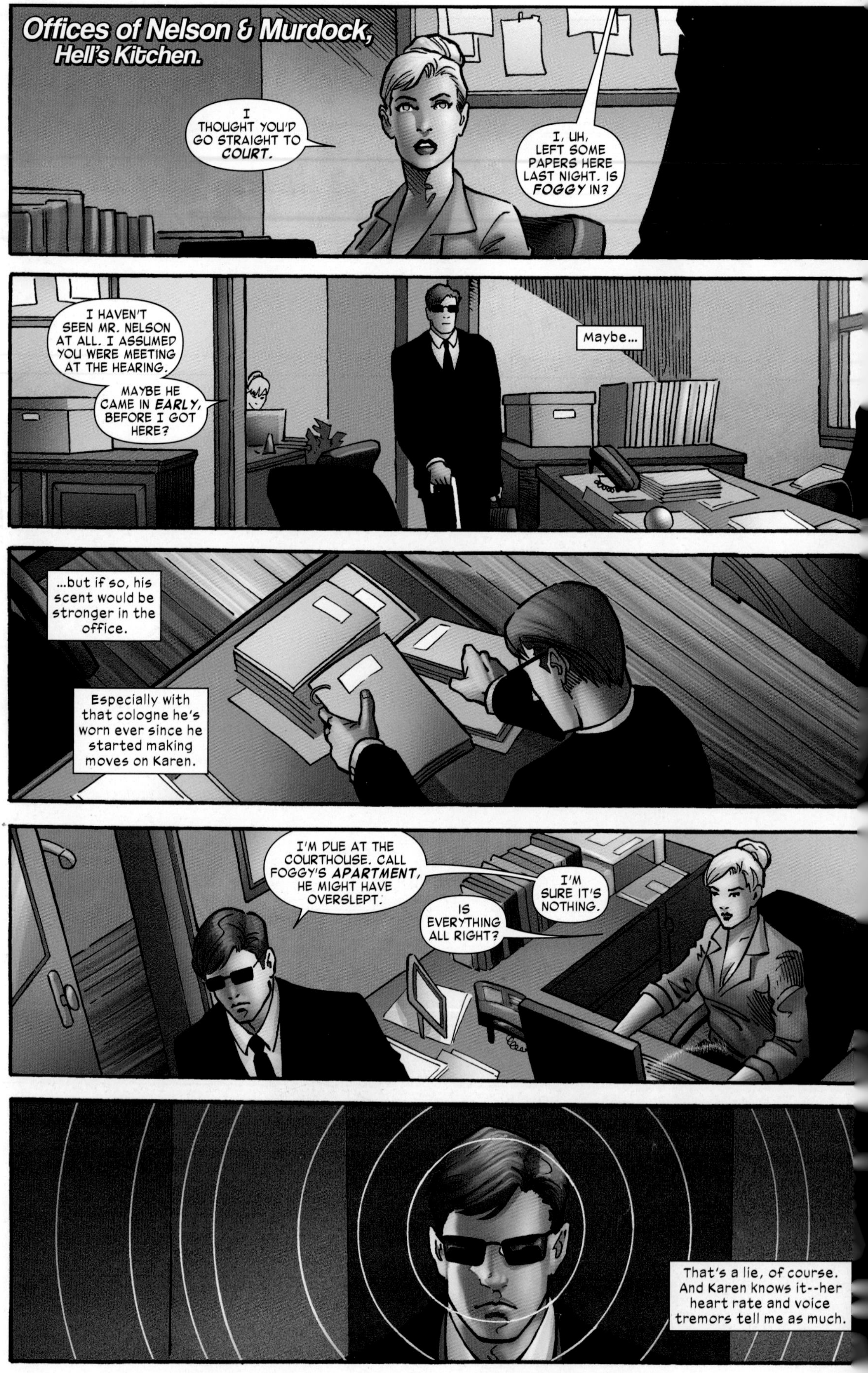
Offices of Nelson & Murdock, Hell's Kitchen.
I THOUGHT YOU'D GO STRAIGHT TO COURT.
I, UH, LEFT SOME PAPERS HERE LAST NIGHT. IS FOGGY IN?
I HAVEN'T SEEN MR. NELSON AT ALL. I ASSUMED YOU WERE MEETING AT THE HEARING.
MAYBE HE CAME IN EARLY, BEFORE I GOT HERE?
Maybe...
...but if so, his scent would be stronger in the office.
Especially with that cologne he's worn ever since he started making moves on Karen.
I'M DUE AT THE COURTHOUSE. CALL FOGGY'S APARTMENT, HE MIGHT HAVE OVERSLEPT.
IS EVERYTHING ALL RIGHT?
I'M SURE IT'S NOTHING.
That's a lie, of course. And Karen knows it--her heart rate and voice tremors tell me as much.

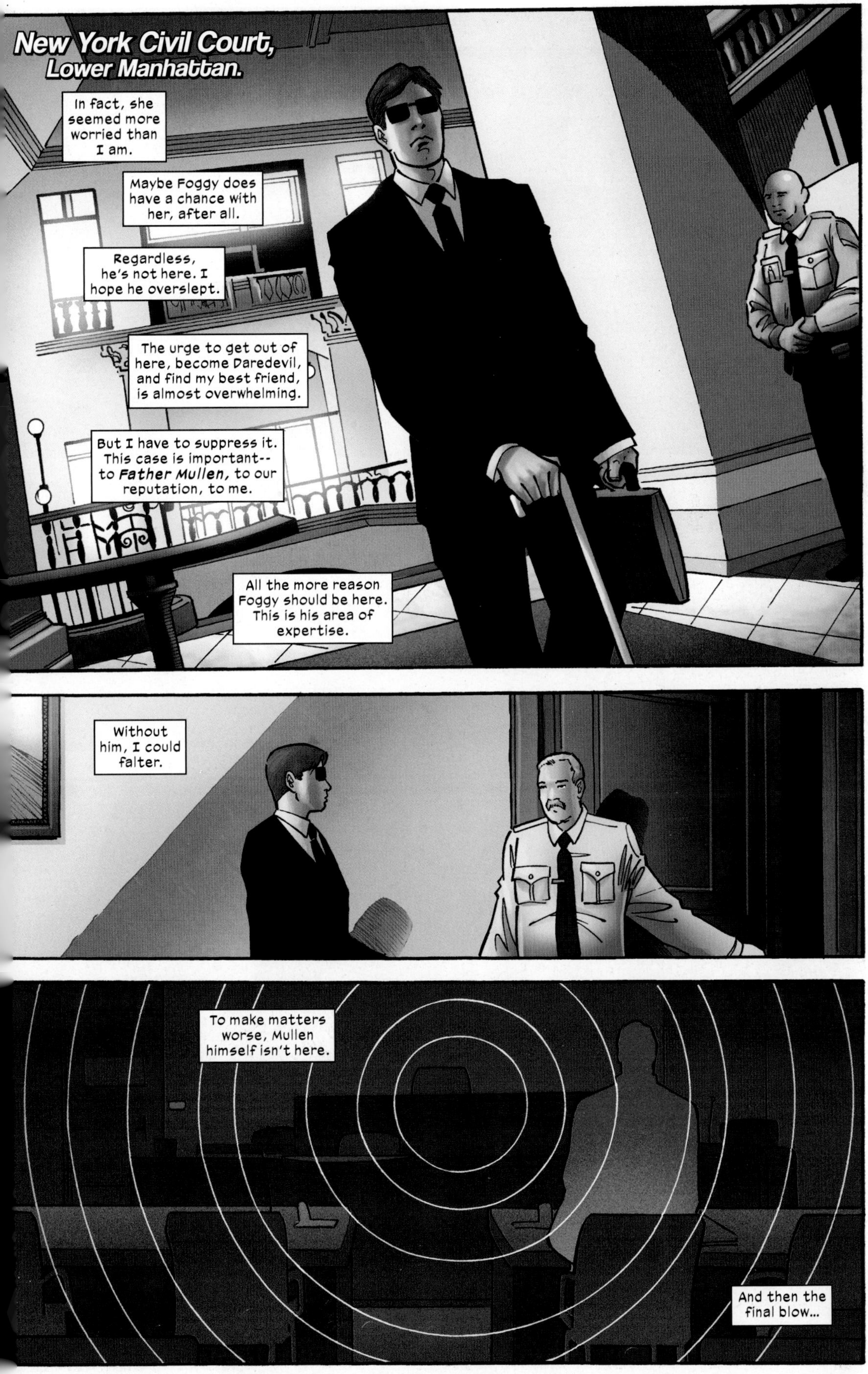
New York Civil Court, Lower Manhattan.
In fact, she seemed more worried than I am.
Maybe Foggy does have a chance with her, after all.
Regardless, he's not here. I hope he overslept.
The urge to get out of here, become Daredevil, and find my best friend, is almost overwhelming.
But I have to suppress it. This case is important-- to Father Mullen, to our reputation, to me.
All the more reason Foggy should be here. This is his area of expertise.
Without him, I could falter.
To make matters worse, Mullen himself isn't here.
And then the final blow...

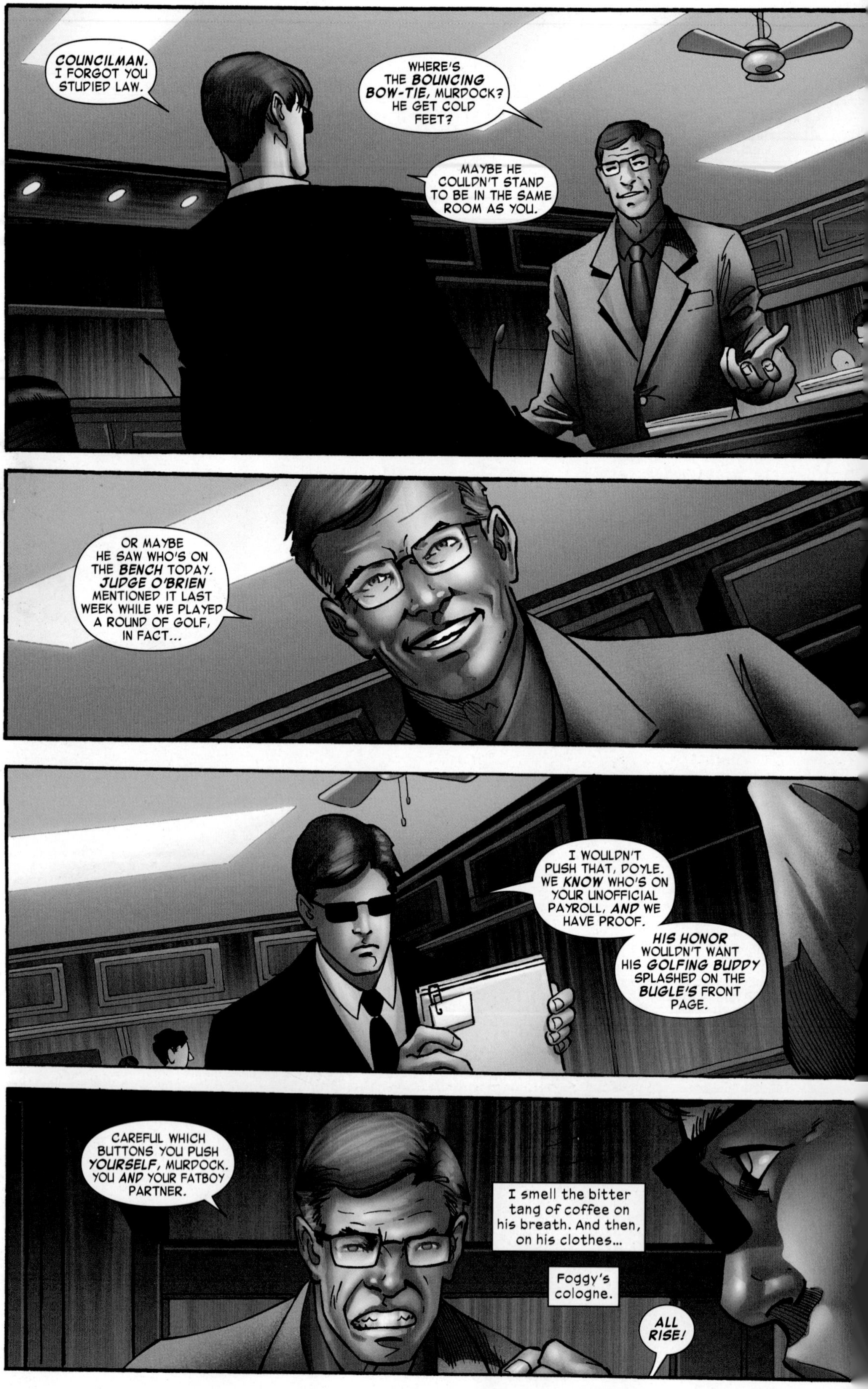
COUNCILMAN. I FORGOT YOU STUDIED LAW.
WHERE'S THE BOUNCING BOW-TIE, MURDOCK? HE GET COLD FEET?
MAYBE HE COULDN'T STAND TO BE IN THE SAME ROOM AS YOU.
OR MAYBE HE SAW WHO'S ON THE BENCH TODAY. JUDGE O'BRIEN MENTIONED IT LAST WEEK WHILE WE PLAYED A ROUND OF GOLF, IN FACT...
I WOULDN'T PUSH THAT, DOYLE. WE KNOW WHO'S ON YOUR UNOFFICIAL PAYROLL, AND WE HAVE PROOF.
HIS HONOR WOULDN'T WANT HIS GOLFING BUDDY SPLASHED ON THE BUGLE'S FRONT PAGE.
CAREFUL WHICH BUTTONS YOU PUSH YOURSELF, MURDOCK. YOU AND YOUR FATBOY PARTNER.
I smell the bitter tang of coffee on his breath. And then, on his clothes...
Foggy's cologne.
ALL RISE!

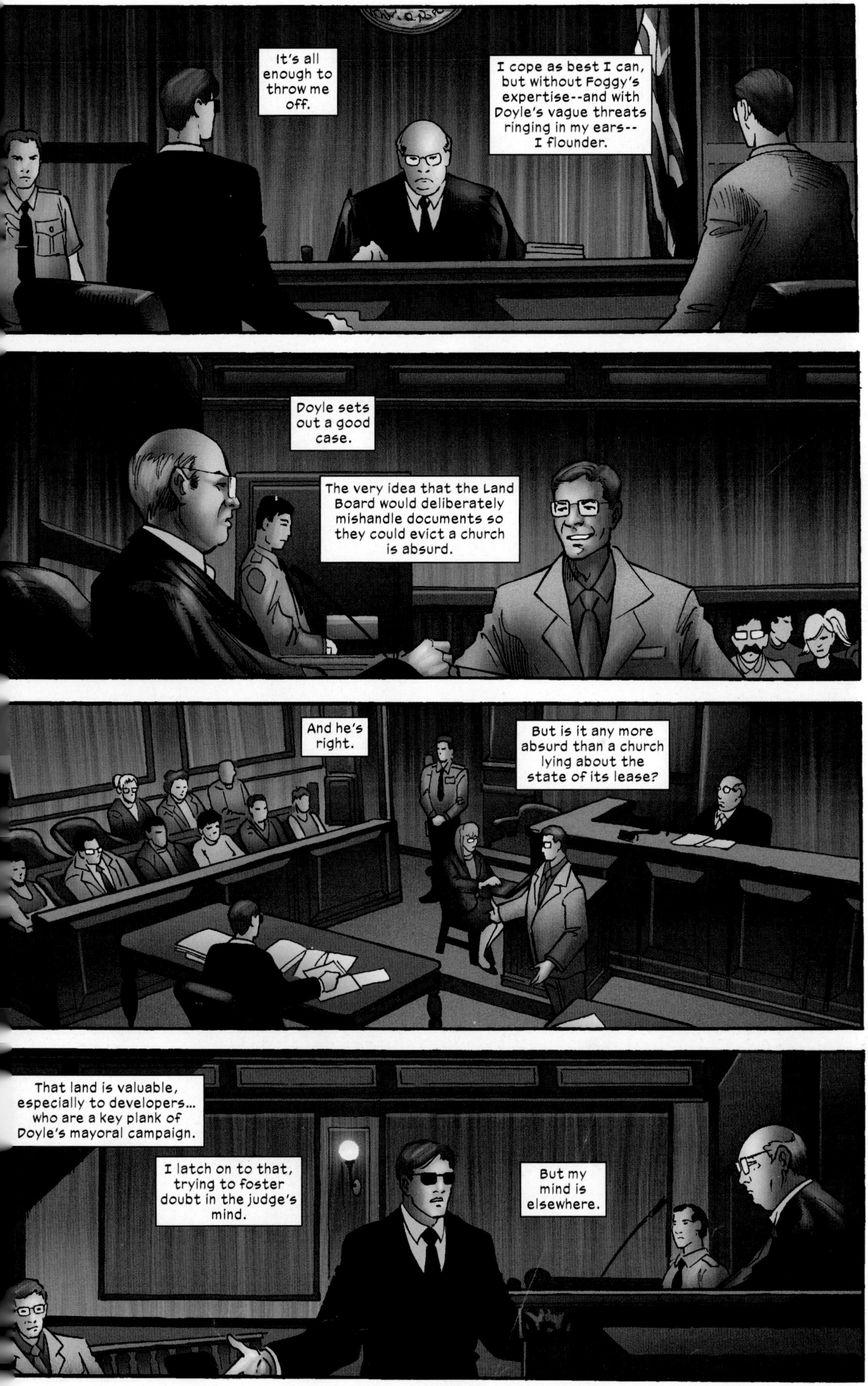
It's all enough to throw me off.
I cope as best I can, but without Foggy's expertise--and with Doyle's vague threats ringing in my ears--I flounder.
Doyle sets out a good case.
The very idea that the Land Board would deliberately mishandle documents so they could evict a church is absurd.
And he's right.
But is it any more absurd than a church lying about the state of its lease?
That land is valuable, especially to developers... who are a key plank of Doyle's mayoral campaign.
I latch on to that, trying to foster doubt in the judge's mind.
But my mind is elsewhere.

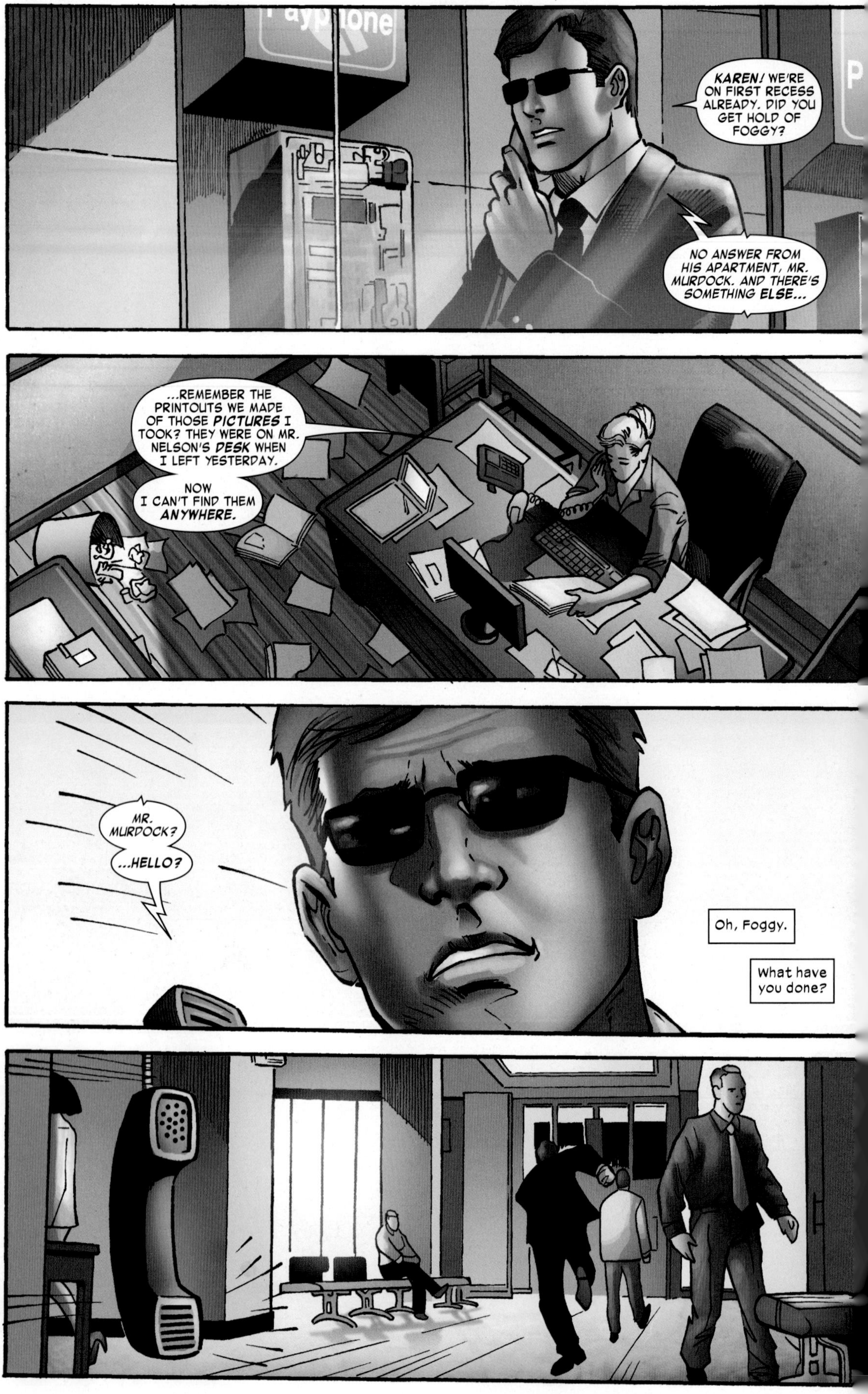
Payphone
KAREN! WE'RE ON FIRST RECESS ALREADY. DID YOU GET HOLD OF FOGGY?
NO ANSWER FROM HIS APARTMENT, MR. MURDOCK. AND THERE'S SOMETHING ELSE...
...REMEMBER THE PRINTOUTS WE MADE OF THOSE PICTURES I TOOK? THEY WERE ON MR. NELSON'S DESK WHEN I LEFT YESTERDAY.
NOW I CAN'T FIND THEM ANYWHERE.
MR. MURDOCK?
...HELLO?
Oh, Foggy.
What have you done?

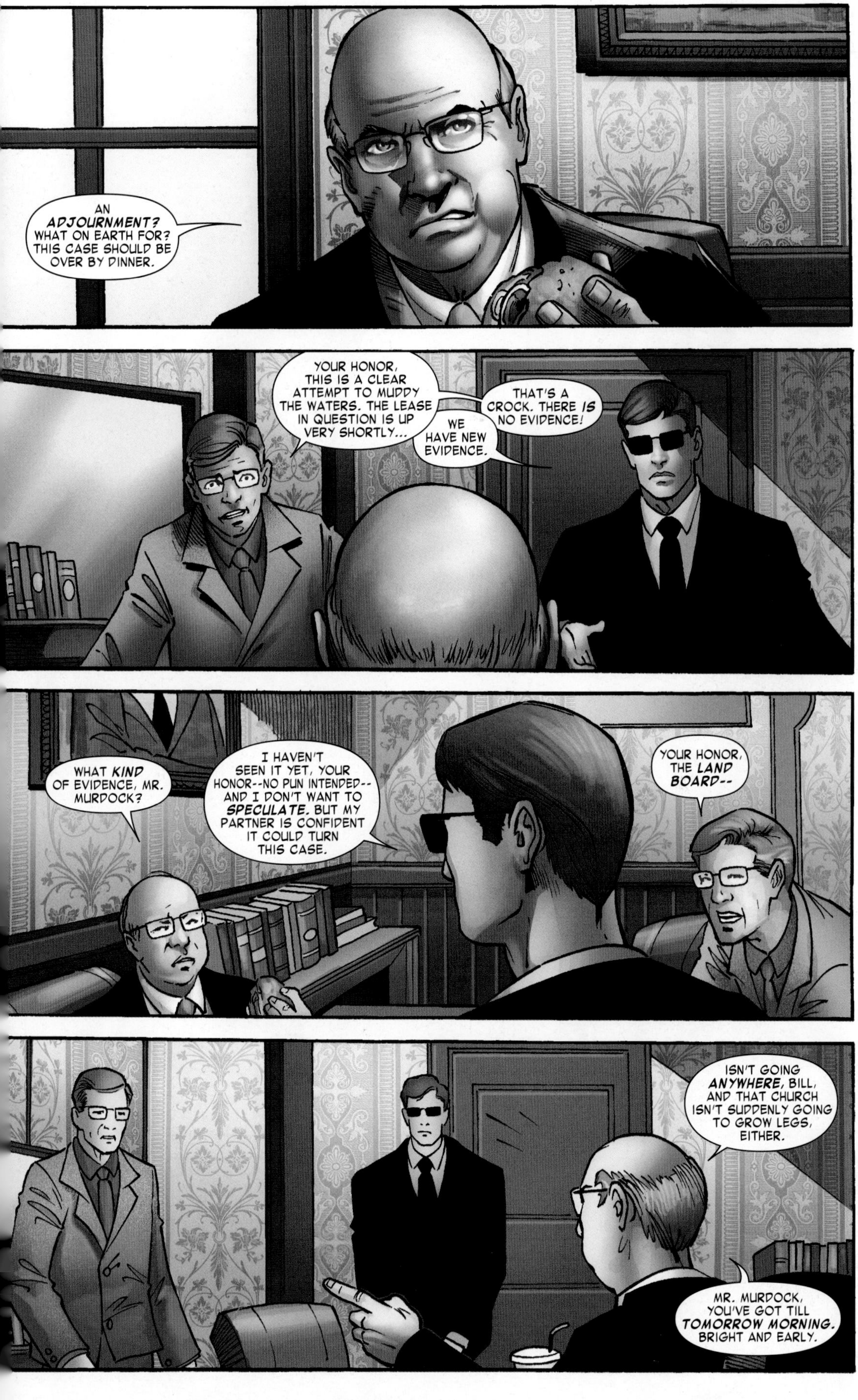
AN ADJOURNMENT? WHAT ON EARTH FOR? THIS CASE SHOULD BE OVER BY DINNER.
YOUR HONOR, THIS IS A CLEAR ATTEMPT TO MUDDY THE WATERS. THE LEASE IN QUESTION IS UP VERY SHORTLY...
WE HAVE NEW EVIDENCE.
THAT'S A CROCK. THERE IS NO EVIDENCE!
WHAT KIND OF EVIDENCE, MR. MURDOCK?
I HAVEN'T SEEN IT YET, YOUR HONOR--NO PUN INTENDED--AND I DON'T WANT TO SPECULATE. BUT MY PARTNER IS CONFIDENT IT COULD TURN THIS CASE.
YOUR HONOR, THE LAND BOARD--
ISN'T GOING ANYWHERE, BILL, AND THAT CHURCH ISN'T SUDDENLY GOING TO GROW LEGS, EITHER.
MR. MURDOCK, YOU'VE GOT TILL TOMORROW MORNING. BRIGHT AND EARLY.

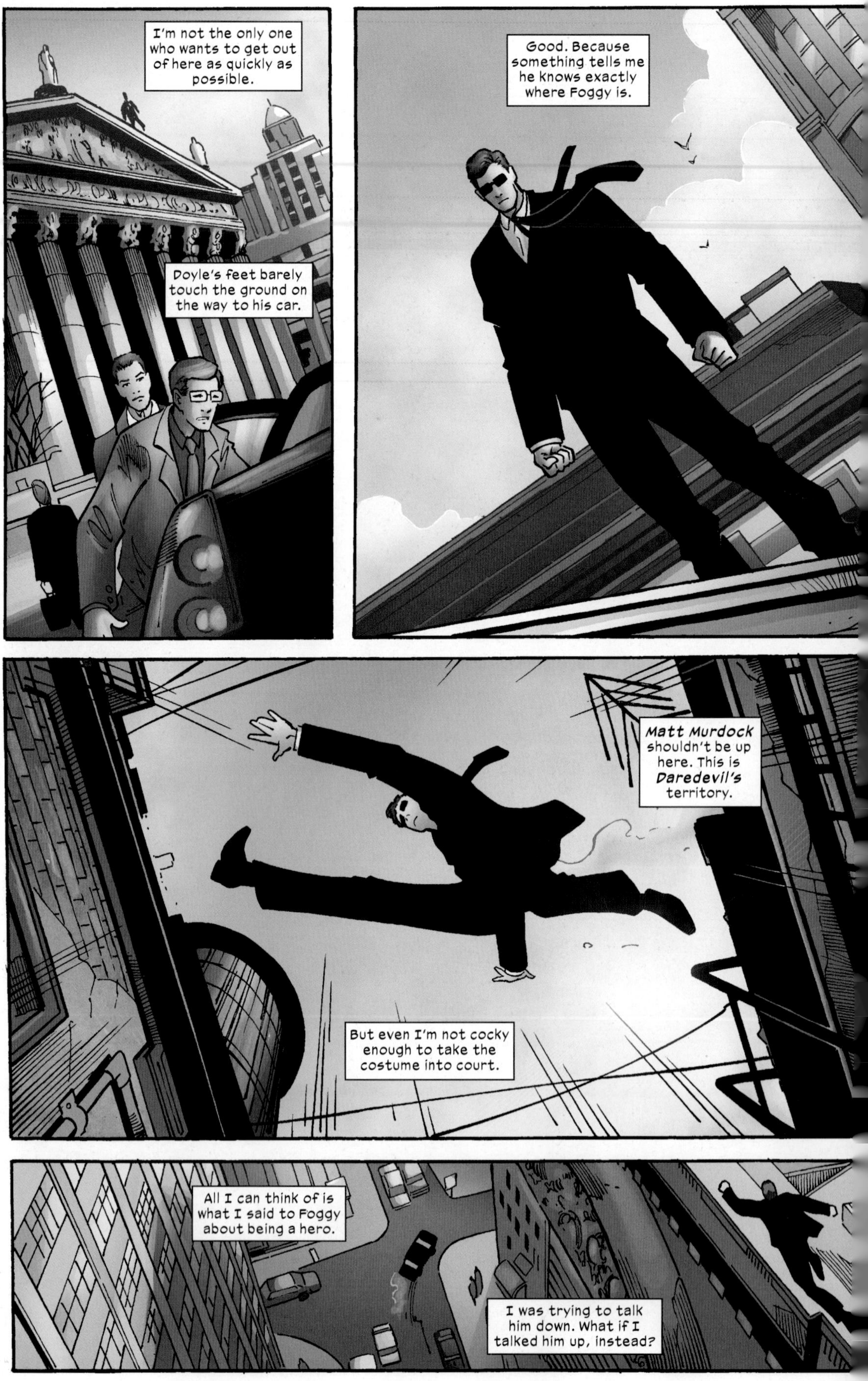
I'm not the only one who wants to get out of here as quickly as possible.
Doyle's feet barely touch the ground on the way to his car.
Good. Because something tells me he knows exactly where Foggy is.
Matt Murdock shouldn't be up here. This is Daredevil's territory.
But even I'm not cocky enough to take the costume into court.
All I can think of is what I said to Foggy about being a hero.
I was trying to talk him down. What if I talked him up, instead?

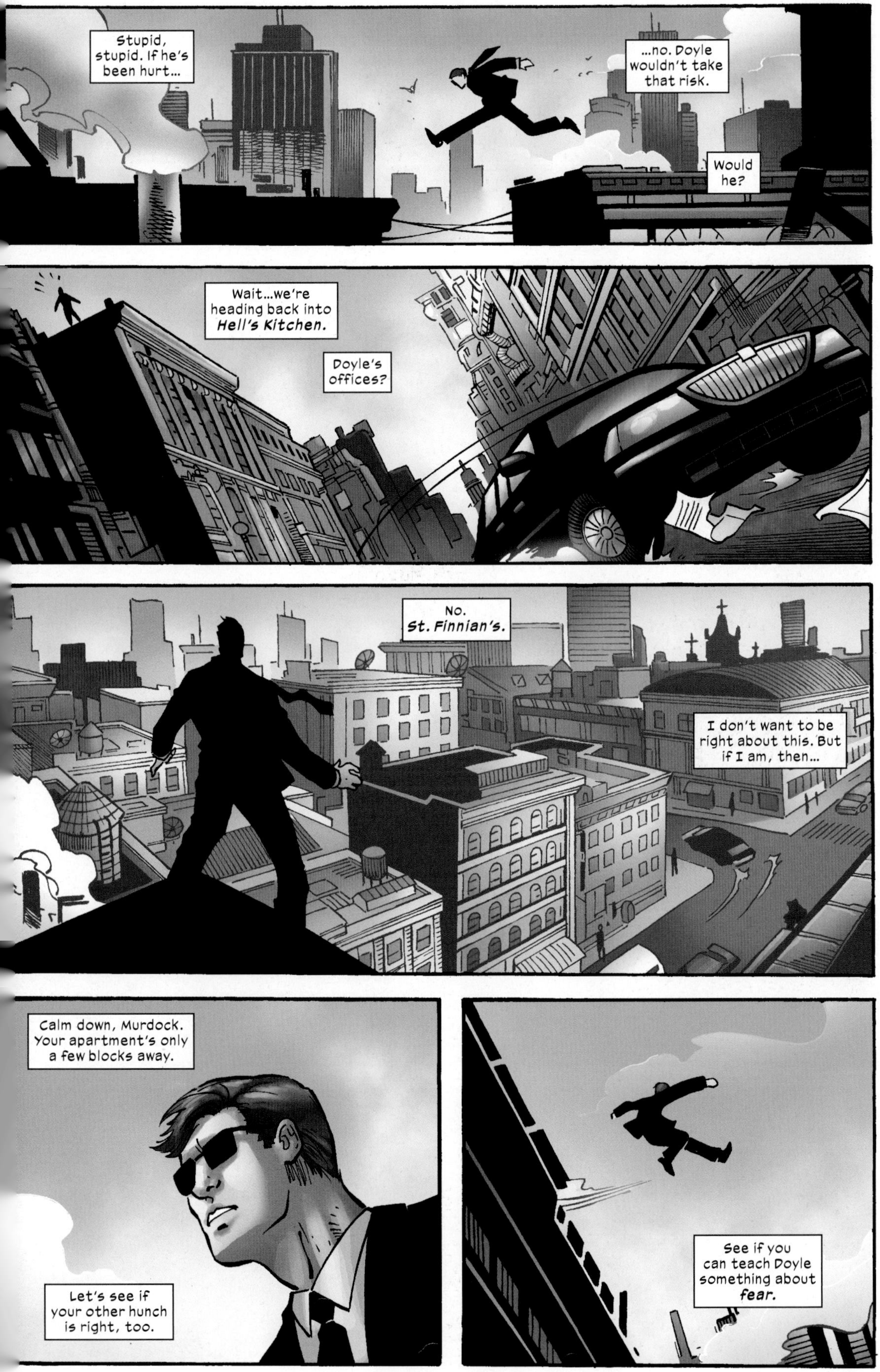
Stupid, stupid. If he's been hurt...
...no. Doyle wouldn't take that risk.
Would he?
Wait...we're heading back into *Hell's Kitchen.*
Doyle's offices?
No. *St. Finnian's.*
I don't want to be right about this. But if I am, then...
Calm down, Murdock. Your apartment's only a few blocks away.
Let's see if your other hunch is right, too.
See if you can teach Doyle something about *fear.*

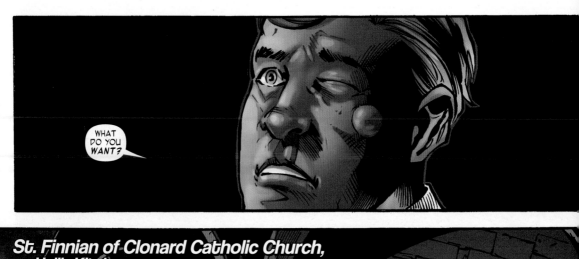

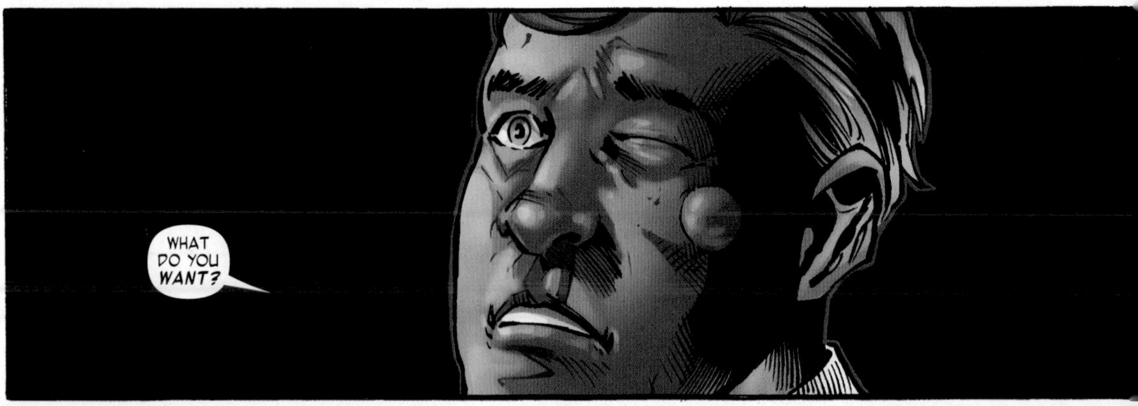
WHAT DO YOU *WANT?*

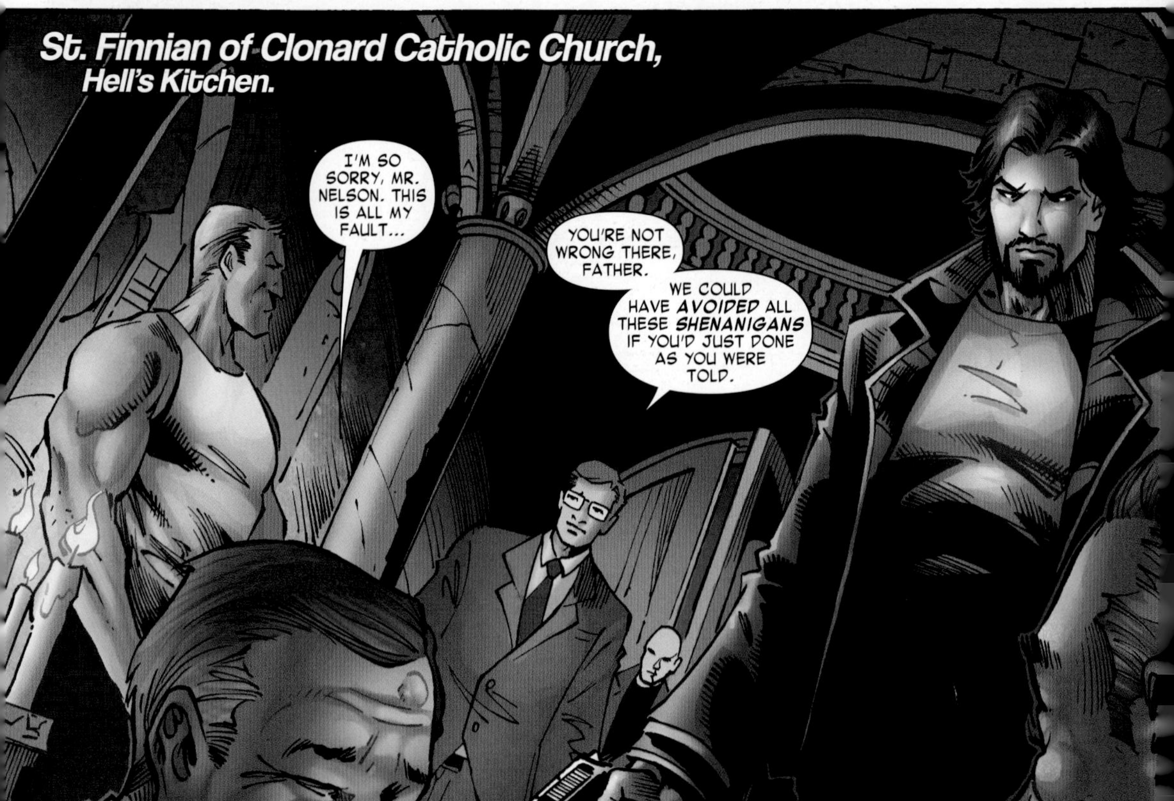
St. Finnian of Clonard Catholic Church,
Hell's Kitchen.
I'M SO SORRY, MR. NELSON. THIS IS ALL MY FAULT...
YOU'RE NOT WRONG THERE, FATHER.
WE COULD HAVE *AVOIDED* ALL THESE *SHENANIGANS* IF YOU'D JUST DONE AS YOU WERE TOLD.

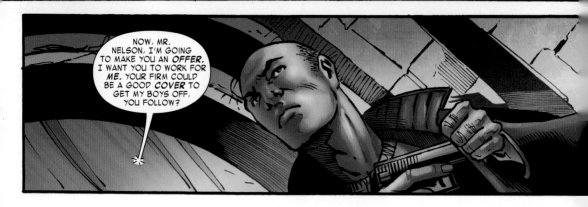

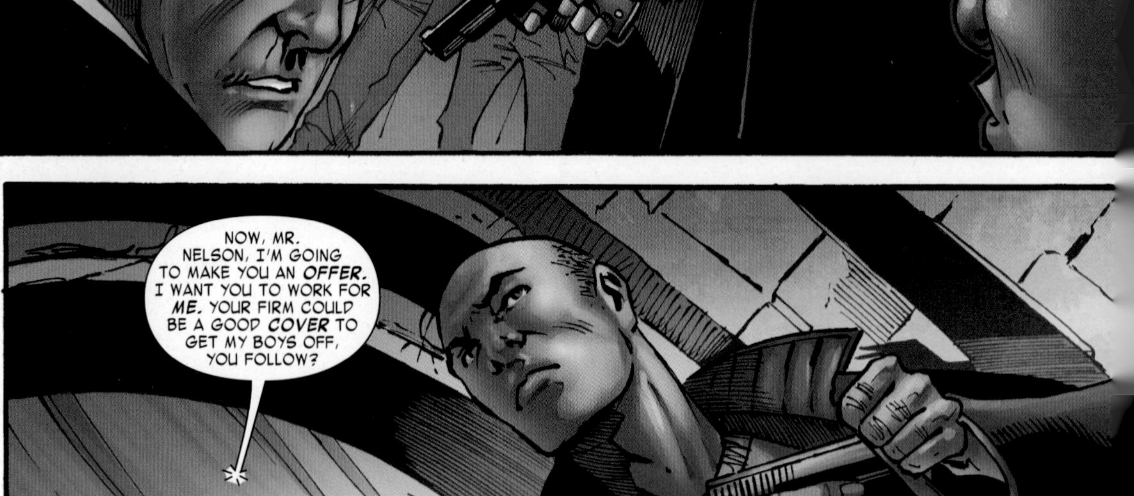
NOW, MR. NELSON, I'M GOING TO MAKE YOU AN *OFFER.* I WANT YOU TO WORK FOR *ME.* YOUR FIRM COULD BE A GOOD *COVER* TO GET MY BOYS OFF, YOU FOLLOW?

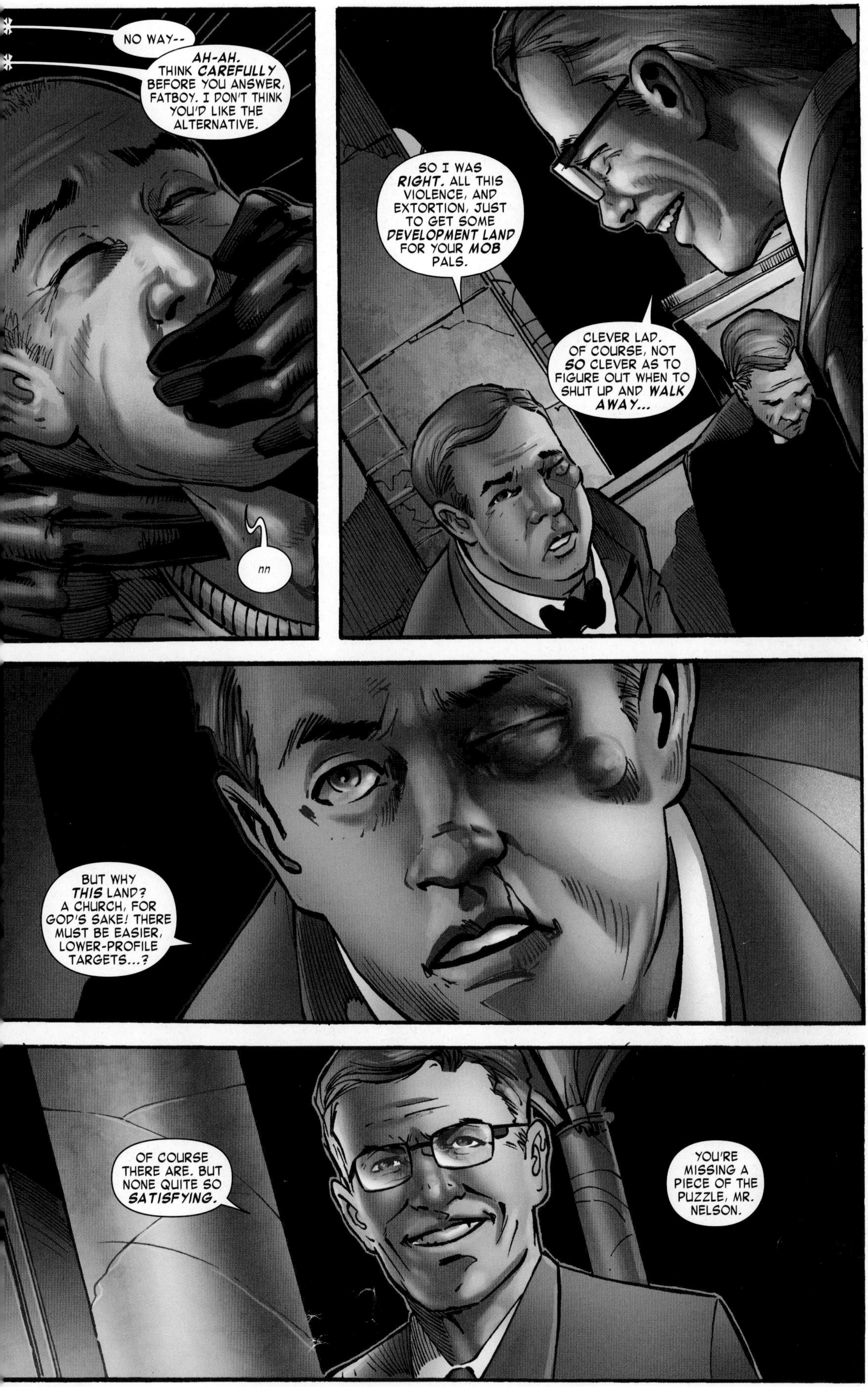
NO WAY--
AH-AH. THINK CAREFULLY BEFORE YOU ANSWER, FATBOY. I DON'T THINK YOU'D LIKE THE ALTERNATIVE.
nn
SO I WAS RIGHT. ALL THIS VIOLENCE, AND EXTORTION, JUST TO GET SOME DEVELOPMENT LAND FOR YOUR MOB PALS.
CLEVER LAD. OF COURSE, NOT SO CLEVER AS TO FIGURE OUT WHEN TO SHUT UP AND WALK AWAY...
BUT WHY THIS LAND? A CHURCH, FOR GOD'S SAKE! THERE MUST BE EASIER, LOWER-PROFILE TARGETS...?
OF COURSE THERE ARE. BUT NONE QUITE SO SATISFYING.
YOU'RE MISSING A PIECE OF THE PUZZLE, MR. NELSON.

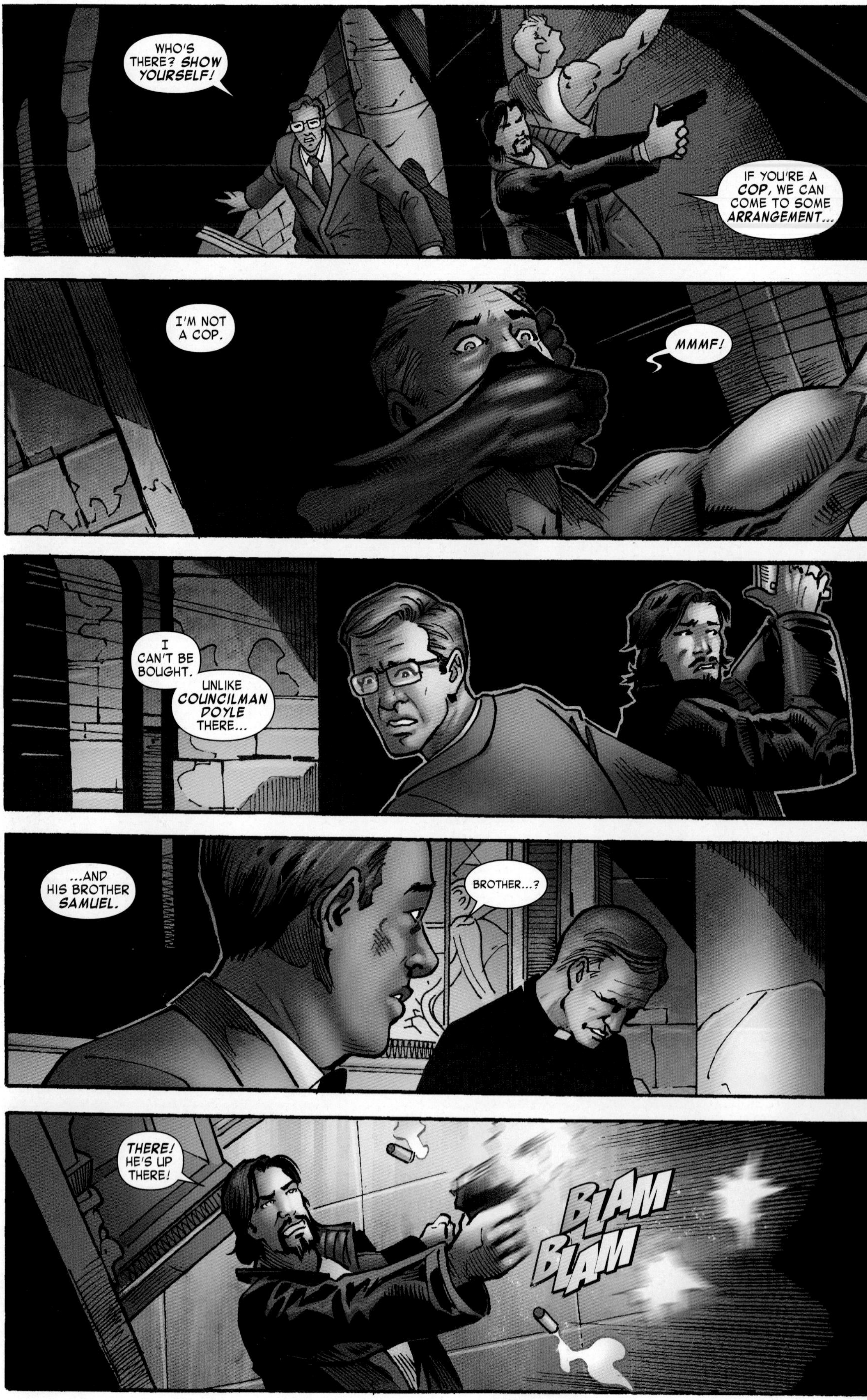
WHO'S THERE? SHOW YOURSELF!
IF YOU'RE A COP, WE CAN COME TO SOME ARRANGEMENT...
I'M NOT A COP.
MMMF!
I CAN'T BE BOUGHT.
UNLIKE COUNCILMAN DOYLE THERE...
...AND HIS BROTHER SAMUEL.
BROTHER...?
THERE! HE'S UP THERE!
BLAM
BLAM

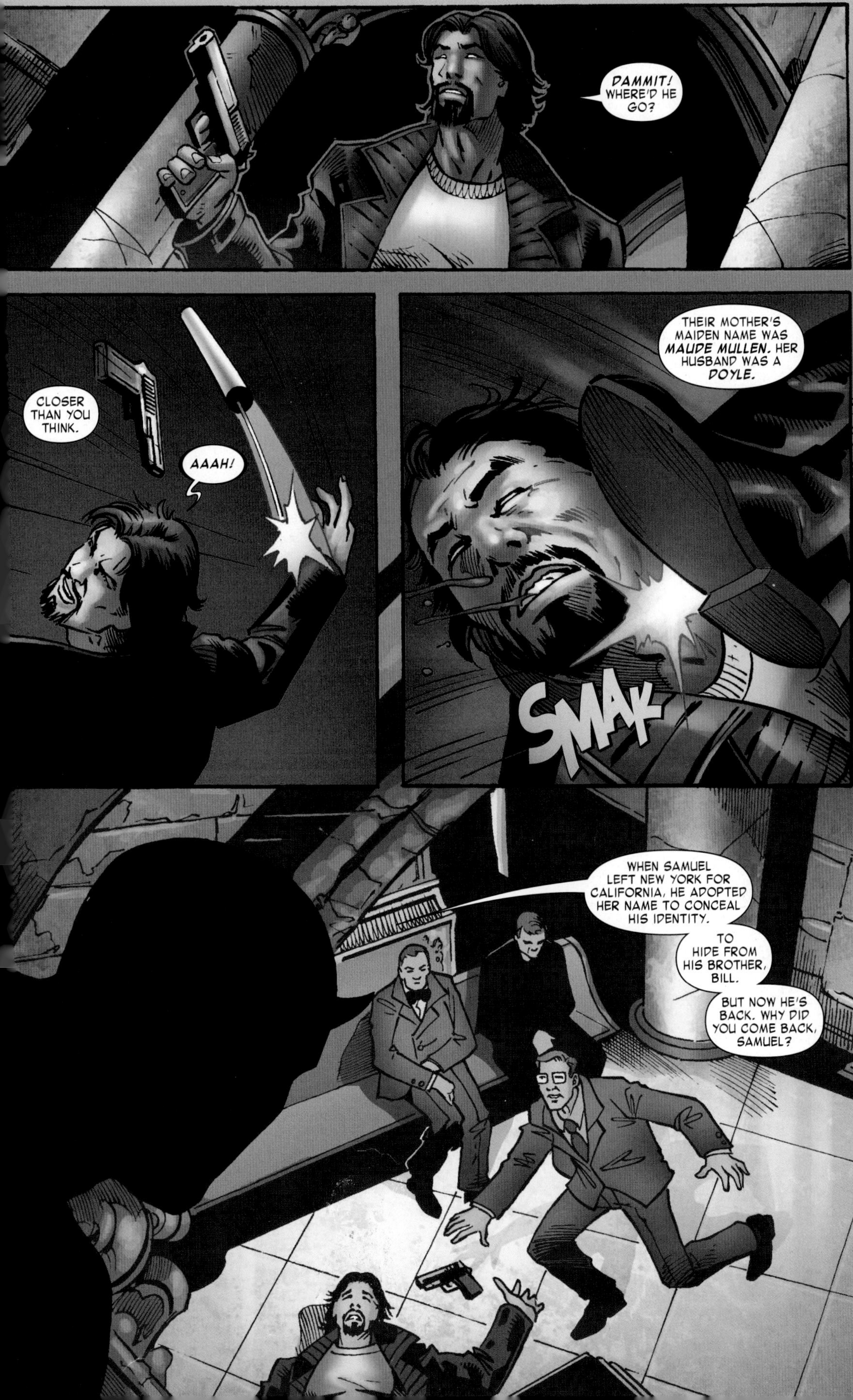
DAMMIT! WHERE'D HE GO?
CLOSER THAN YOU THINK.
AAAH!
THEIR MOTHER'S MAIDEN NAME WAS MAUDE MULLEN. HER HUSBAND WAS A DOYLE.
SMAK
WHEN SAMUEL LEFT NEW YORK FOR CALIFORNIA, HE ADOPTED HER NAME TO CONCEAL HIS IDENTITY.
TO HIDE FROM HIS BROTHER, BILL.
BUT NOW HE'S BACK. WHY DID YOU COME BACK, SAMUEL?

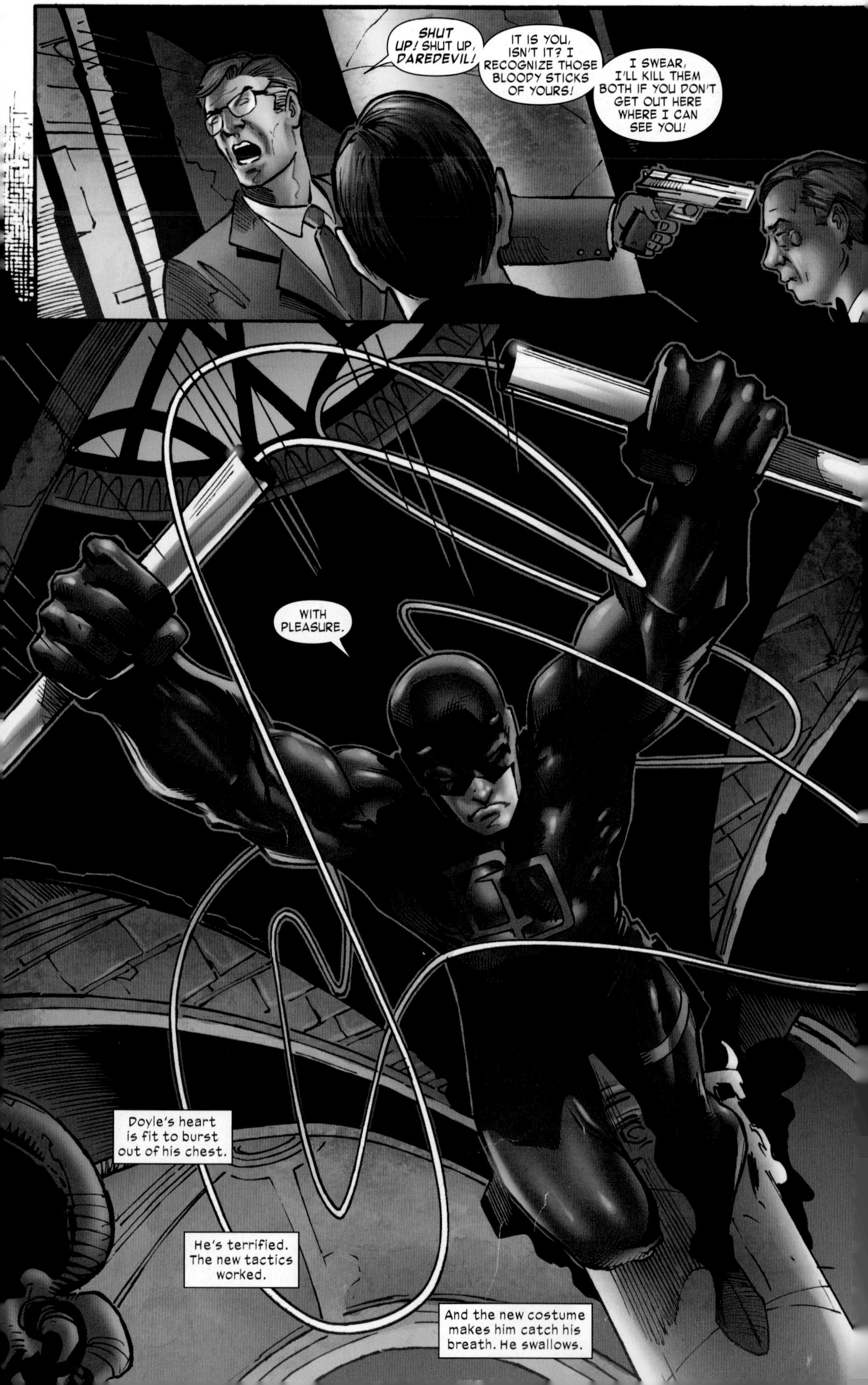
SHUT UP! SHUT UP, DAREDEVIL!
IT IS YOU, ISN'T IT? I RECOGNIZE THOSE BLOODY STICKS OF YOURS!
I SWEAR, I'LL KILL THEM BOTH IF YOU DON'T GET OUT HERE WHERE I CAN SEE YOU!
WITH PLEASURE.
Doyle's heart is fit to burst out of his chest.
He's terrified. The new tactics worked.
And the new costume makes him catch his breath. He swallows.

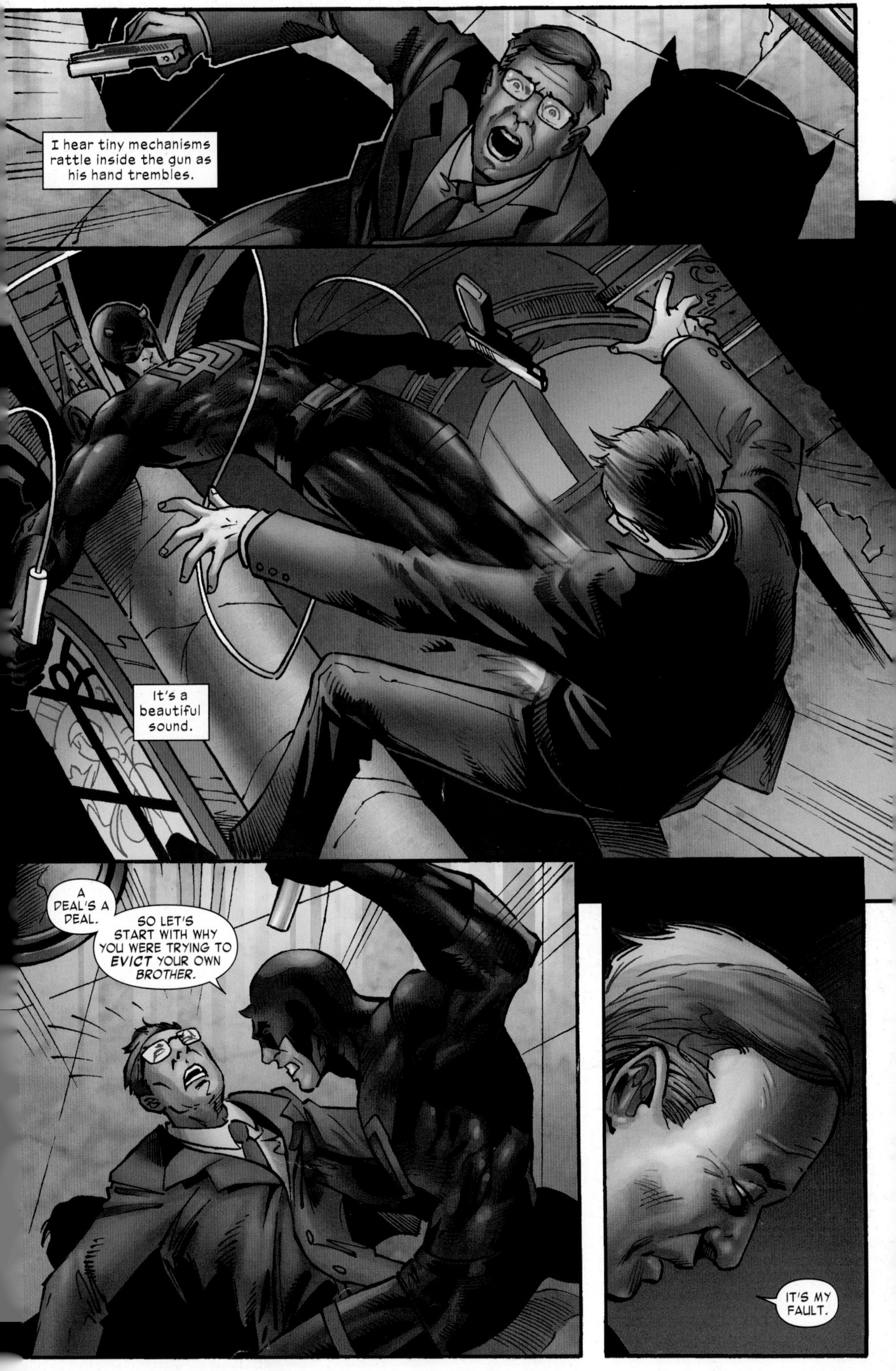
I hear tiny mechanisms rattle inside the gun as his hand trembles.
It's a beautiful sound.
A DEAL'S A DEAL.
SO LET'S START WITH WHY YOU WERE TRYING TO EVICT YOUR OWN BROTHER.
IT'S MY FAULT.

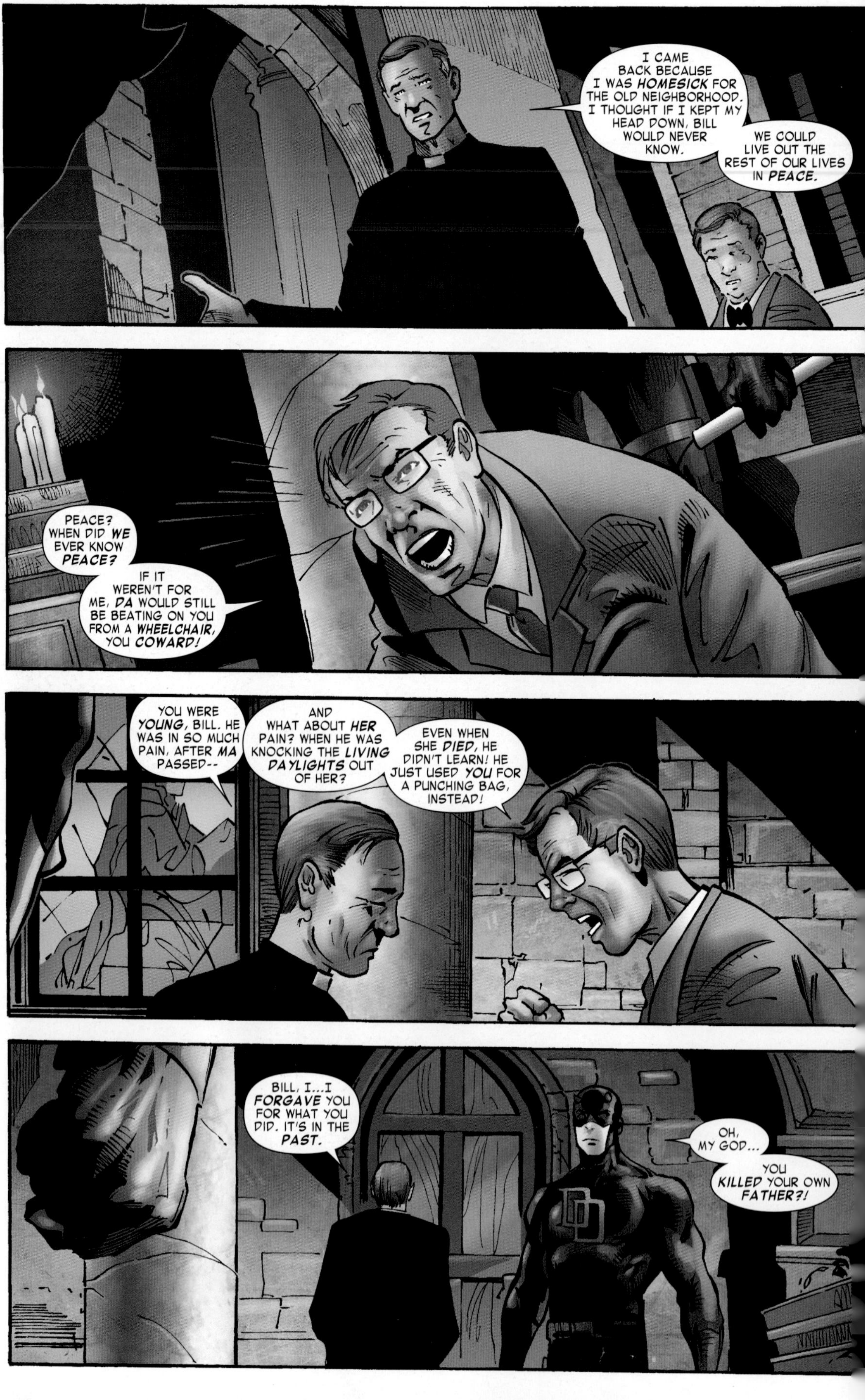
I CAME BACK BECAUSE I WAS HOMESICK FOR THE OLD NEIGHBORHOOD. I THOUGHT IF I KEPT MY HEAD DOWN, BILL WOULD NEVER KNOW.
WE COULD LIVE OUT THE REST OF OUR LIVES IN PEACE.
PEACE? WHEN DID WE EVER KNOW PEACE?
IF IT WEREN'T FOR ME, DA WOULD STILL BE BEATING ON YOU FROM A WHEELCHAIR, YOU COWARD!
YOU WERE YOUNG, BILL. HE WAS IN SO MUCH PAIN, AFTER MA PASSED--
AND WHAT ABOUT HER PAIN? WHEN HE WAS KNOCKING THE LIVING DAYLIGHTS OUT OF HER?
EVEN WHEN SHE DIED, HE DIDN'T LEARN! HE JUST USED YOU FOR A PUNCHING BAG, INSTEAD!
BILL, I...I FORGAVE YOU FOR WHAT YOU DID. IT'S IN THE PAST.
OH, MY GOD...
YOU KILLED YOUR OWN FATHER?!

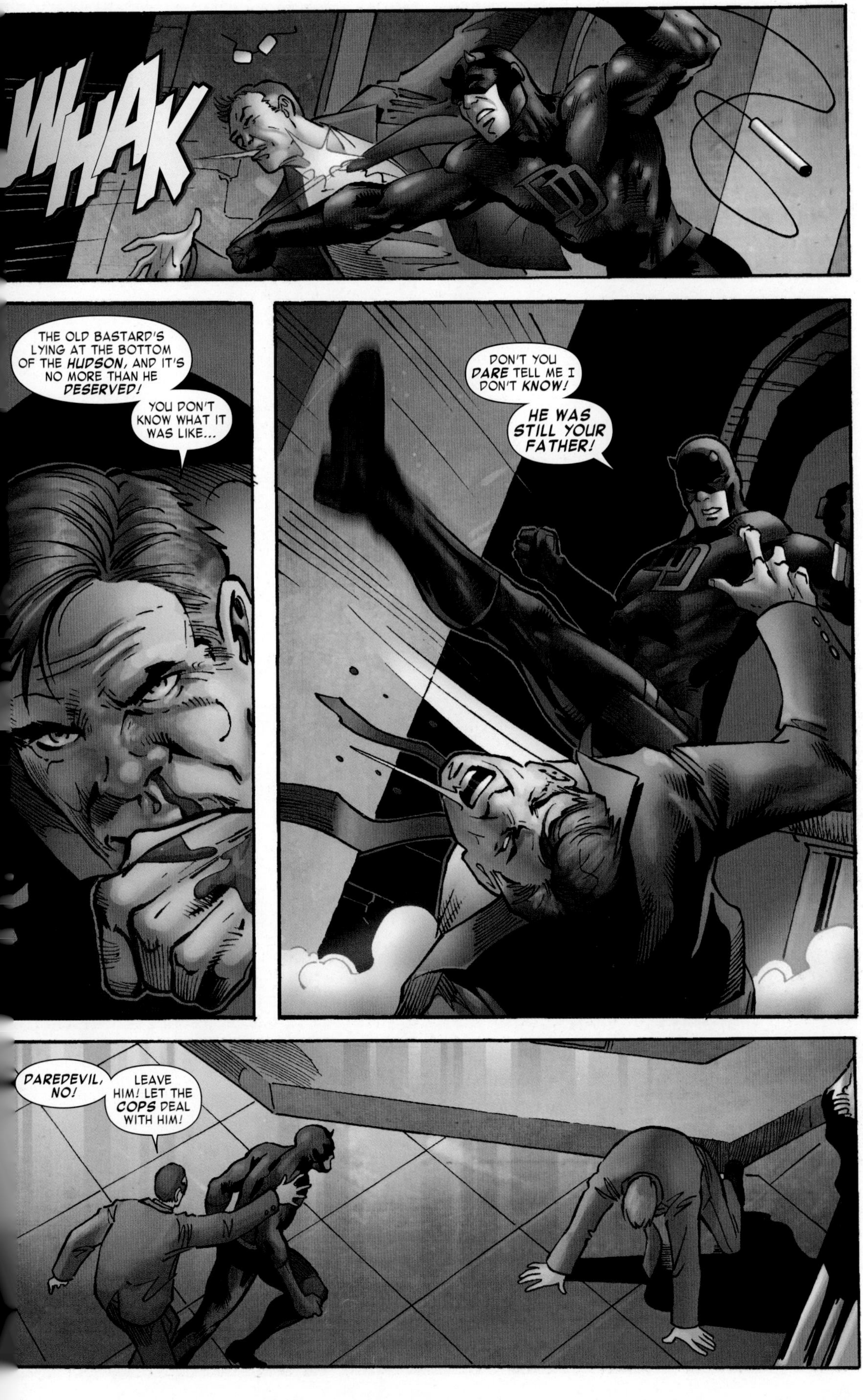
WHAK
THE OLD BASTARD'S LYING AT THE BOTTOM OF THE HUDSON, AND IT'S NO MORE THAN HE DESERVED!
YOU DON'T KNOW WHAT IT WAS LIKE...
DON'T YOU DARE TELL ME I DON'T KNOW!
HE WAS STILL YOUR FATHER!
DAREDEVIL, NO!
LEAVE HIM! LET THE COPS DEAL WITH HIM!

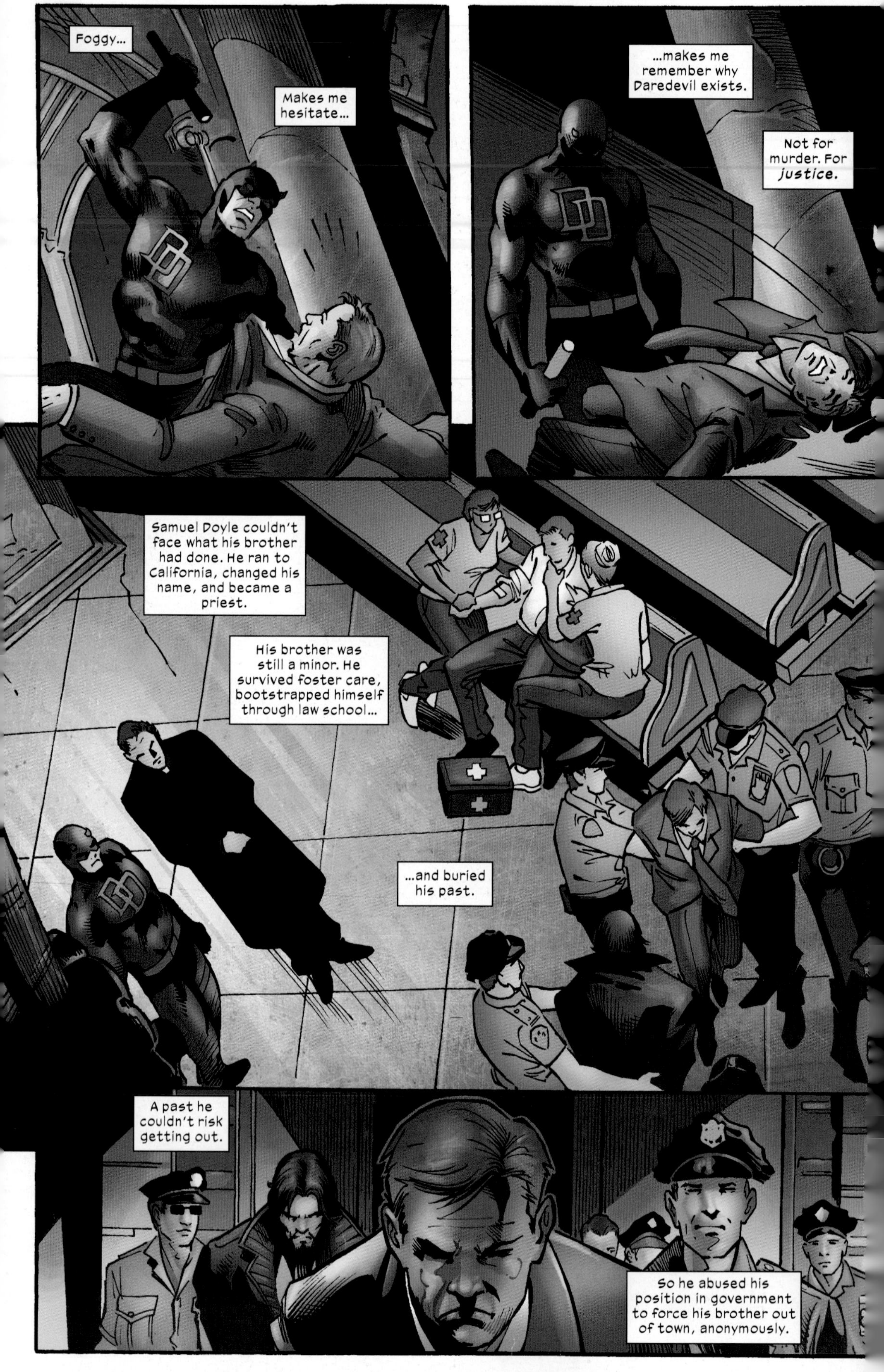
Foggy...
Makes me hesitate...
...makes me remember why Daredevil exists.
Not for murder. For *justice.*
Samuel Doyle couldn't face what his brother had done. He ran to California, changed his name, and became a priest.
His brother was still a minor. He survived foster care, bootstrapped himself through law school...
...and buried his past.
A past he couldn't risk getting out.
So he abused his position in government to force his brother out of town, anonymously.

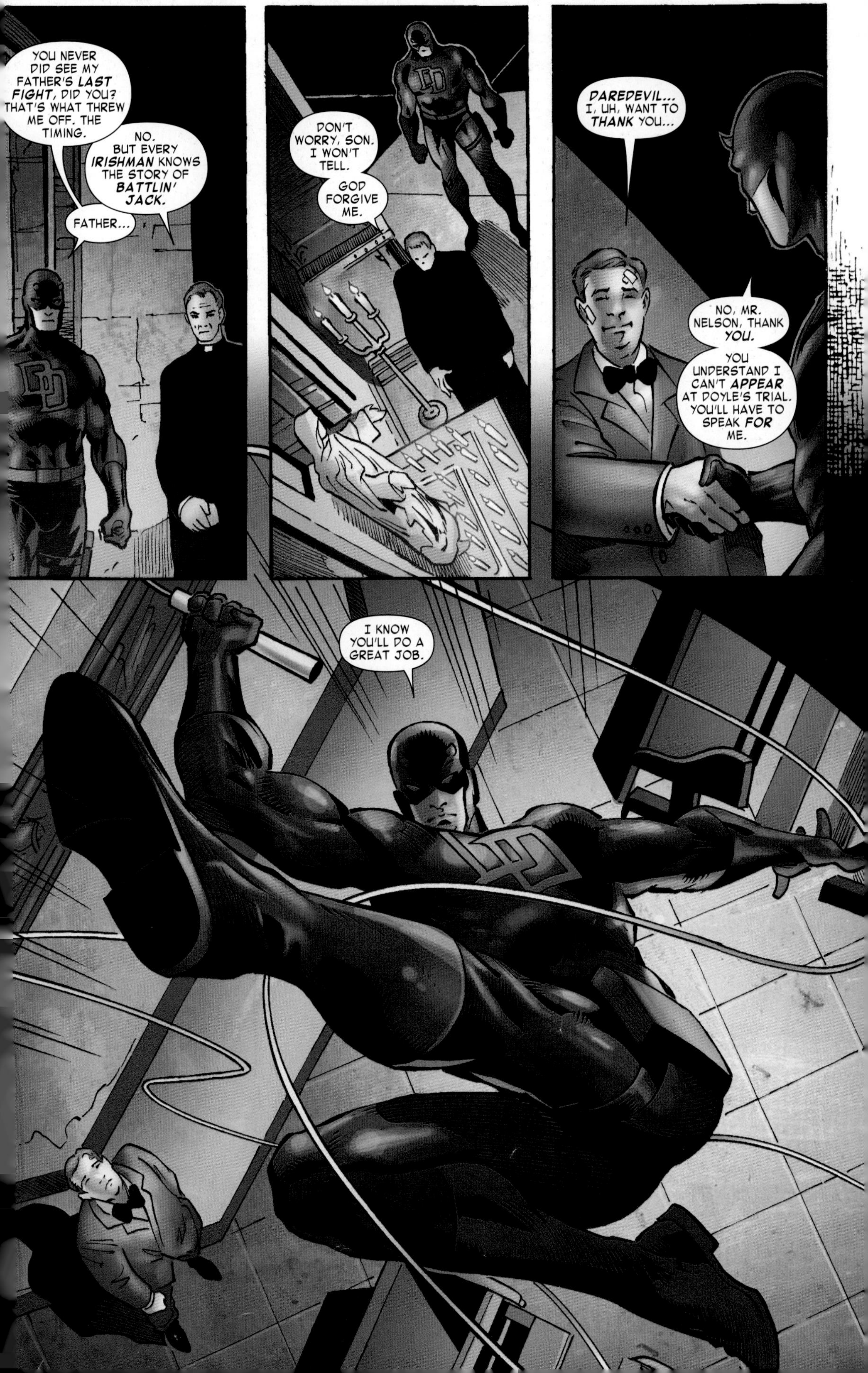

YOU NEVER DID SEE MY FATHER'S **LAST FIGHT**, DID YOU? THAT'S WHAT THREW ME OFF. THE TIMING.
NO. BUT EVERY **IRISHMAN** KNOWS THE STORY OF **BATTLIN' JACK.**
FATHER...
DON'T WORRY, SON. I WON'T TELL.
GOD FORGIVE ME.
DAREDEVIL... I, UH, WANT TO **THANK** YOU...
NO, MR. NELSON, THANK **YOU.**
YOU UNDERSTAND I CAN'T **APPEAR** AT DOYLE'S TRIAL. YOU'LL HAVE TO SPEAK **FOR** ME.
I KNOW YOU'LL DO A GREAT JOB.

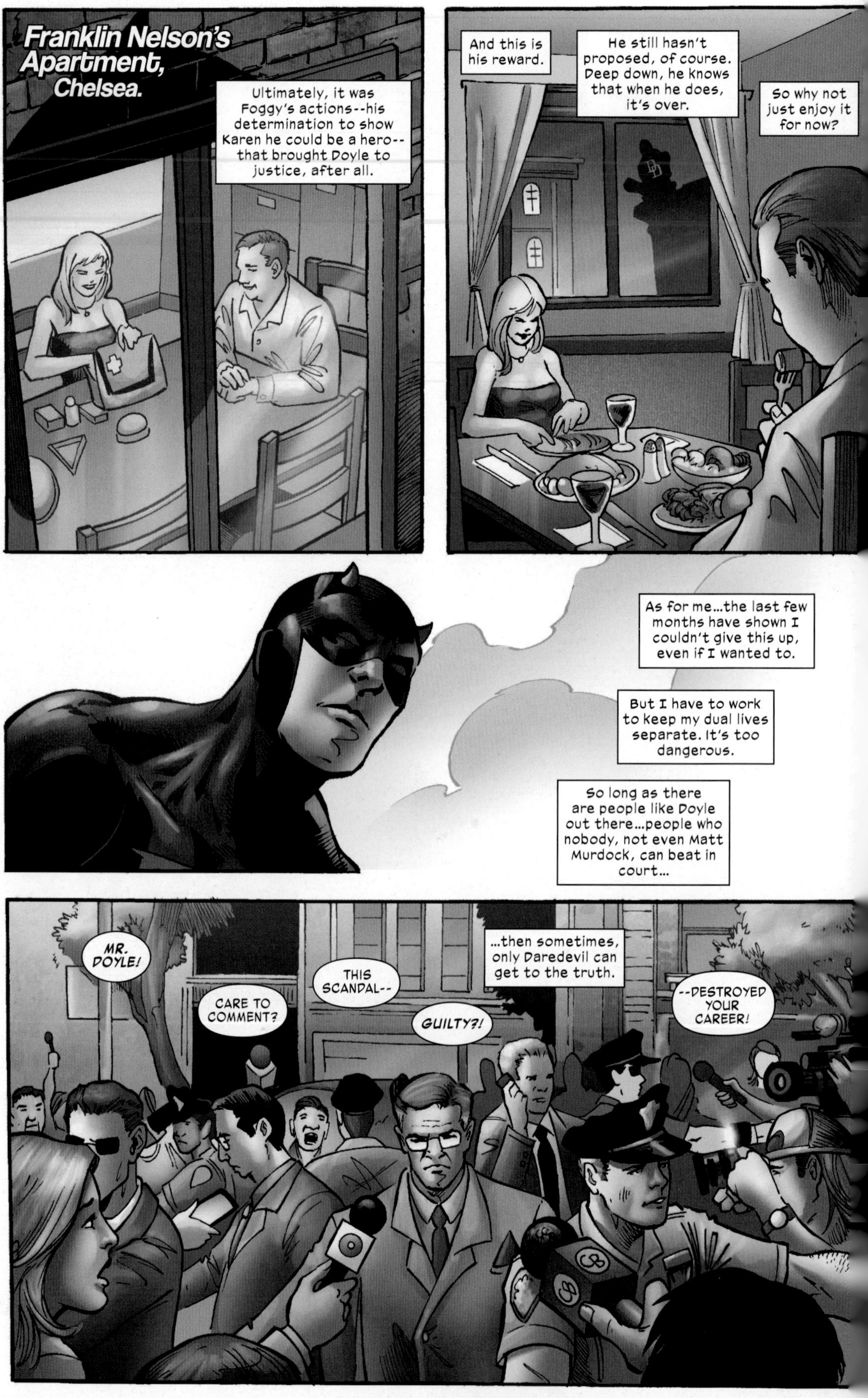
Franklin Nelson's Apartment, Chelsea.
Ultimately, it was Foggy's actions--his determination to show Karen he could be a hero--that brought Doyle to justice, after all.
And this is his reward.
He still hasn't proposed, of course. Deep down, he knows that when he does, it's over.
So why not just enjoy it for now?
As for me...the last few months have shown I couldn't give this up, even if I wanted to.
But I have to work to keep my dual lives separate. It's too dangerous.
So long as there are people like Doyle out there...people who nobody, not even Matt Murdock, can beat in court...
...then sometimes, only Daredevil can get to the truth.
MR. DOYLE!
CARE TO COMMENT?
THIS SCANDAL--
GUILTY?!
--DESTROYED YOUR CAREER!

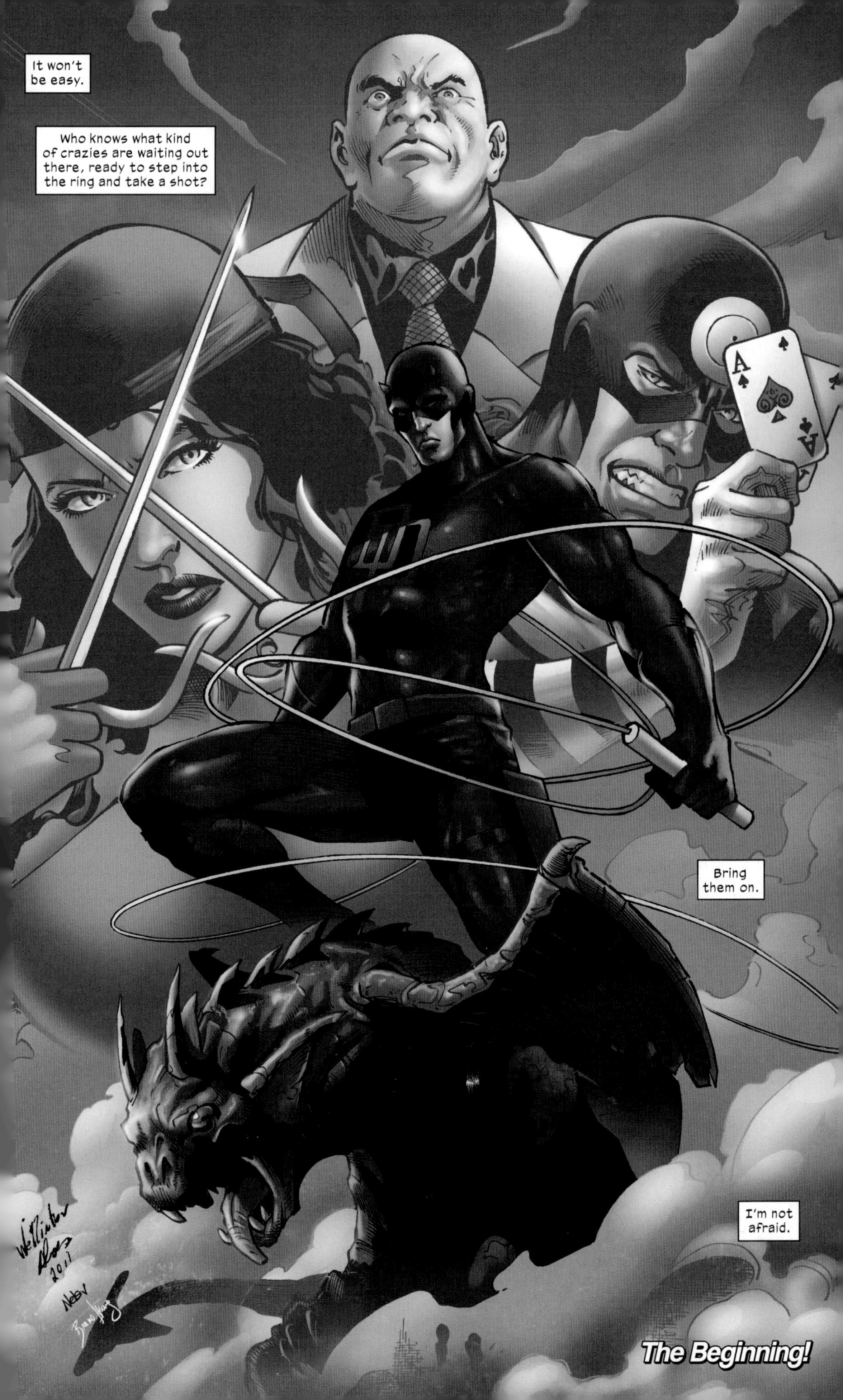
It won't be easy.
Who knows what kind of crazies are waiting out there, ready to step into the ring and take a shot?
Bring them on.
I'm not afraid.
The Beginning!

WHERE ARE THEY NOW? *DAREDEVIL (2011) #1* WRITER MARK WAID JOINS ARTISTS PAOLO RIVERA AND MARCOS MARTIN FOR A NEW SPIN ON DAREDEVIL THAT WILL LEAVE YOU GASPING FOR AIR! IF MATT MURDOCK COULD SEE WHAT HE WAS DOING...HE'D BE TERRIFIED.

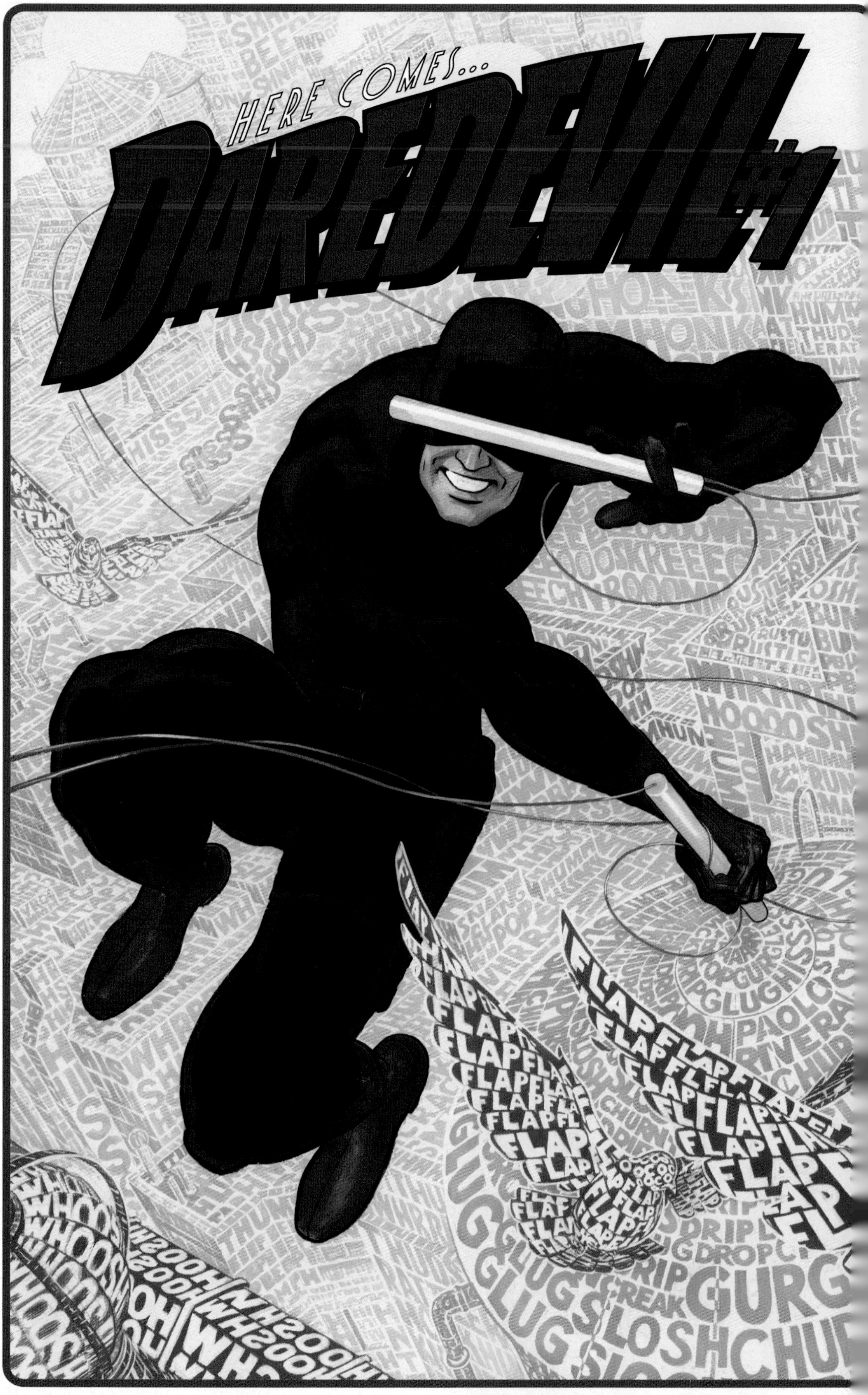

HERE COMES...
DAREDEVIL #1

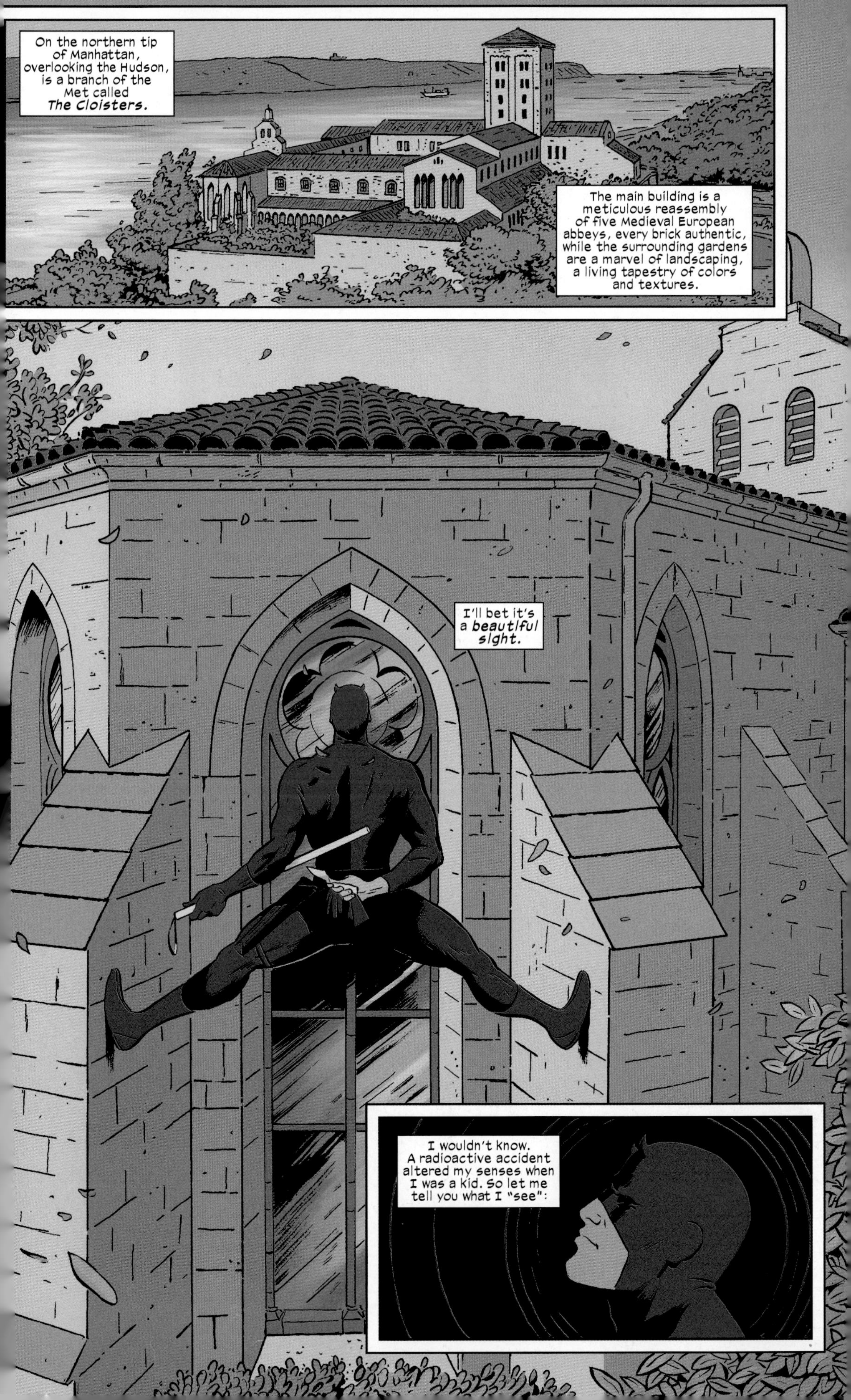
On the northern tip of Manhattan, overlooking the Hudson, is a branch of the Met called *The Cloisters.*
The main building is a meticulous reassembly of five Medieval European abbeys, every brick authentic, while the surrounding gardens are a marvel of landscaping, a living tapestry of colors and textures.
I'll bet it's a *beautiful sight.*
I wouldn't know. A radioactive accident altered my senses when I was a kid. So let me tell you what I "see":

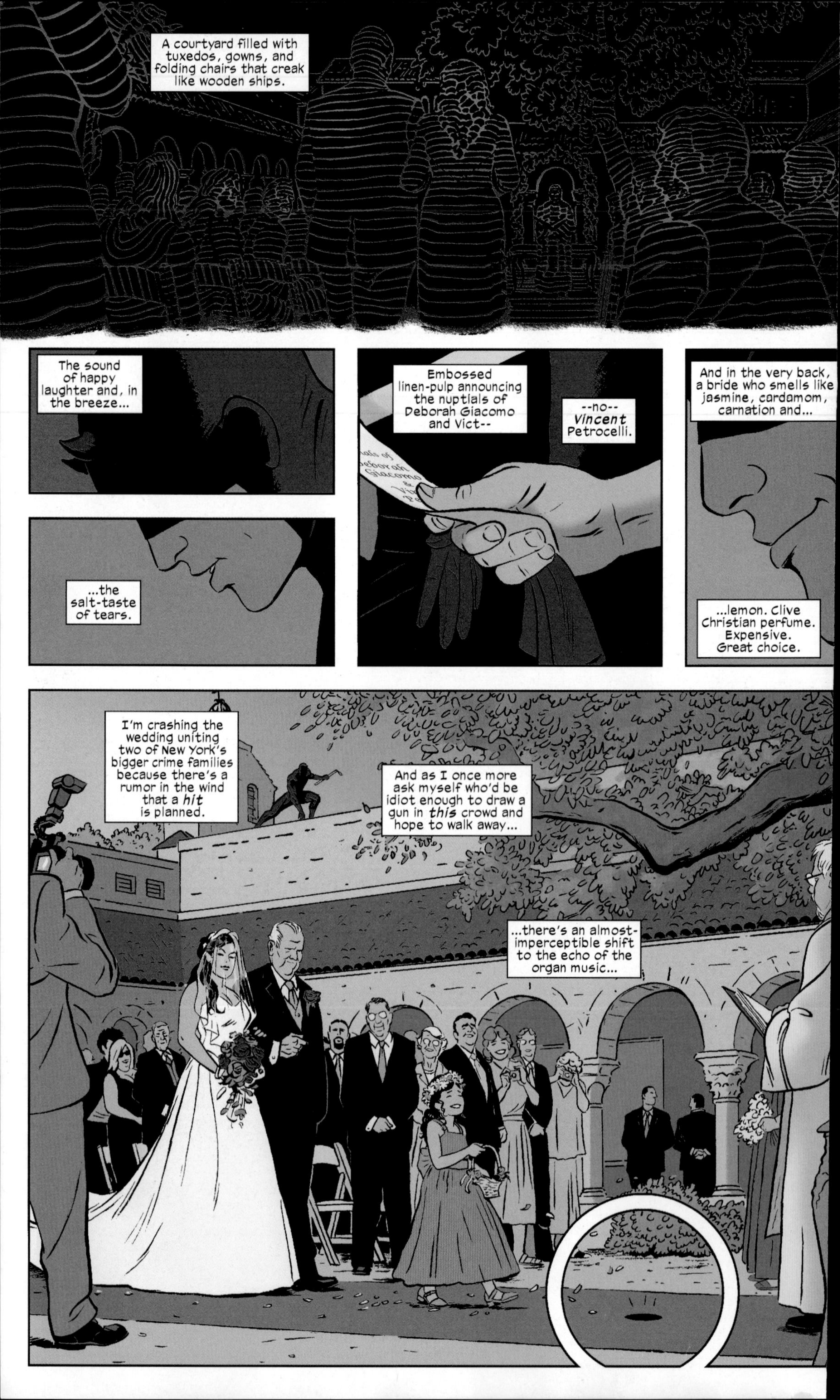
A courtyard filled with tuxedos, gowns, and folding chairs that creak like wooden ships.
The sound of happy laughter and, in the breeze...
...the salt-taste of tears.
Embossed linen-pulp announcing the nuptials of Deborah Giacomo and Vict--
--no-- *Vincent* Petrocelli.
And in the very back, a bride who smells like jasmine, cardamom, carnation and...
...lemon. Clive Christian perfume. Expensive. Great choice.
I'm crashing the wedding uniting two of New York's bigger crime families because there's a rumor in the wind that a *hit* is planned.
And as I once more ask myself who'd be idiot enough to draw a gun in *this* crowd and hope to walk away...
...there's an almost-imperceptible shift to the echo of the organ music...

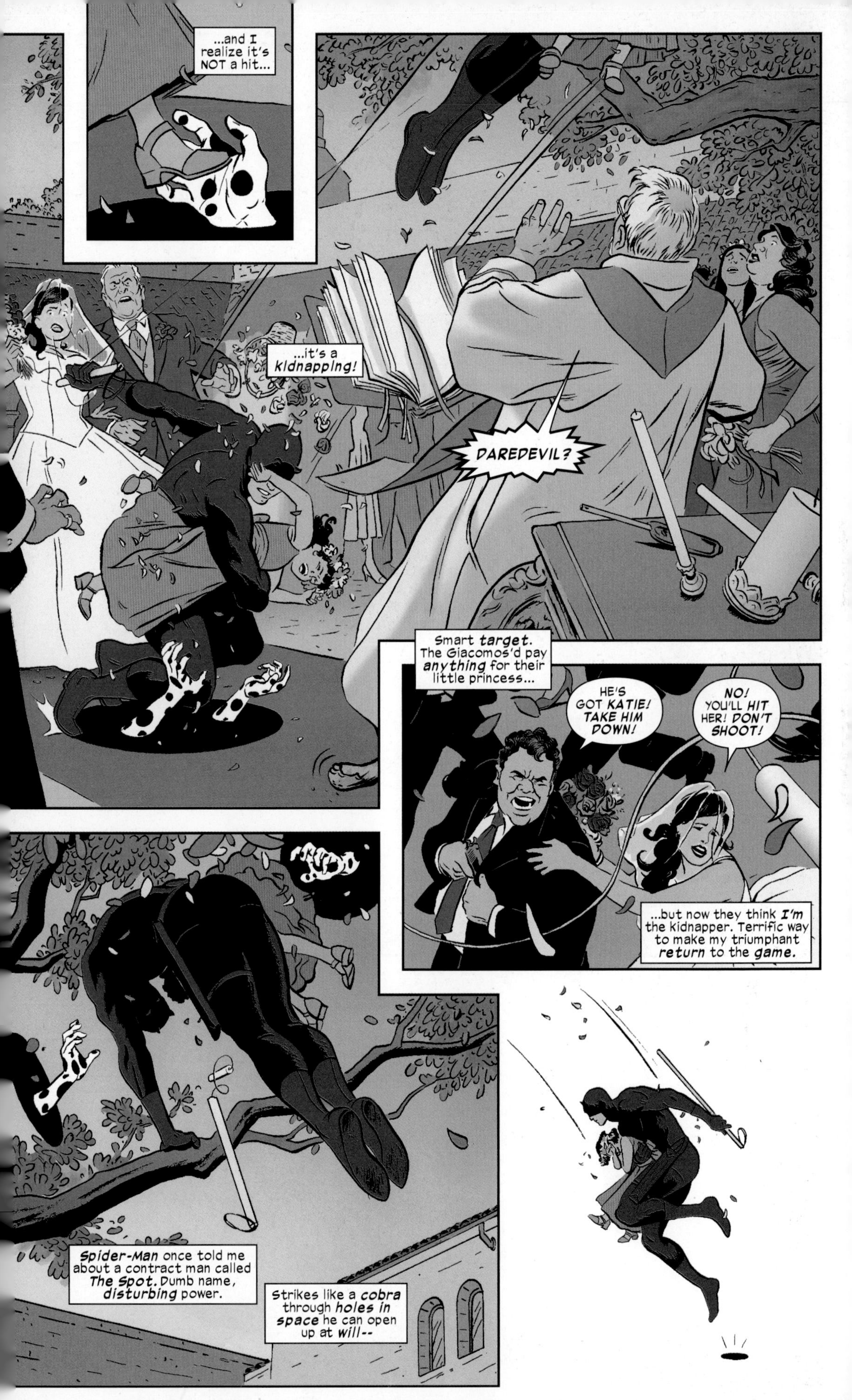

...and I realize it's NOT a hit...
...it's a kidnapping!
DAREDEVIL?
Smart target. The Giacomos'd pay anything for their little princess...
HE'S GOT KATIE! TAKE HIM DOWN!
NO! YOU'LL HIT HER! DON'T SHOOT!
...but now they think I'm the kidnapper. Terrific way to make my triumphant return to the game.
Spider-Man once told me about a contract man called The Spot. Dumb name, disturbing power.
Strikes like a cobra through holes in space he can open up at will--

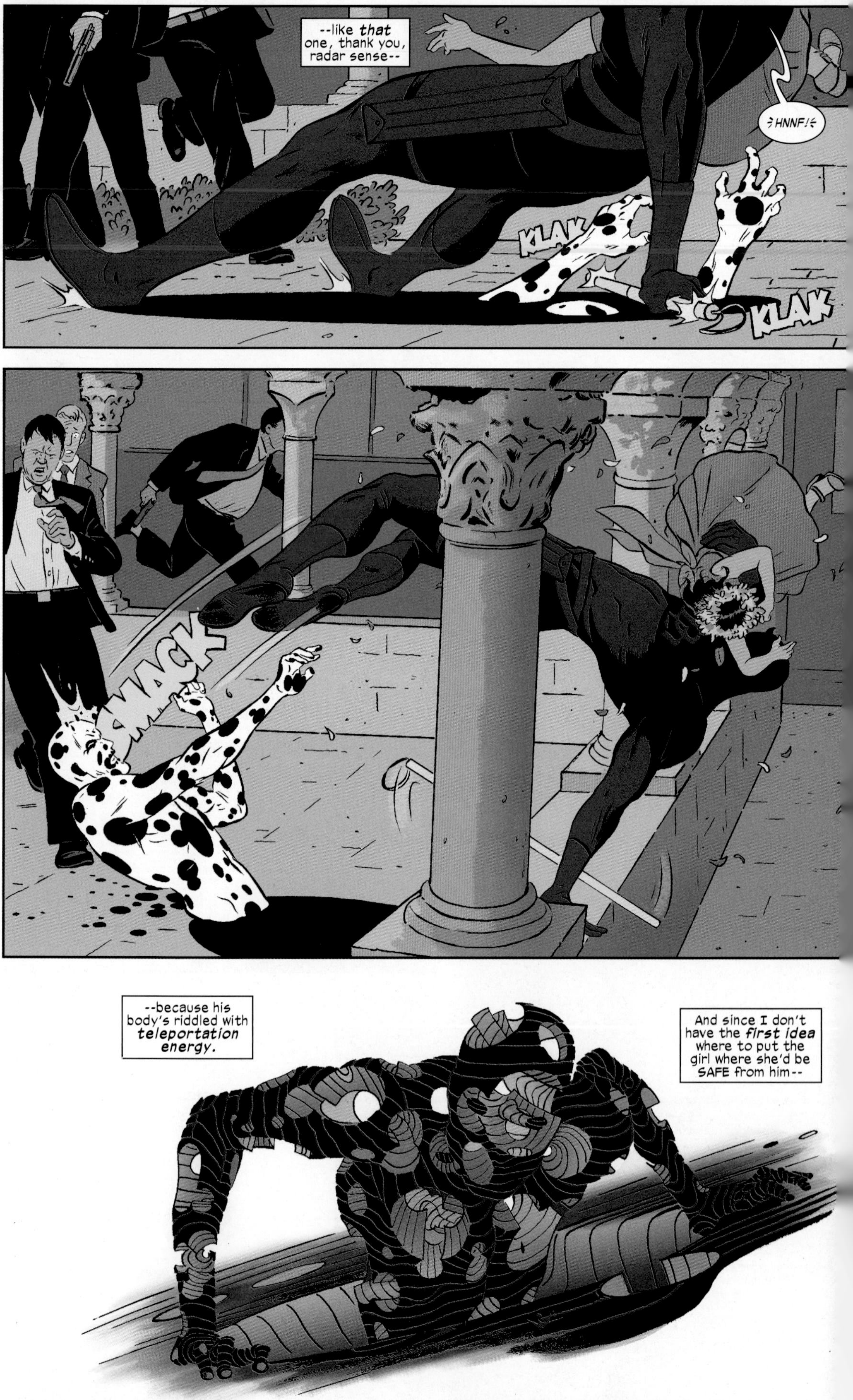
--like *that* one, thank you, radar sense--
HNNF!
KLAK
KLAK
SMACK
--because his body's riddled with *teleportation energy.*
And since I don't have the *first idea* where to put the girl where she'd be SAFE from him--

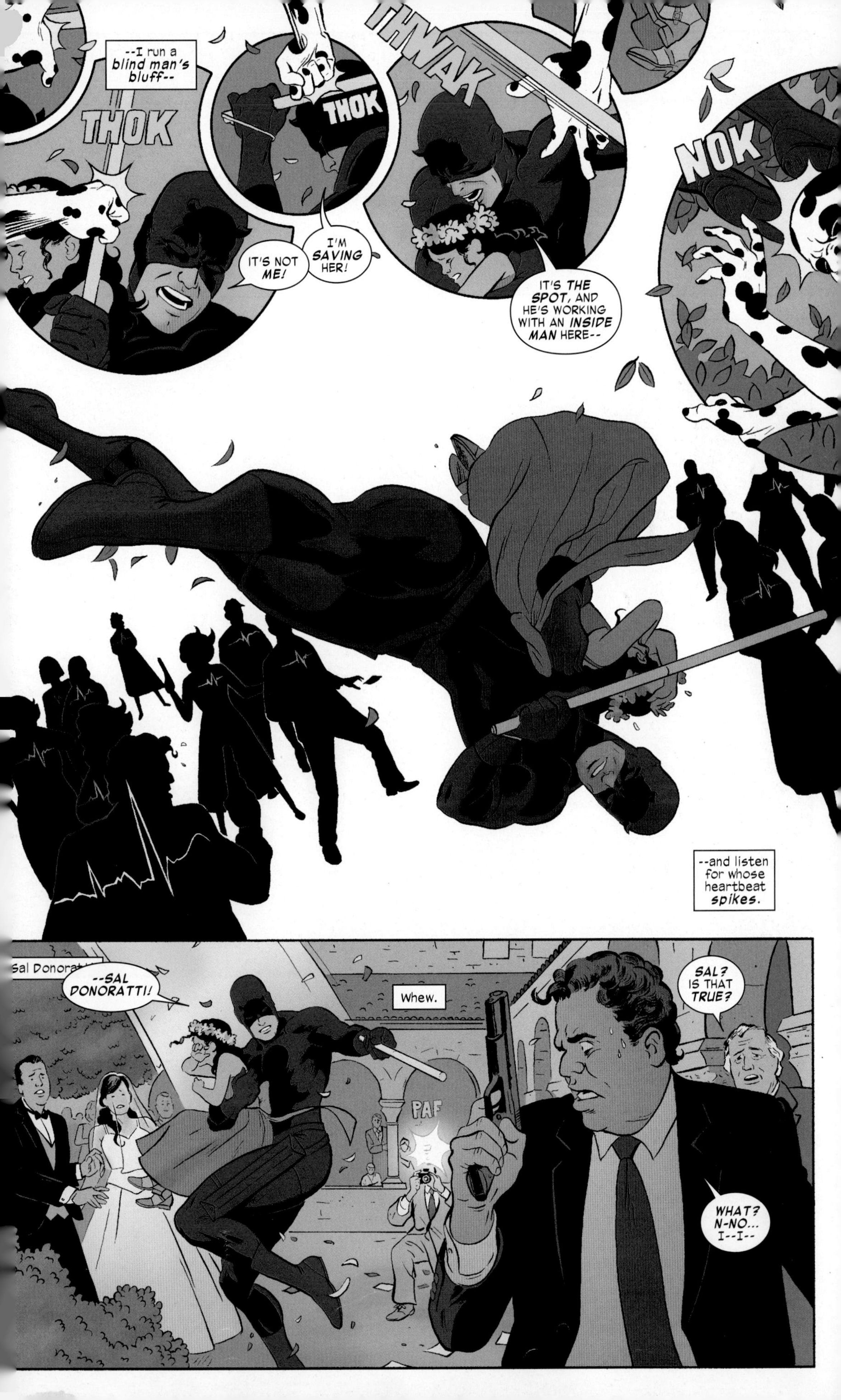
--I run a blind man's bluff--
THOK
IT'S NOT ME!
THOK
I'M SAVING HER!
THWAK
IT'S THE SPOT, AND HE'S WORKING WITH AN INSIDE MAN HERE--
NOK
--and listen for whose heartbeat spikes.
Sal Donorat
--SAL DONORATTI!
Whew.
PAF
SAL? IS THAT TRUE?
WHAT? N-NO... I--I--

That bought me a moment.

...OH, CHRIST!

HOW'D YOU KNOW, YOU COSTUMED FREAK? HOW?

LOOK, IT WAS HIS IDEA, NOT MINE, OKAY? YOU WANT THE SPOT? I'LL TELL YOU EVERYTHING I KNOW!

UNCLE SAL?

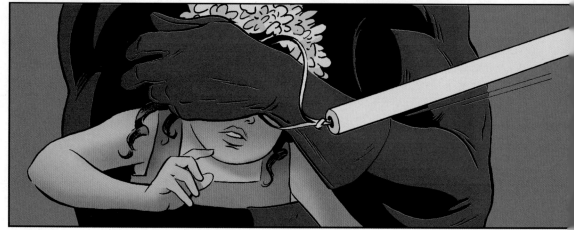

KRAK

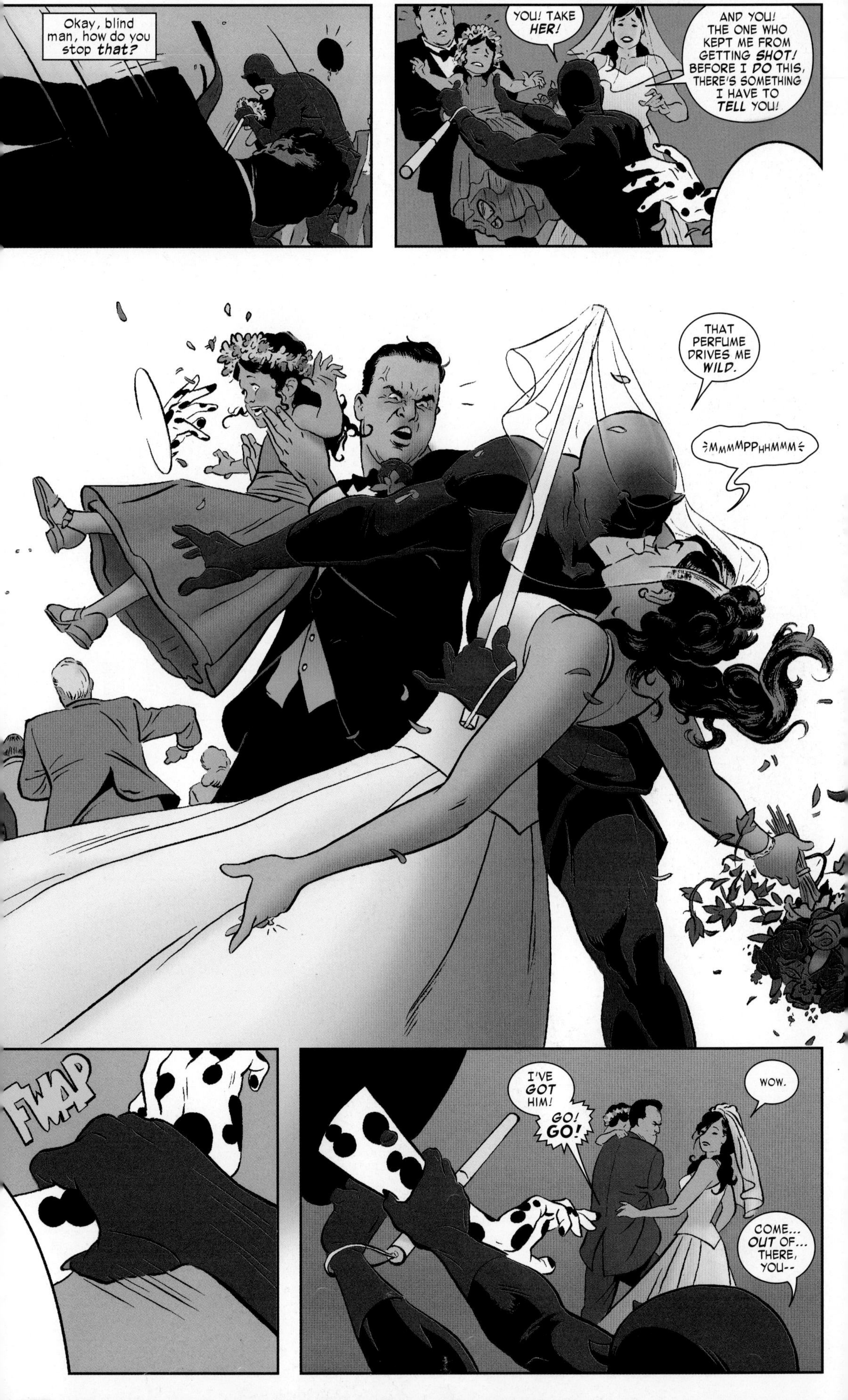
Okay, blind man, how do you stop *that?*
YOU! TAKE *HER!*
AND YOU! THE ONE WHO KEPT ME FROM GETTING *SHOT!* BEFORE I *DO* THIS, THERE'S SOMETHING I HAVE TO *TELL* YOU!
THAT PERFUME DRIVES ME *WILD.*
MMMMPPHHMMM
FWAP
I'VE *GOT* HIM!
GO! GO!
WOW.
COME... *OUT* OF... THERE, YOU--

YAAAAAA

Didn't-- *expect* that--!

Whatever's-- on the other *side*--like jagged *ice*--!

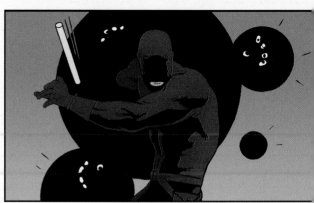

?

What the holy hell am I *dealing* with--?

I could just let go and *run*.

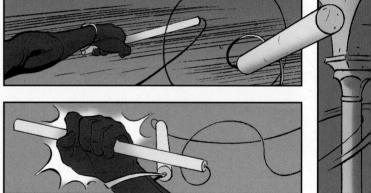

Yeah, right.

DAILY BUGLE

FINAL ★★★★

🎺

SINCE 1897 ★★★★★
$1.00 (in NYC)
$1.50 (outside city)

NEW YORK'S FINEST DAILY NEWSPAPER

SIDE: ROX STOX ON THE RISE; URICH ON JAMESON'S FALLING POLL NUMBERS; WINTERS ON PUNISHER COPYCAT; RUMOR: METS CONTACT GRIMM; MORE

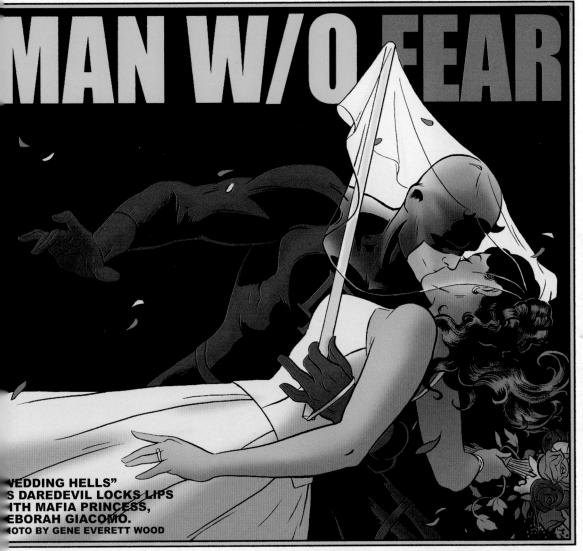

MAN W/O FEAR

"WEDDING HELLS"
S DAREDEVIL LOCKS LIPS
ITH MAFIA PRINCESS,
EBORAH GIACOMO.
HOTO BY GENE EVERETT WOOD

DD K.O.s
Spot
P.O.s Mob

ARK WAID
WRITER

PAOLO RIVERA
PENCILER

JOE RIVERA
INKER

JAVIER RODRIGUEZ
COLOR ARTIST

C'S JOE CARAMAGNA
LETTERER

ELLIE PYLE
ASST. EDITOR

STEPHEN WACKER
EDITOR

AXEL ALONSO
EDITOR IN CHIEF

JOE QUESADA
CHIEF CREATIVE OFFICER

DAN BUCKLEY
PUBLISHER

ALAN FINE
EXEC. PRODUCER

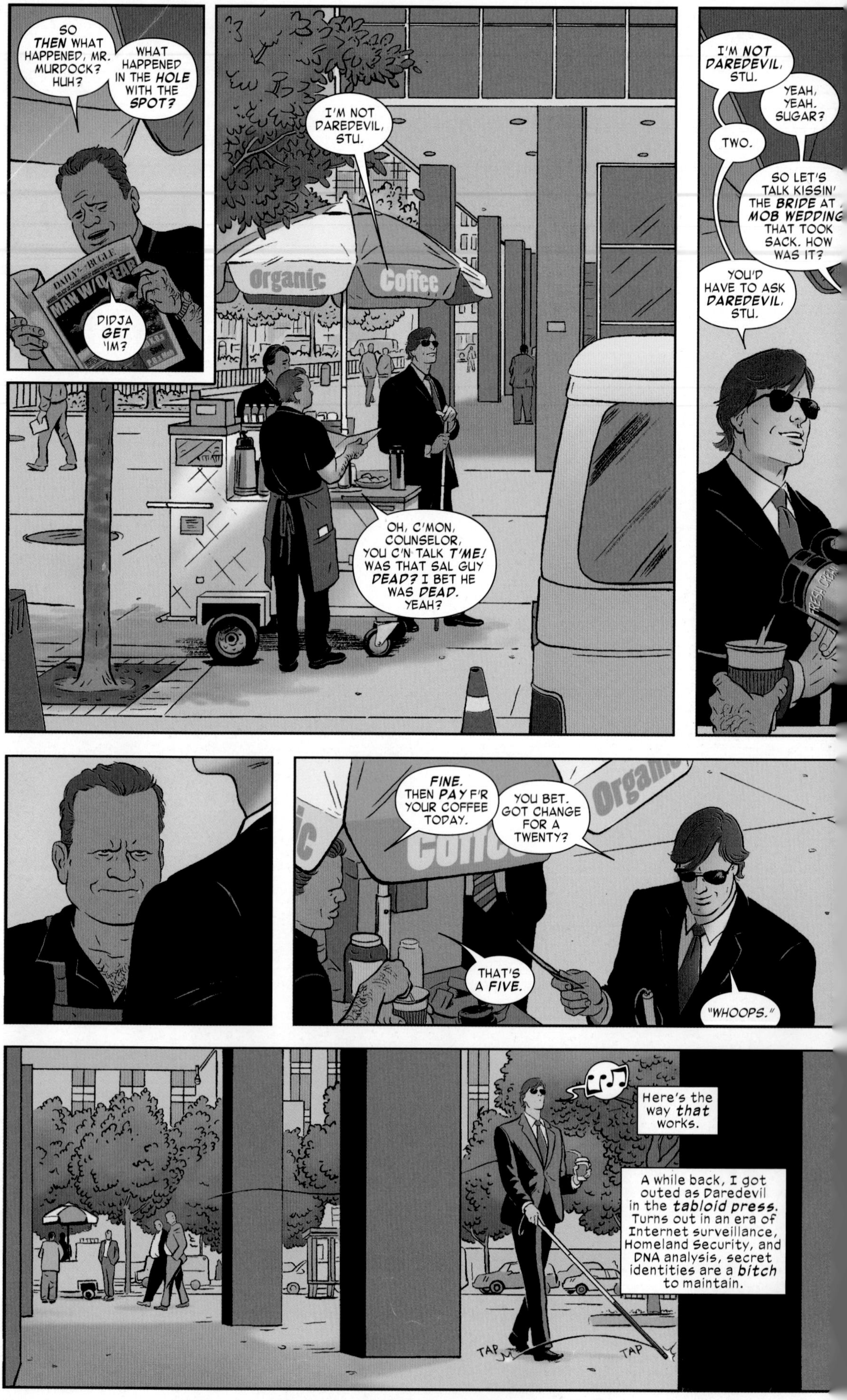

SO THEN WHAT HAPPENED, MR. MURDOCK? HUH?
WHAT HAPPENED IN THE HOLE WITH THE SPOT?
DAILY BUGLE
MAN W/O FEAR
DIDJA GET 'IM?
I'M NOT DAREDEVIL, STU.
Organic
Coffee
OH, C'MON, COUNSELOR, YOU C'N TALK T'ME! WAS THAT SAL GUY DEAD? I BET HE WAS DEAD. YEAH?
I'M NOT DAREDEVIL, STU.
YEAH, YEAH. SUGAR?
TWO.
SO LET'S TALK KISSIN' THE BRIDE AT MOB WEDDING THAT TOOK SACK. HOW WAS IT?
YOU'D HAVE TO ASK DAREDEVIL, STU.
FINE. THEN PAY F'R YOUR COFFEE TODAY.
YOU BET. GOT CHANGE FOR A TWENTY?
THAT'S A FIVE.
"WHOOPS."
Here's the way that works.
A while back, I got outed as Daredevil in the tabloid press. Turns out in an era of Internet surveillance, Homeland Security, and DNA analysis, secret identities are a bitch to maintain.
TAP
TAP

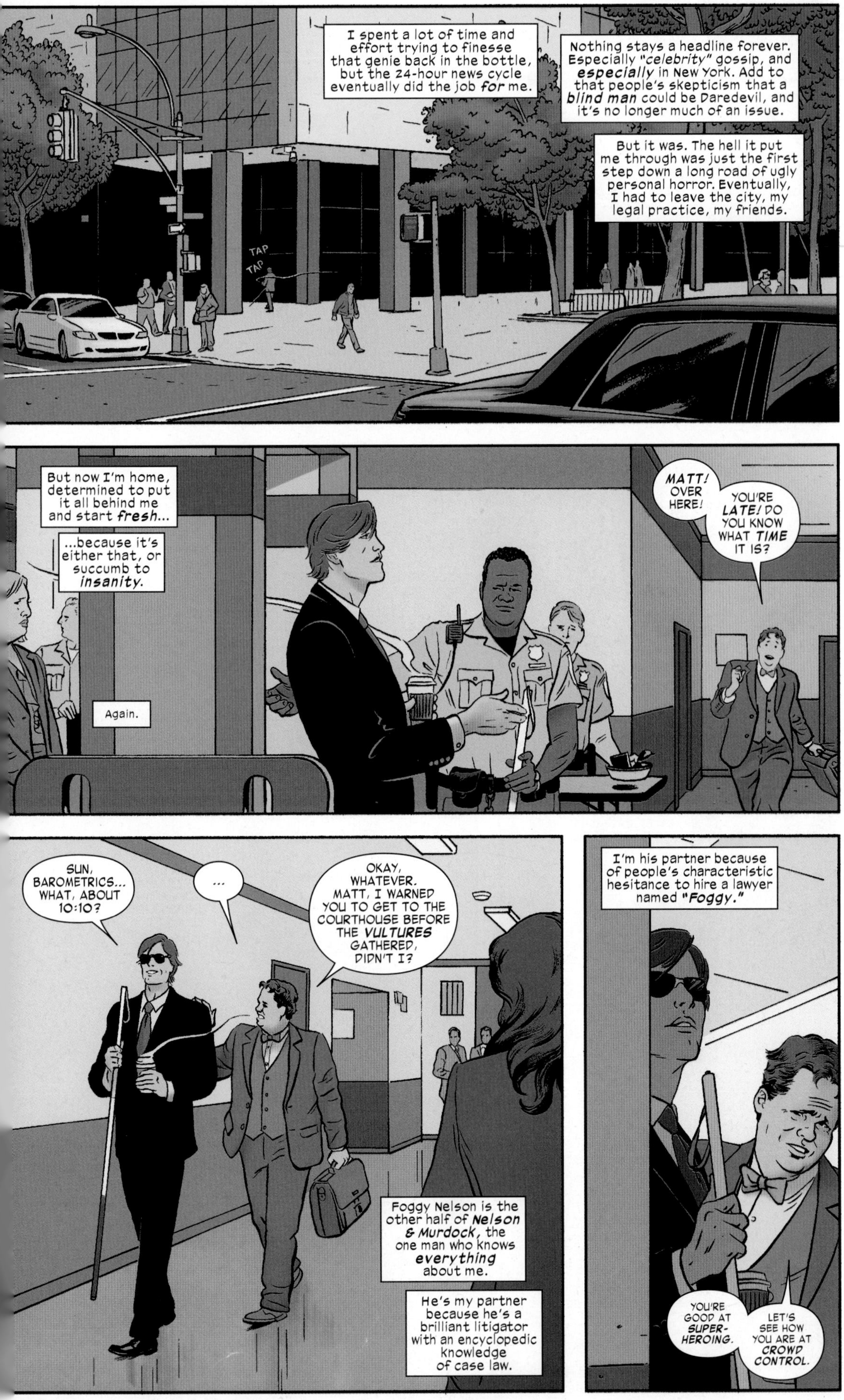
I spent a lot of time and effort trying to finesse that genie back in the bottle, but the 24-hour news cycle eventually did the job for me.
Nothing stays a headline forever. Especially "celebrity" gossip, and especially in New York. Add to that people's skepticism that a blind man could be Daredevil, and it's no longer much of an issue.
But it was. The hell it put me through was just the first step down a long road of ugly personal horror. Eventually, I had to leave the city, my legal practice, my friends.
TAP
TAP
But now I'm home, determined to put it all behind me and start fresh...
...because it's either that, or succumb to insanity.
Again.
MATT! OVER HERE!
YOU'RE LATE! DO YOU KNOW WHAT TIME IT IS?
SUN, BAROMETRICS... WHAT, ABOUT 10:10?
...
OKAY, WHATEVER. MATT, I WARNED YOU TO GET TO THE COURTHOUSE BEFORE THE VULTURES GATHERED, DIDN'T I?
Foggy Nelson is the other half of Nelson & Murdock, the one man who knows everything about me.
He's my partner because he's a brilliant litigator with an encyclopedic knowledge of case law.
I'm his partner because of people's characteristic hesitance to hire a lawyer named "Foggy."
YOU'RE GOOD AT SUPER-HEROING.
LET'S SEE HOW YOU ARE AT CROWD CONTROL.

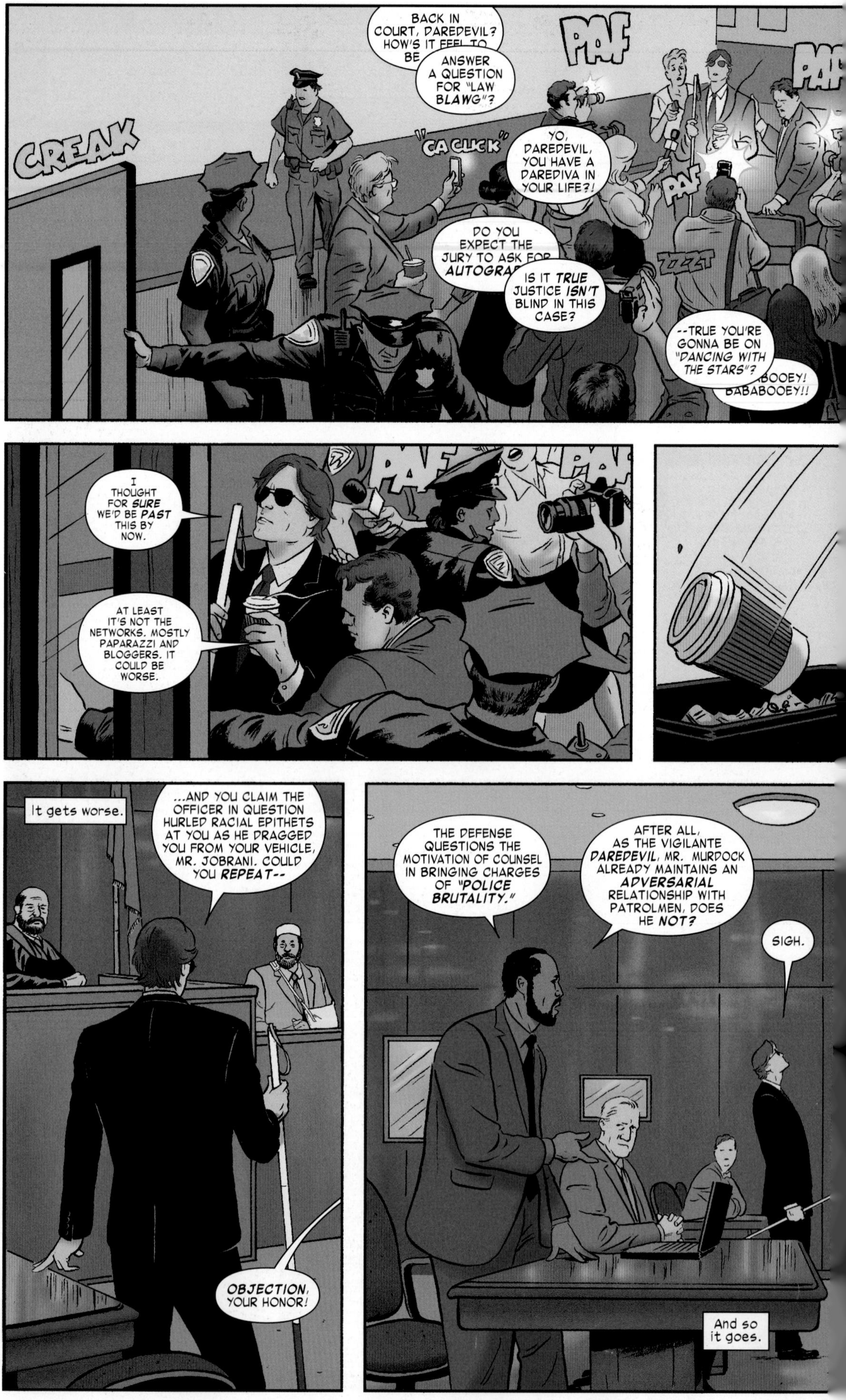
CREAK
BACK IN COURT, DAREDEVIL? HOW'S IT FEEL TO BE
ANSWER A QUESTION FOR "LAW BLAWG"?
PAF
PAF
"CA CLICK"
YO, DAREDEVIL, YOU HAVE A DAREDIVA IN YOUR LIFE?!
PAF
DO YOU EXPECT THE JURY TO ASK FOR AUTOGRA
IS IT TRUE JUSTICE ISN'T BLIND IN THIS CASE?
--TRUE YOU'RE GONNA BE ON "DANCING WITH THE STARS"?
BABOOEY! BABABOOEY!!
I THOUGHT FOR SURE WE'D BE PAST THIS BY NOW.
AT LEAST IT'S NOT THE NETWORKS. MOSTLY PAPARAZZI AND BLOGGERS. IT COULD BE WORSE.
It gets worse.
...AND YOU CLAIM THE OFFICER IN QUESTION HURLED RACIAL EPITHETS AT YOU AS HE DRAGGED YOU FROM YOUR VEHICLE, MR. JOBRANI. COULD YOU REPEAT--
OBJECTION, YOUR HONOR!
THE DEFENSE QUESTIONS THE MOTIVATION OF COUNSEL IN BRINGING CHARGES OF "POLICE BRUTALITY."
AFTER ALL, AS THE VIGILANTE DAREDEVIL, MR. MURDOCK ALREADY MAINTAINS AN ADVERSARIAL RELATIONSHIP WITH PATROLMEN, DOES HE NOT?
SIGH.
And so it goes.

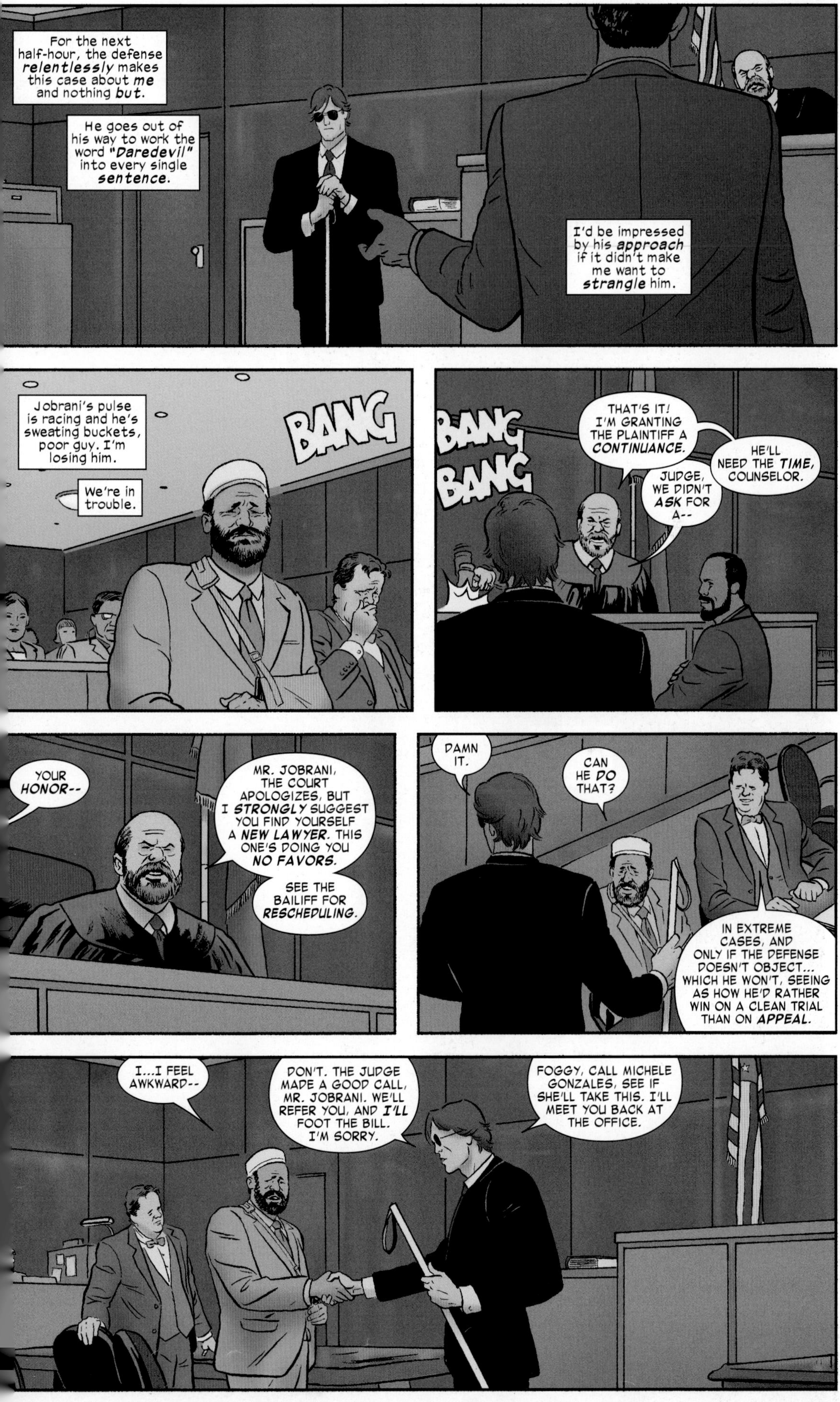
For the next half-hour, the defense *relentlessly* makes this case about *me* and nothing *but*.
He goes out of his way to work the word *"Daredevil"* into every single *sentence*.
I'd be impressed by his *approach* if it didn't make me want to *strangle* him.
Jobrani's pulse is racing and he's sweating buckets, poor guy. I'm losing him.
We're in trouble.
BANG
BANG
BANG
THAT'S IT! I'M GRANTING THE PLAINTIFF A *CONTINUANCE.*
JUDGE, WE DIDN'T *ASK* FOR A--
HE'LL NEED THE *TIME,* COUNSELOR.
YOUR *HONOR*--
MR. JOBRANI, THE COURT APOLOGIZES, BUT I *STRONGLY* SUGGEST YOU FIND YOURSELF A *NEW LAWYER.* THIS ONE'S DOING YOU *NO FAVORS.*
SEE THE BAILIFF FOR *RESCHEDULING.*
DAMN IT.
CAN HE *DO* THAT?
IN EXTREME CASES, AND ONLY IF THE DEFENSE DOESN'T OBJECT... WHICH HE WON'T, SEEING AS HOW HE'D RATHER WIN ON A CLEAN TRIAL THAN ON *APPEAL.*
I...I FEEL AWKWARD--
DON'T. THE JUDGE MADE A GOOD CALL, MR. JOBRANI. WE'LL REFER YOU, AND *I'LL* FOOT THE BILL. I'M SORRY.
FOGGY, CALL MICHELE GONZALES, SEE IF SHE'LL TAKE THIS. I'LL MEET YOU BACK AT THE OFFICE.

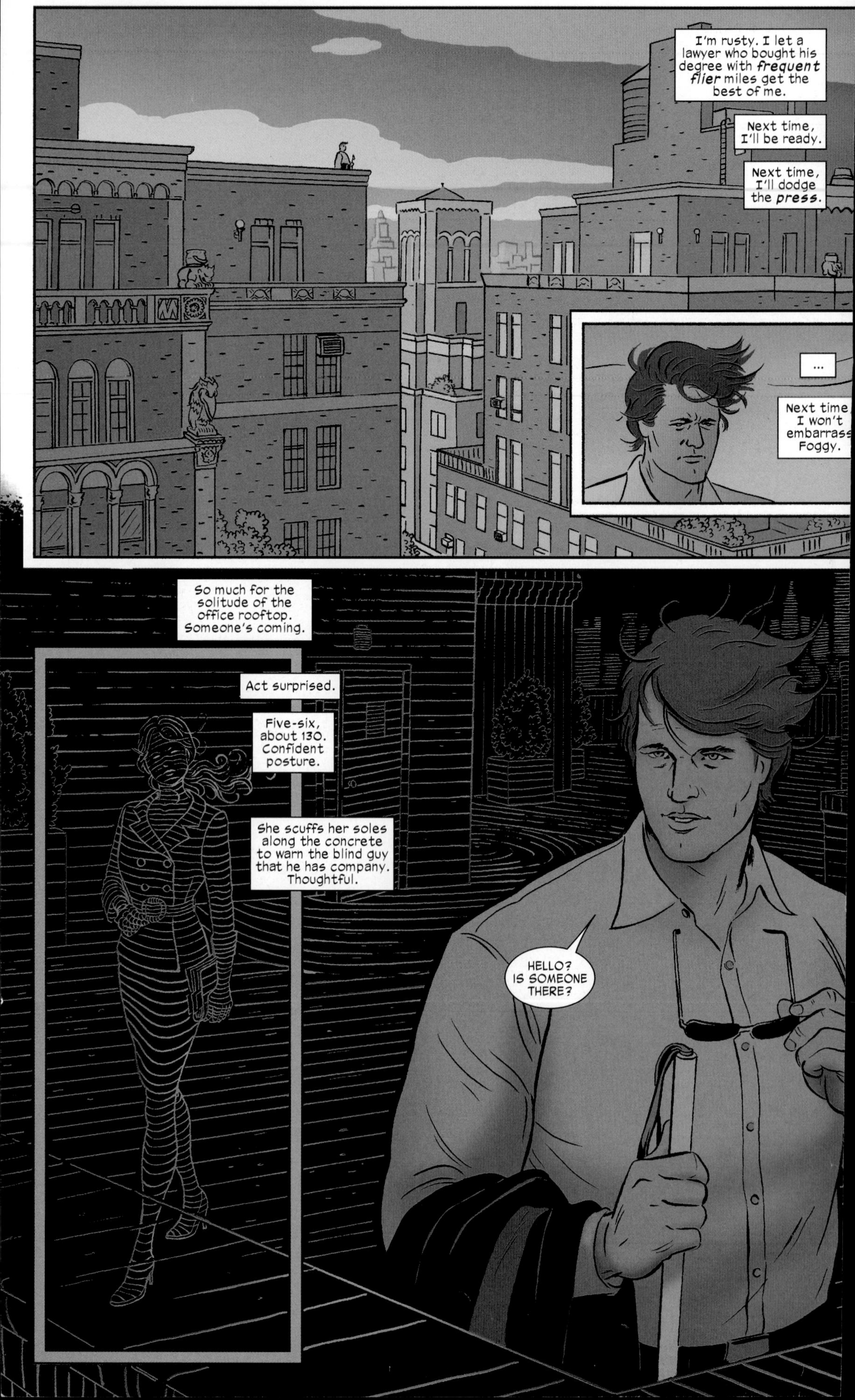

I'm rusty. I let a lawyer who bought his degree with *frequent flier* miles get the best of me.
Next time, I'll be ready.
Next time, I'll dodge the *press*.
...
Next time, I won't embarrass Foggy.
So much for the solitude of the office rooftop. Someone's coming.
Act surprised.
Five-six, about 130. Confident posture.
She scuffs her soles along the concrete to warn the blind guy that he has company. Thoughtful.
HELLO? IS SOMEONE THERE?

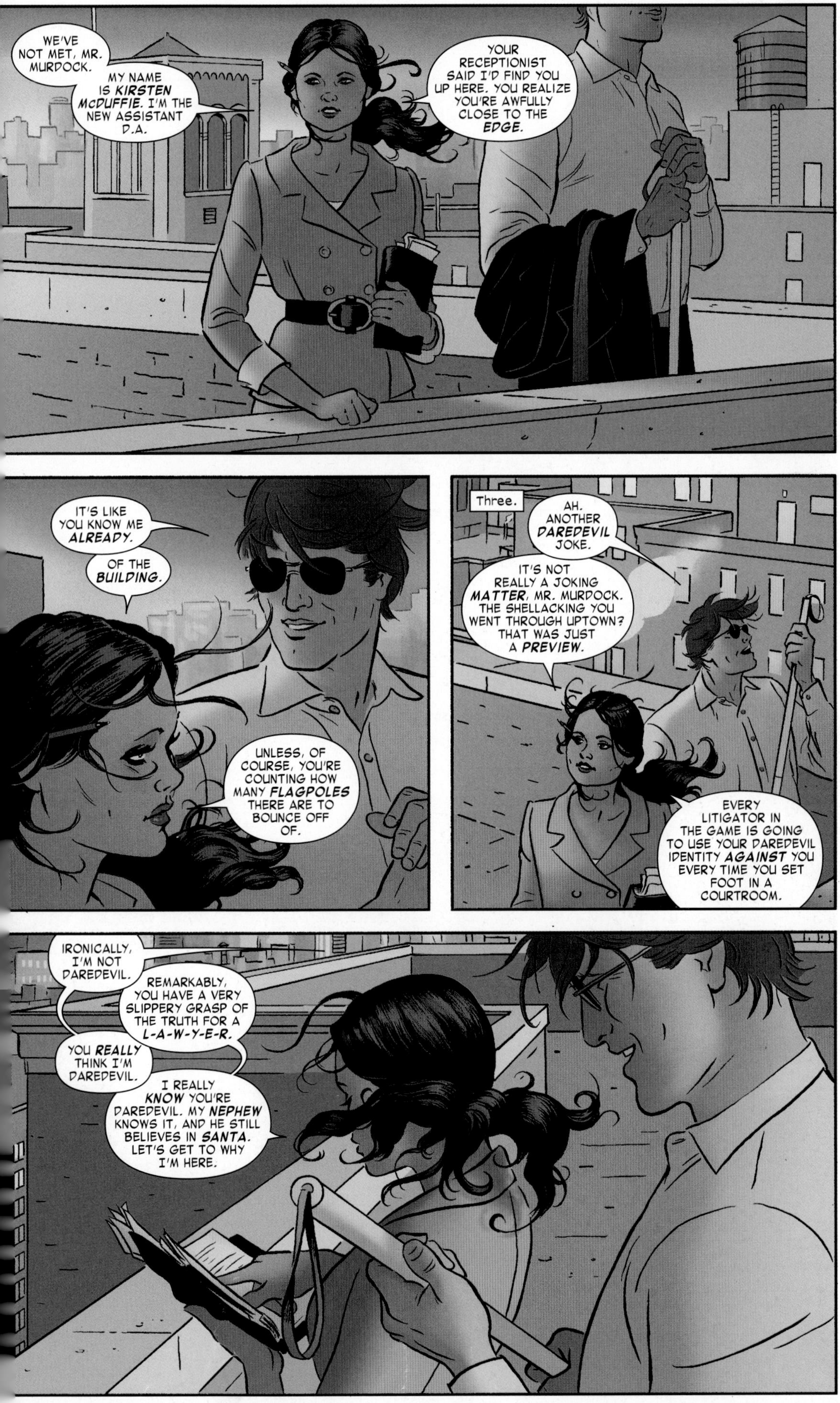

WE'VE NOT MET, MR. MURDOCK.
MY NAME IS KIRSTEN McDUFFIE. I'M THE NEW ASSISTANT D.A.
YOUR RECEPTIONIST SAID I'D FIND YOU UP HERE. YOU REALIZE YOU'RE AWFULLY CLOSE TO THE EDGE.
IT'S LIKE YOU KNOW ME ALREADY.
OF THE BUILDING.
UNLESS, OF COURSE, YOU'RE COUNTING HOW MANY FLAGPOLES THERE ARE TO BOUNCE OFF OF.
Three.
AH. ANOTHER DAREDEVIL JOKE.
IT'S NOT REALLY A JOKING MATTER, MR. MURDOCK. THE SHELLACKING YOU WENT THROUGH UPTOWN? THAT WAS JUST A PREVIEW.
EVERY LITIGATOR IN THE GAME IS GOING TO USE YOUR DAREDEVIL IDENTITY AGAINST YOU EVERY TIME YOU SET FOOT IN A COURTROOM.
IRONICALLY, I'M NOT DAREDEVIL.
REMARKABLY, YOU HAVE A VERY SLIPPERY GRASP OF THE TRUTH FOR A L-A-W-Y-E-R.
YOU REALLY THINK I'M DAREDEVIL.
I REALLY KNOW YOU'RE DAREDEVIL. MY NEPHEW KNOWS IT, AND HE STILL BELIEVES IN SANTA. LET'S GET TO WHY I'M HERE.

LOOK, EVEN THE D.A.'S OFFICE CAN'T ORDER YOU NOT TO ENTER A COURTROOM. NOT OFFICIALLY.

BUT NOW THAT YOU'RE BACK IN NEW YORK AND, PRESUMABLY, CHARTING A FUTURE, WE DO...

...ENCOURAGE YOU TO CONSIDER WHAT A LIABILITY YOU ARE TO YOUR CLIENTS AND TO AN ALREADY-OVERBURDENED JUDICIAL SYSTEM.

MM-HMM. DO YOU GIVE THIS SAME SPEECH TO ALL THE OTHER LAWYERS WHO AREN'T DAREDEVIL?

OW!

DID YOU JUST THROW SOMETHING AT ME?

THOK

YEAH. A CHANCE TO COME CLEAN.

GIVE WEIG TO WHAT SAID, M MURDOC

CLAP

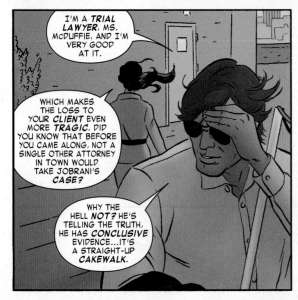

I'M A TRIAL LAWYER, MS. MCDUFFIE, AND I'M VERY GOOD AT IT.

WHICH MAKES THE LOSS TO YOUR CLIENT EVEN MORE TRAGIC. DID YOU KNOW THAT BEFORE YOU CAME ALONG, NOT A SINGLE OTHER ATTORNEY IN TOWN WOULD TAKE JOBRANI'S CASE?

WHY THE HELL NOT? HE'S TELLING THE TRUTH, HE HAS CONCLUSIVE EVIDENCE...IT'S A STRAIGHT-UP CAKEWALK.

ARE YOU INTIMATING THAT SOMETHING SCARED THEM OFF? WHY? WHO?

IF I WERE DAREDEVIL, THOSE ARE CERTAINLY THE QUESTIONS I'D BE ASKING.

JUST SAYIN'.

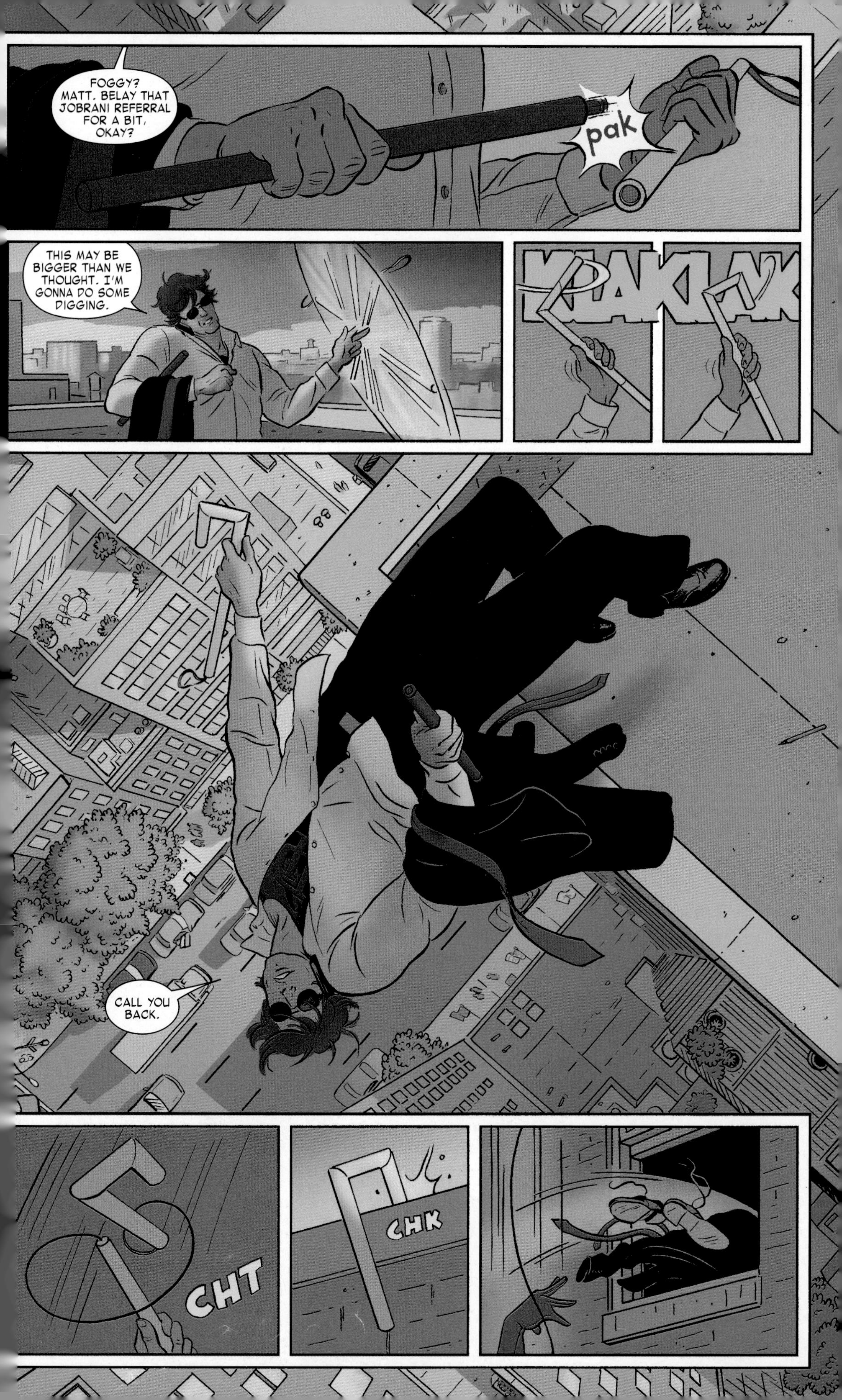
FOGGY? MATT. BELAY THAT JOBRANI REFERRAL FOR A BIT, OKAY?
pak
THIS MAY BE BIGGER THAN WE THOUGHT. I'M GONNA DO SOME DIGGING.
KLAKKLAK
CALL YOU BACK.
CHT
CHK

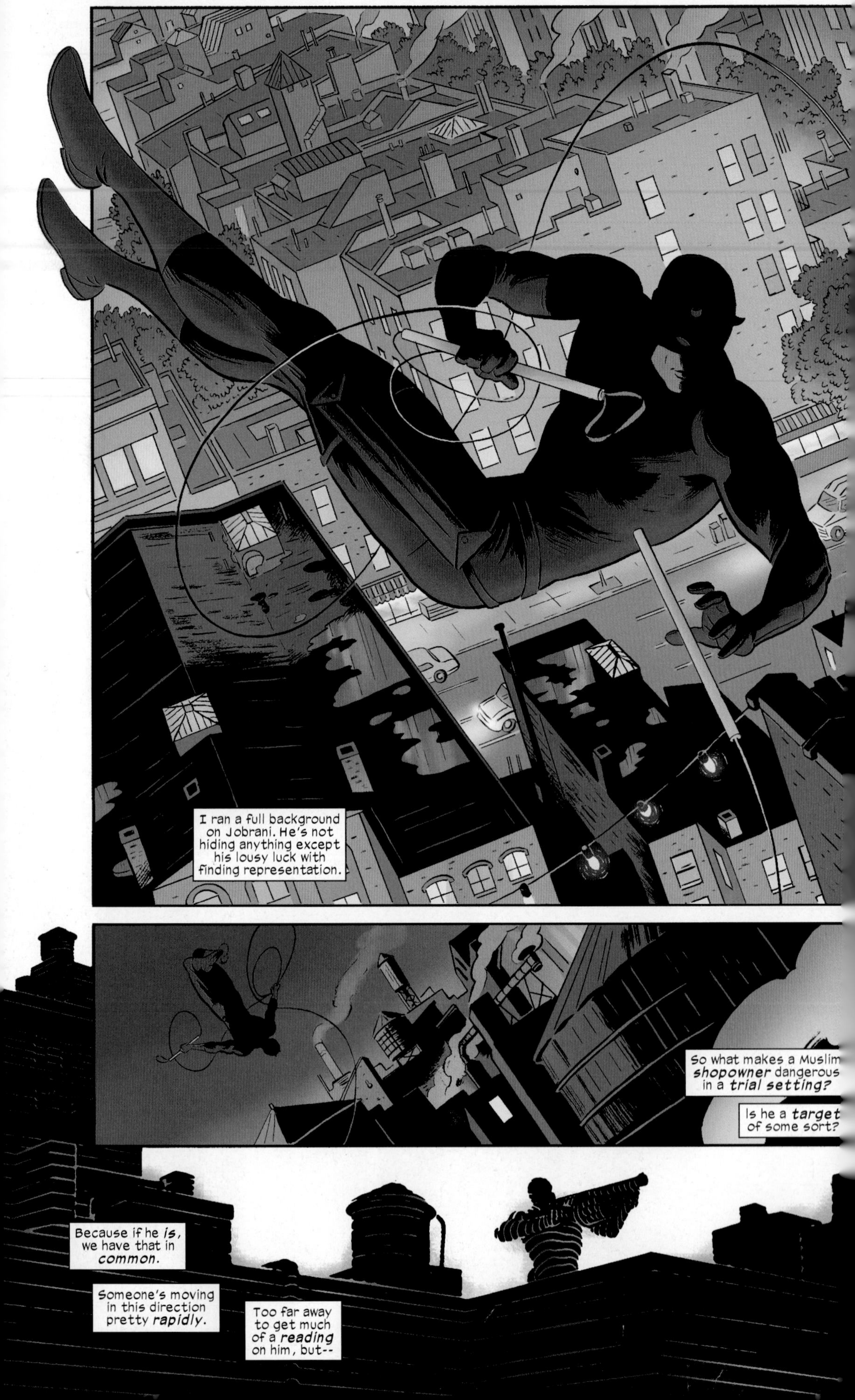
I ran a full background on Jobrani. He's not hiding anything except his lousy luck with finding representation.
So what makes a Muslim shopowner dangerous in a trial setting?
Is he a target of some sort?
Because if he is, we have that in common.
Someone's moving in this direction pretty rapidly.
Too far away to get much of a reading on him, but--

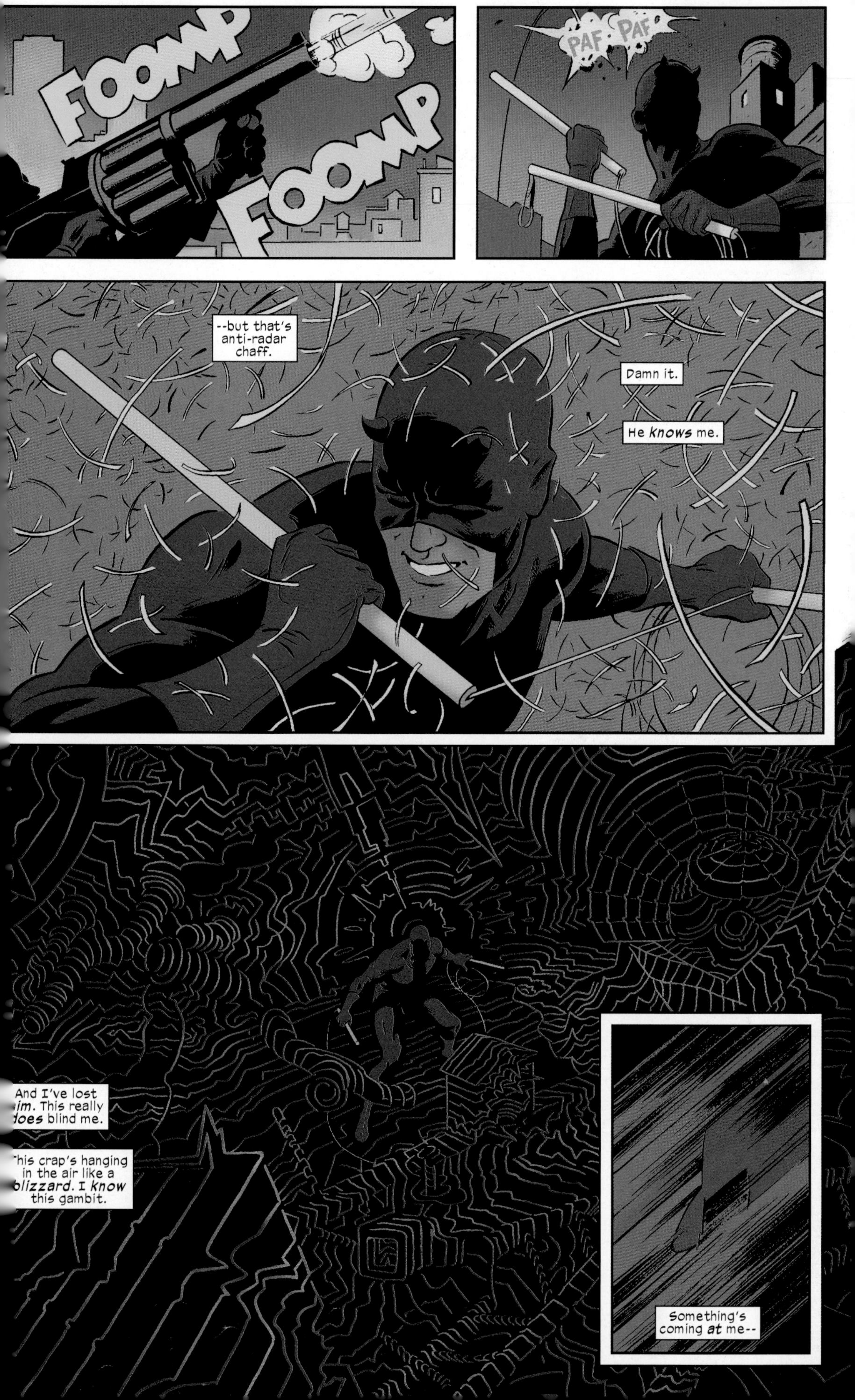

FOOMP
FOOMP
PAF PAF
--but that's anti-radar chaff.
Damn it.
He *knows* me.
And I've lost *im*. This really *does* blind me.
This crap's hanging in the air like a *blizzard*. I *know* this gambit.
Something's coming *at* me--

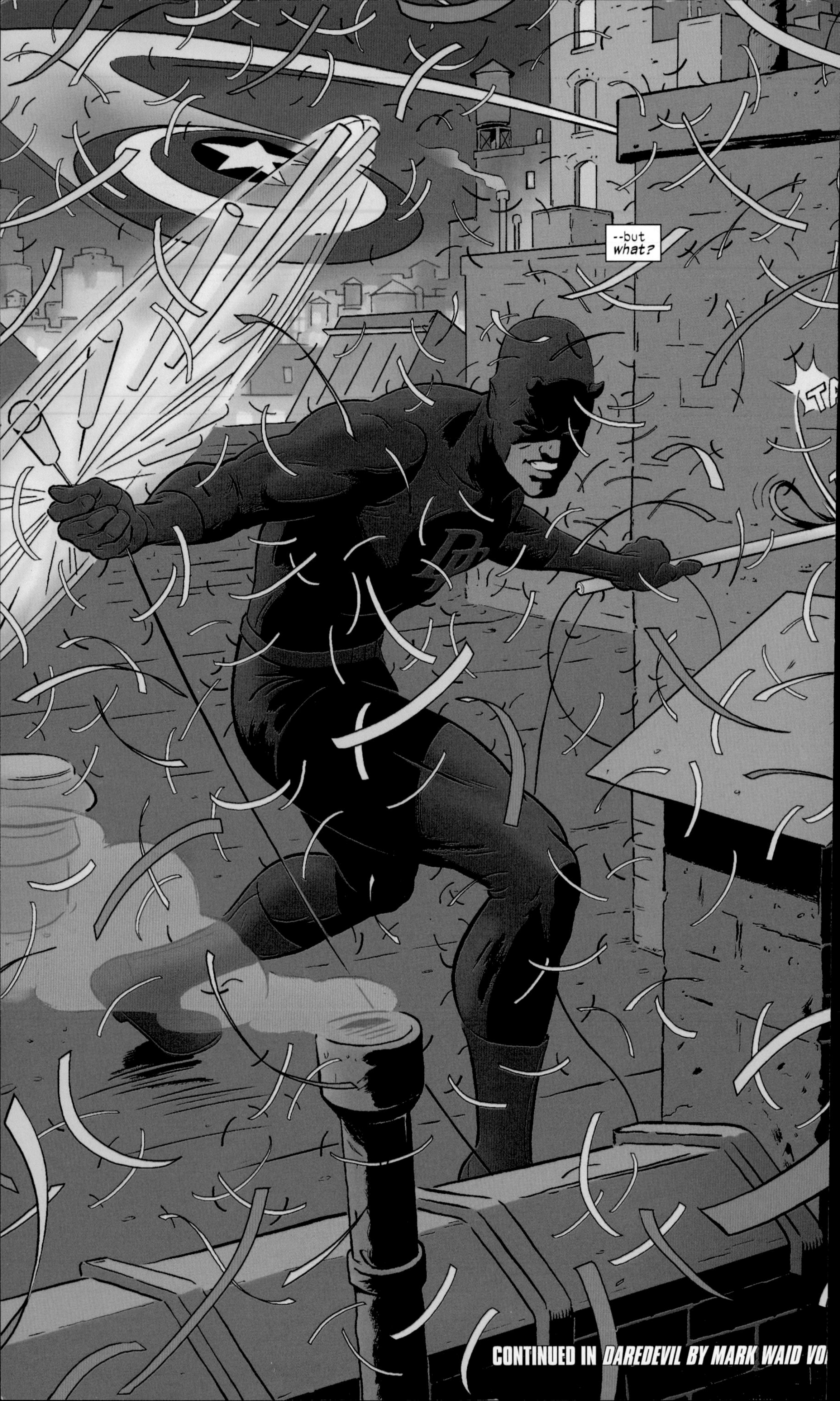
--but what?

CONTINUED IN *DAREDEVIL BY MARK WAID VO*

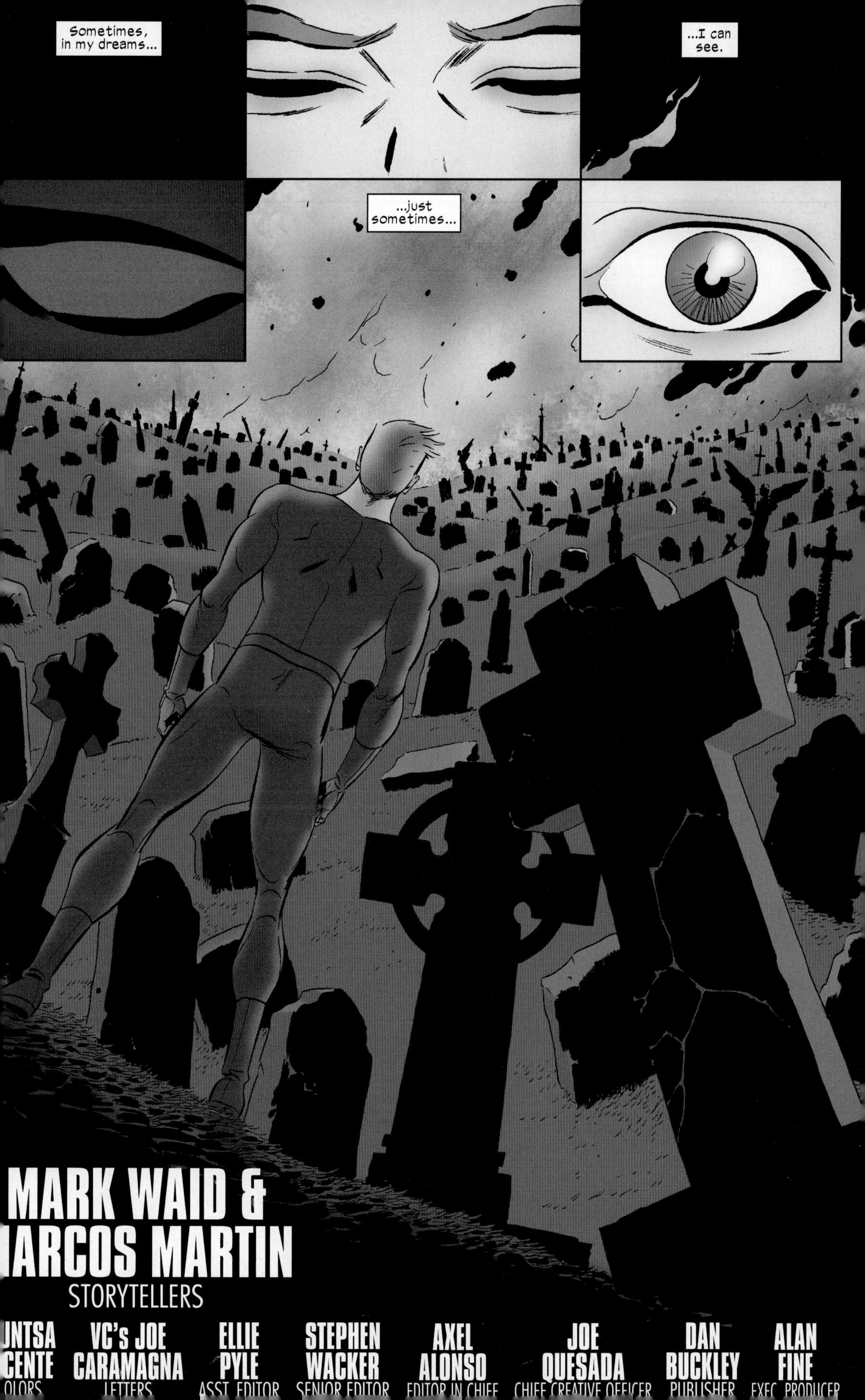

Sometimes, in my dreams...
...I can see.
...just sometimes...
MARK WAID &
ARCOS MARTIN
STORYTELLERS
NTSA
CENTE
OLORS
VC's JOE
CARAMAGNA
LETTERS
ELLIE
PYLE
ASST. EDITOR
STEPHEN
WACKER
SENIOR EDITOR
AXEL
ALONSO
EDITOR IN CHIEF
JOE
QUESADA
CHIEF CREATIVE OFFICER
DAN
BUCKLEY
PUBLISHER
ALAN
FINE
EXEC. PRODUCER

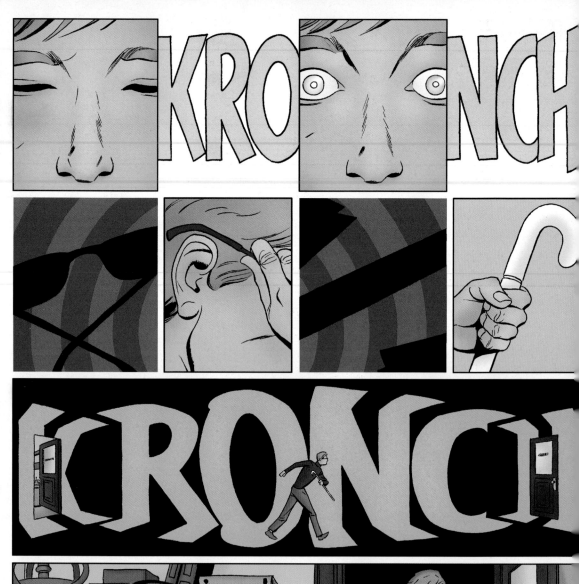

KRO   NCH

KRONCH

WHAT?

WE TALKED ABOUT THIS.

SORRY. SORRY. SORRY. TODAY'S THE DAY, RIGHT?

⸮KAAF⸮ YEP. AND YOU'RE COMING WITH.

PLOOF

E? NO. CAN'T. O TIME. TOO MUCH TO DO.

REBUILDING *NELSON & MURDOCK* IS AN *EXPENSIVE PROPOSITION,* MY FRIEND.

SO RIGHT NOW, WE ARE A *VOLUME BUSINESS.*

I'VE GOT BRIEFS TO FILE, CLERKS TO CALL, DEPOSITIONS TO CHECK, AFFIDA--

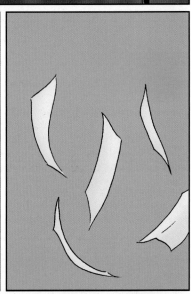

YOU ARE A *MYSTERY.*

I AM AN *OPEN BOOK.*

EVEN BOOKS *TRAVEL.* I DON'T UNDERSTAND HOW YOU CAN BE SO *SEDENTARY* AND SO *COOPED-UP* AND SO...SO...

RESPONSIBLE?

...*NUMB.* OH, MY *GOD,* FOGGY...WE LIVE IN *NEW YORK.*

THE GREATEST CITY ON *EARTH.*

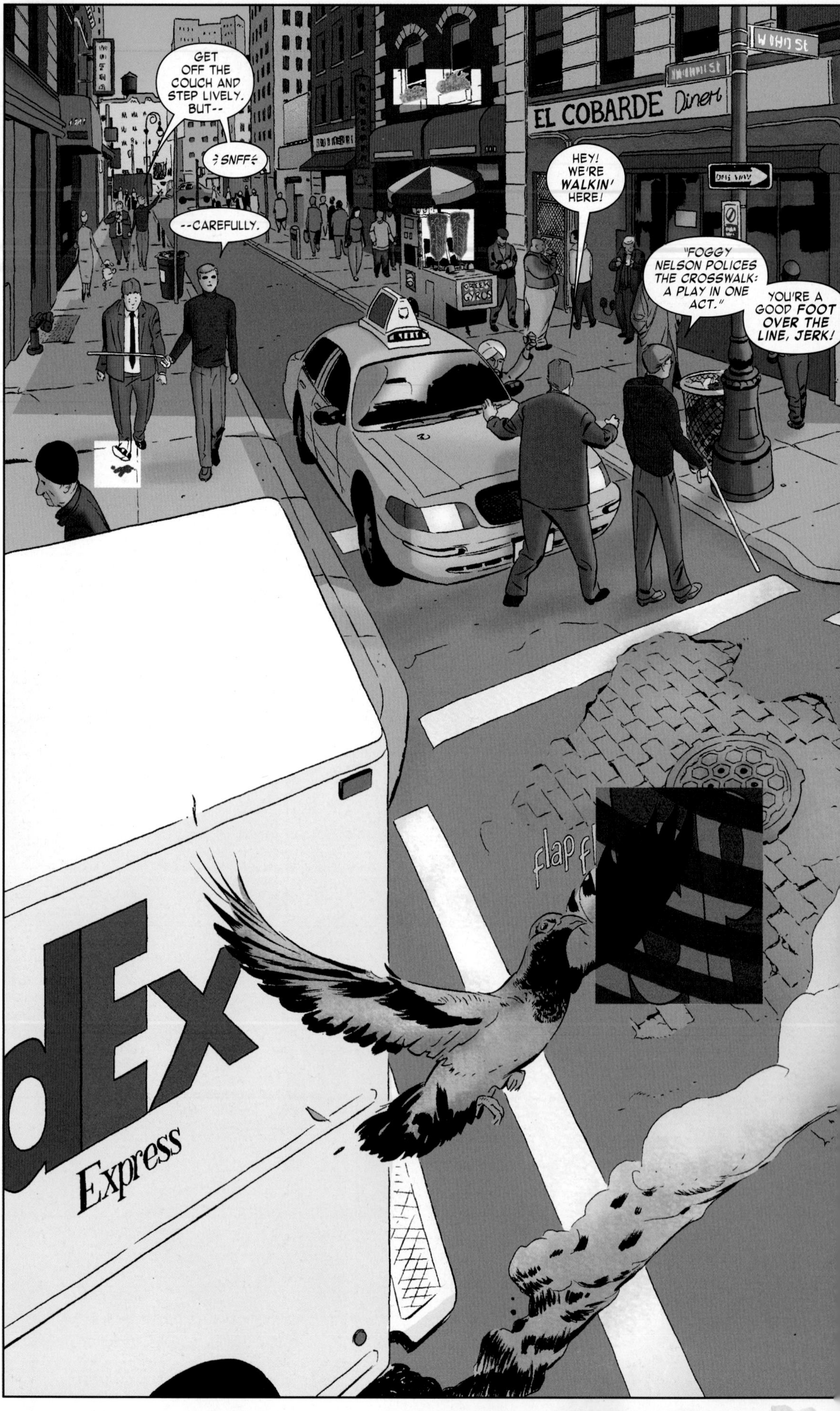
GET OFF THE COUCH AND STEP LIVELY. BUT--
SNFF
--CAREFULLY.
EL COBARDE Diner
HEY! WE'RE WALKIN' HERE!
"FOGGY NELSON POLICES THE CROSSWALK: A PLAY IN ONE ACT."
YOU'RE A GOOD FOOT OVER THE LINE, JERK!
flap fl
dEx
Express

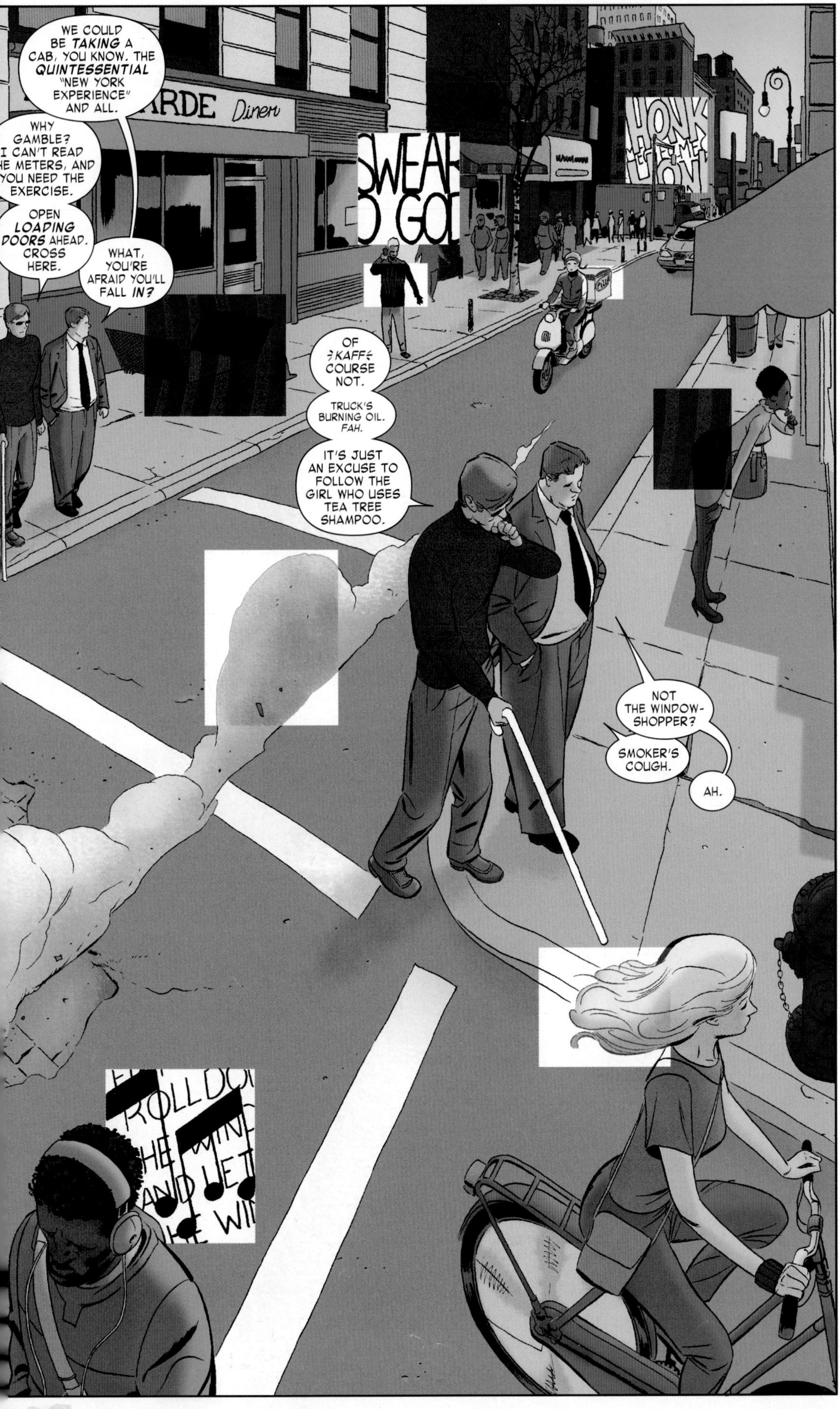
WE COULD BE ***TAKING*** A CAB, YOU KNOW. THE ***QUINTESSENTIAL*** "NEW YORK EXPERIENCE" AND ALL.
WHY GAMBLE? I CAN'T READ HE METERS, AND YOU NEED THE EXERCISE.
OPEN ***LOADING DOORS*** AHEAD. CROSS HERE.
WHAT, YOU'RE AFRAID YOU'LL FALL ***IN?***
SWEAR
HONK
OF ‡*KAFF*‡ COURSE NOT.
TRUCK'S BURNING OIL. *FAH.*
IT'S JUST AN EXCUSE TO FOLLOW THE GIRL WHO USES TEA TREE SHAMPOO.
NOT THE WINDOW-SHOPPER?
SMOKER'S COUGH.
AH.

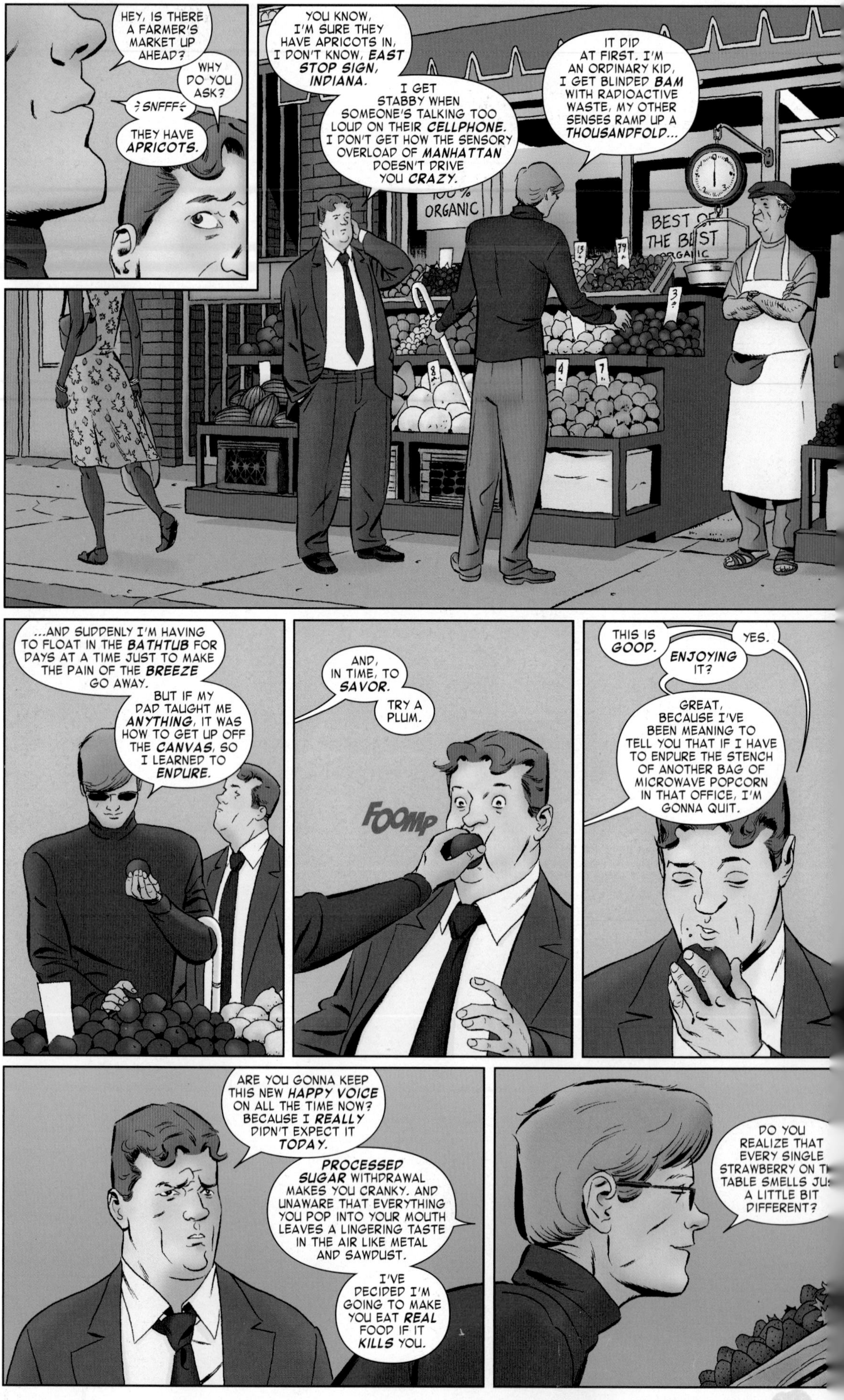

HEY, IS THERE A FARMER'S MARKET UP AHEAD?
WHY DO YOU ASK?
SNFFF
THEY HAVE APRICOTS.
YOU KNOW, I'M SURE THEY HAVE APRICOTS IN, I DON'T KNOW, EAST STOP SIGN, INDIANA.
I GET STABBY WHEN SOMEONE'S TALKING TOO LOUD ON THEIR CELLPHONE. I DON'T GET HOW THE SENSORY OVERLOAD OF MANHATTAN DOESN'T DRIVE YOU CRAZY.
IT DID AT FIRST. I'M AN ORDINARY KID, I GET BLINDED BAM WITH RADIOACTIVE WASTE, MY OTHER SENSES RAMP UP A THOUSANDFOLD...
ORGANIC
BEST OF THE BEST
...AND SUDDENLY I'M HAVING TO FLOAT IN THE BATHTUB FOR DAYS AT A TIME JUST TO MAKE THE PAIN OF THE BREEZE GO AWAY.
BUT IF MY DAD TAUGHT ME ANYTHING, IT WAS HOW TO GET UP OFF THE CANVAS, SO I LEARNED TO ENDURE.
AND, IN TIME, TO SAVOR.
TRY A PLUM.
FOOMP
THIS IS GOOD.
YES.
ENJOYING IT?
GREAT, BECAUSE I'VE BEEN MEANING TO TELL YOU THAT IF I HAVE TO ENDURE THE STENCH OF ANOTHER BAG OF MICROWAVE POPCORN IN THAT OFFICE, I'M GONNA QUIT.
ARE YOU GONNA KEEP THIS NEW HAPPY VOICE ON ALL THE TIME NOW? BECAUSE I REALLY DIDN'T EXPECT IT TODAY.
PROCESSED SUGAR WITHDRAWAL MAKES YOU CRANKY. AND UNAWARE THAT EVERYTHING YOU POP INTO YOUR MOUTH LEAVES A LINGERING TASTE IN THE AIR LIKE METAL AND SAWDUST.
I'VE DECIDED I'M GOING TO MAKE YOU EAT REAL FOOD IF IT KILLS YOU.
DO YOU REALIZE THAT EVERY SINGLE STRAWBERRY ON TH TABLE SMELLS JUS A LITTLE BIT DIFFERENT?

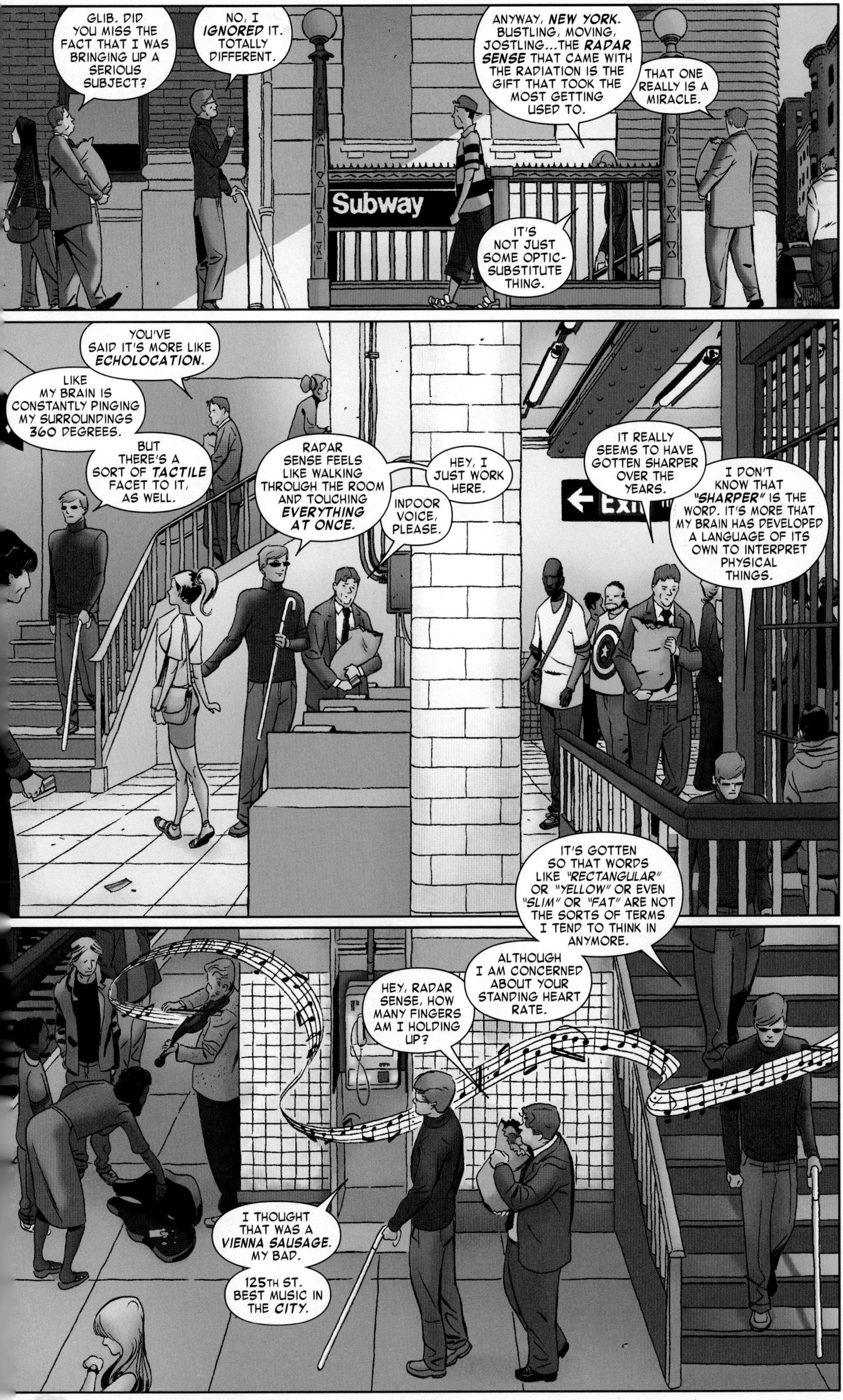
GLIB. DID YOU MISS THE FACT THAT I WAS BRINGING UP A SERIOUS SUBJECT?
NO, I IGNORED IT. TOTALLY DIFFERENT.
ANYWAY, NEW YORK. BUSTLING, MOVING, JOSTLING...THE RADAR SENSE THAT CAME WITH THE RADIATION IS THE GIFT THAT TOOK THE MOST GETTING USED TO.
THAT ONE REALLY IS A MIRACLE.
Subway
IT'S NOT JUST SOME OPTIC-SUBSTITUTE THING.
YOU'VE SAID IT'S MORE LIKE ECHOLOCATION.
LIKE MY BRAIN IS CONSTANTLY PINGING MY SURROUNDINGS 360 DEGREES.
BUT THERE'S A SORT OF TACTILE FACET TO IT, AS WELL.
RADAR SENSE FEELS LIKE WALKING THROUGH THE ROOM AND TOUCHING EVERYTHING AT ONCE.
HEY, I JUST WORK HERE.
INDOOR VOICE, PLEASE.
IT REALLY SEEMS TO HAVE GOTTEN SHARPER OVER THE YEARS.
I DON'T KNOW THAT "SHARPER" IS THE WORD. IT'S MORE THAT MY BRAIN HAS DEVELOPED A LANGUAGE OF ITS OWN TO INTERPRET PHYSICAL THINGS.
IT'S GOTTEN SO THAT WORDS LIKE "RECTANGULAR" OR "YELLOW" OR EVEN "SLIM" OR "FAT" ARE NOT THE SORTS OF TERMS I TEND TO THINK IN ANYMORE.
ALTHOUGH I AM CONCERNED ABOUT YOUR STANDING HEART RATE.
HEY, RADAR SENSE, HOW MANY FINGERS AM I HOLDING UP?
I THOUGHT THAT WAS A VIENNA SAUSAGE. MY BAD.
125TH ST. BEST MUSIC IN THE CITY.

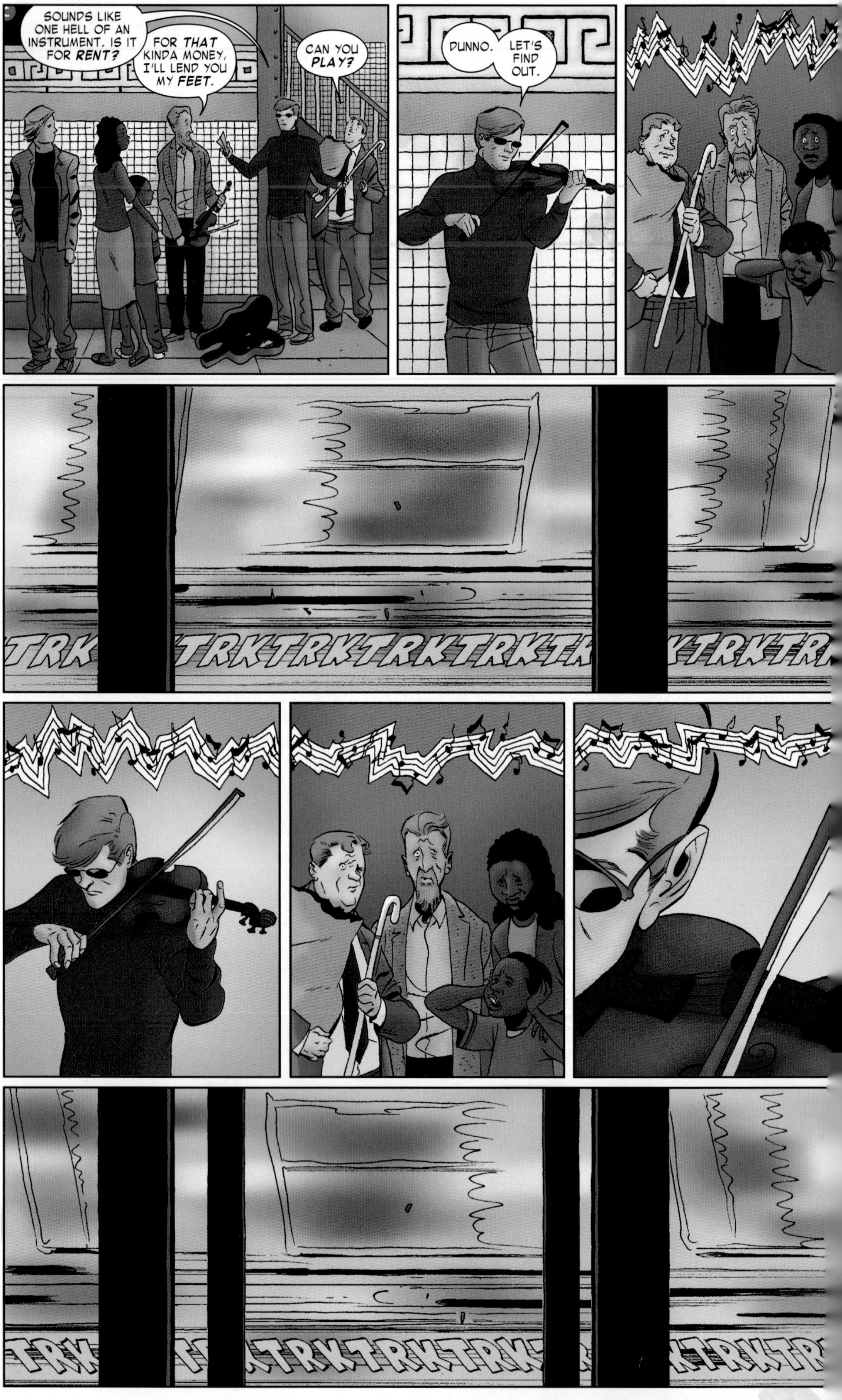

SOUNDS LIKE ONE HELL OF AN INSTRUMENT. IS IT FOR RENT?
FOR THAT KINDA MONEY, I'LL LEND YOU MY FEET.
CAN YOU PLAY?
DUNNO.
LET'S FIND OUT.
TRKTRKTRKTRKTRKTRKTRKTRKTRK
TRKTRKTRKTRKTRKTRKTRKTR

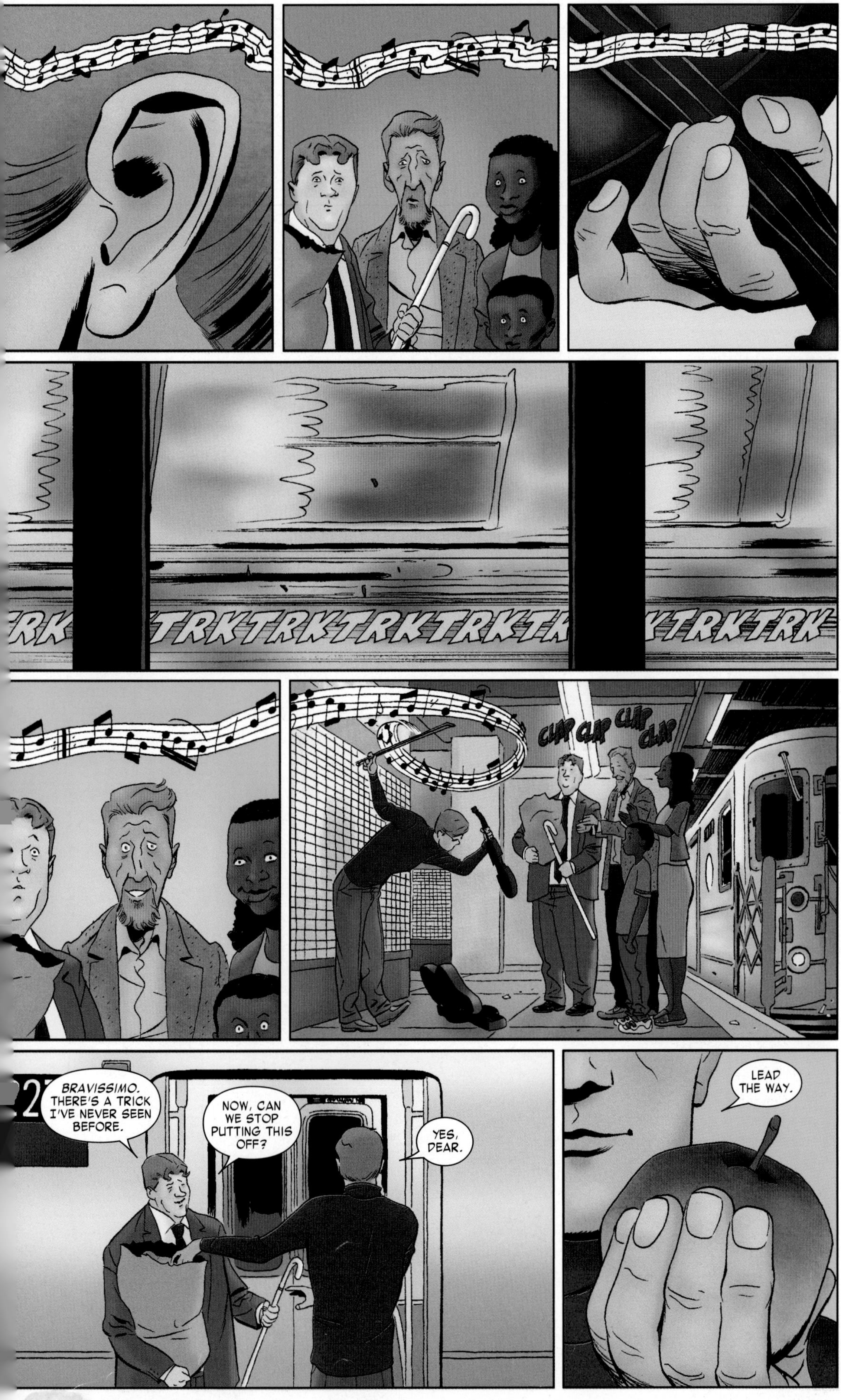
TRKTRKTRKTRKTRKTRKTRKTRK
CLAP CLAP CLAP CLAP
BRAVISSIMO. THERE'S A TRICK I'VE NEVER SEEN BEFORE.
NOW, CAN WE STOP PUTTING THIS OFF?
YES, DEAR.
LEAD THE WAY.

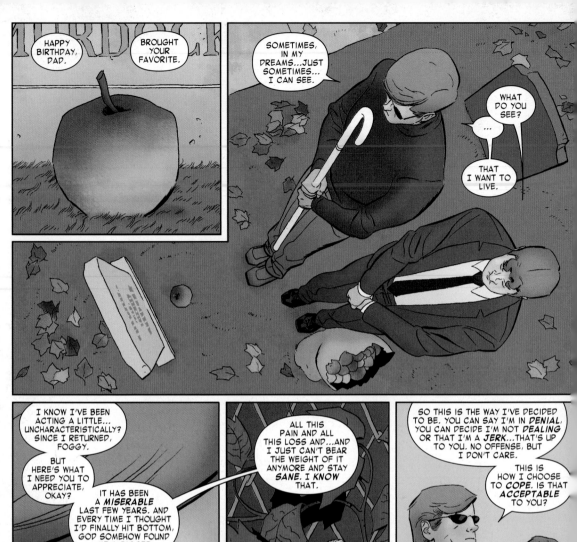

HAPPY BIRTHDAY, DAD.

BROUGHT YOUR FAVORITE.

SOMETIMES, IN MY DREAMS...JUST SOMETIMES... I CAN SEE.

WHAT DO YOU SEE?

...

THAT I WANT TO LIVE.

I KNOW I'VE BEEN ACTING A LITTLE... UNCHARACTERISTICALLY? SINCE I RETURNED, FOGGY.

BUT HERE'S WHAT I NEED YOU TO APPRECIATE, OKAY?

IT HAS BEEN A *MISERABLE* LAST FEW YEARS. AND EVERY TIME I THOUGHT I'D FINALLY HIT BOTTOM, GOD SOMEHOW FOUND ME A BIGGER *SHOVEL.*

ALL THIS PAIN AND ALL THIS LOSS AND...AND I JUST CAN'T BEAR THE WEIGHT OF IT ANYMORE AND STAY *SANE.* I *KNOW* THAT.

SO THIS IS THE WAY I'VE DECIDED TO BE. YOU CAN SAY I'M IN *DENIAL,* YOU CAN DECIDE I'M NOT *DEALING* OR THAT I'M A *JERK...*THAT'S UP TO YOU. NO OFFENSE, BUT I DON'T CARE.

THIS IS HOW I CHOOSE TO *COPE.* IS THAT *ACCEPTABLE* TO YOU?

I'M NOT SURE...

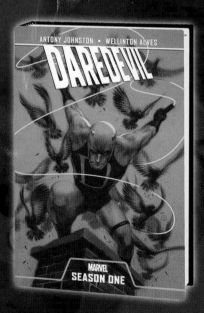

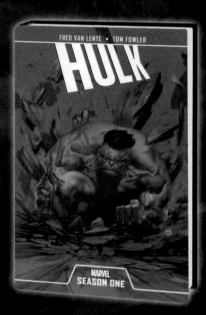